Claus 2013

D0969232

1998 Edition

Acknowledgments p. iv
Warren Hale
Bob Messerschmidt
Daniel Chazin

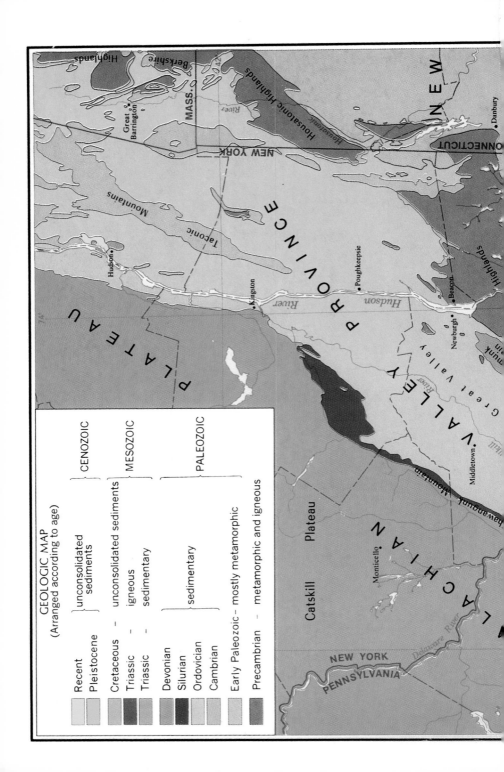

GEOLOGIC MAP
(Arranged according to age)

Recent — unconsolidated sediments | CENOZOIC
Pleistocene — unconsolidated sediments

Cretaceous — unconsolidated sediments | MESOZOIC
Triassic — igneous
Triassic — sedimentary

Devonian — sedimentary | PALEOZOIC
Silurian
Ordovician
Cambrian

Early Paleozoic — mostly metamorphic

Precambrian — metamorphic and igneous

Highlands
Berkshire
Highlands
MASS.
Great
Barrington
NEW YORK
Housatonic Highlands
Housatonic River
CONNECTICUT
Danbury
NEW
Taconic Mountains
Hudson
Kingston
Poughkeepsie
Highlands
Beacon
PROVINCE
Hudson River
VALLEY
Newburgh
Great Valley
Wallkill
PLATEAU
76°
Shawangunk Mountain
Middletown
VALLEY
Catskill Plateau
Monticello
APPALACHIAN
Delaware River
NEW YORK
PENNSYLVANIA

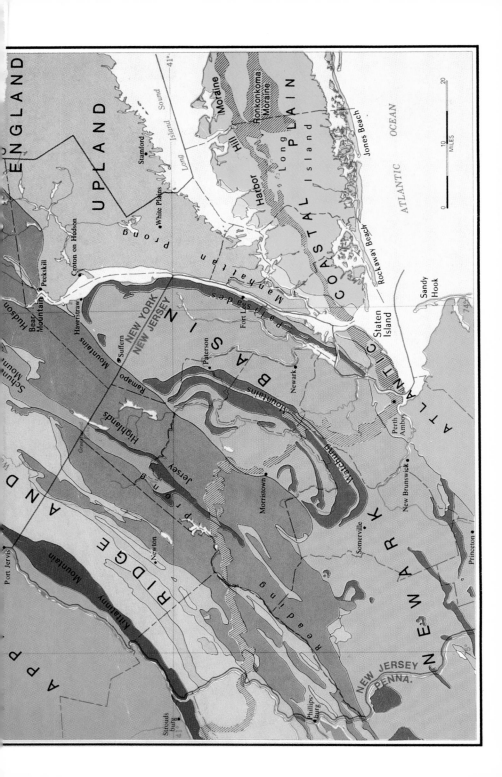

NEW JERSEY WALK BOOK

NEW JERSEY
WALK BOOK

A COMPANION TO THE NEW YORK WALK BOOK

NEW YORK–NEW JERSEY TRAIL CONFERENCE
1998

PUBLISHED BY
NEW YORK-NEW JERSEY TRAIL CONFERENCE
G.P.O. BOX 2250
NEW YORK, NEW YORK 10116

Library of Congress Cataloging-in-Publication Data
New Jersey walk book. — 1st ed.
       314 p.   cm.
    "A companion to the New York walk book."
    Includes bibliographical references (p.) and index.
    ISBN 1-880775-05-0
    1. Hiking—New Jersey—Guidebooks. 2. Trails—New Jersey—
Guidebooks. 3. New Jersey—Guidebooks. I. New York-New Jersey
Trail Conference. II New York walk book.
GV199.42.N5N494 1998
917.4904'43—dc21   98-44411
                                               CIP

Illustrations by Robert L. Dickinson, Richard Edes Harrison, Jack Fagan, Erik M. Gendell,
    Susan K. Gray
Cover photograph - Jim Coon
Cover & text design - Pollard Design
Book design, layout & typesetting - Nora Porter

Although the authors and publisher have tried to make the information as accurate as possible, they accept no responsibility for any loss, injury or inconvenience sustained by any person using this book.

CONTENTS

MAPS

GEOLOGY OF THE LOWER HUDSON VALLEY *(frontis)*

TRAIL MAPS
(b a c k   o f   b o o k)

PREFACE

New Jersey—in spite of its reputation as a bedroom community for commuters—offers open space and opportunities for outdoor recreation. Since 1923, the hiking trails in the region have been described in five editions of the *New York Walk Book*. By 1998, with an increasing number of trails available, it was time that New Jersey trails had a book of their own—the *New Jersey Walk Book*. Trampers of all levels will find a variety of hiking opportunities—from a level stroll along a paved converted railbed, to a hike beside a mountain stream, to a scramble over rocks that ends in a spectacular view. Some of the trails in the region, such as those in Cheesequake State Park or the Pine Barrens, lead hikers through ecologically interesting areas. Others, like the Cannonball Trail and the Paulinskill Valley Trail, are steeped in history. Still others, like the Highlands Trail and the Four Birds Trail, which were built in the mid-1990s, exemplify the work of today's volunteer trail builders.

It is hoped that the *New Jersey Walk Book* will be eagerly received by hikers, just as the previous editions of the *New York Walk Book* have been. Both inexperienced and experienced hikers can continue to rely on these companion volumes. To the beginner, they will be a rich source of information, while to the experienced hiker, they will be a reference book, a reminder of what has changed, and a guide to new areas to explore.

Built upon the previous editions of the *New York Walk Book*, these companion volumes reflect the changes that the world has seen since 1923. Thanks to the advent of personal computers and desktop publishing, the Trail Conference can self-publish the volumes, which gives greater control over both the content and the timing of future editions.

Users of older editions of the *New York Walk Book* will notice other major modifications. Chapters covering areas for which the Trail Conference has a separate, comprehensive publication have been trimmed back, and references are made to that other book. More of the smaller parks, particularly those at the county level, are included. These areas are likely to be of special interest to the beginning hiker as well as to those senior citizens who still want to hike and are looking for new places to go. These smaller trail systems are also great for quick fitness walks. Long-distance trails are in a chapter of their own, a return to the way the Appalachian Trail was presented in the 1934 edition. Rail trails, which are frequently accessible to the handicapped, are included for the first time.

In keeping with the spirit of the older editions of the *New York Walk Book*, much of the original artwork by Robert L. Dickinson has been used. To update the book, new drawings have been added.

The world has changed since the first edition of the *New York Walk Book* was published in 1923. What seems to remain the same is the interest in trails and the need to hike—whether to enjoy nature, to stay in shape, to socialize, or to savor views. Within these pages are many hours of reading and even more hours of exploration. Whatever your reason for hiking, somewhere there is a trail that you can enjoy by yourself or with others.

Jane Daniels
Editor
New Jersey Walk Book

ACKNOWLEDGMENTS

The first edition of the *New Jersey Walk Book* would not be possible without the contributions of members, friends, and partners of the New York-New Jersey Trail Conference. Many people, including those who contributed to the earlier editions of the *New York Walk Book* and are now deceased, wrote the words in this edition. Our traditional partners—park managers, superintendents, and regional administrators—helped review material, sometimes on short notice. We also made contacts with county parks and wildlife management area personnel, some for the first time.

Walt Daniels helped in immeasurable ways. He wrote Suggestions for Hikers, compiled the Long Distance chapter, visited sites, measured trails, wrote trail descriptions, provided technical assistance with computers, formatted text, and made sure the text was consistent. Daniel Chazin did text and copy editing, as well as measuring trails and supplying general advice on publishing. They both made major contributions to the project.

Bob Rooke, Ruth Rosenthal, and Glenn Scherer shared their knowledge of the open spaces in New Jersey and saved hours of research time. Dale Timpe and Dan Chazin coordinated changes to the maps and interacted with the cartographers. Auralie Logan, a professional indexer, prepared the index for the book.

The following people donated their time to walk the trails, gather information, check facts, measure trails, write chapters, and recheck material. Their enthusiasm for the project on short notice is commendable. They are:

Fr. Fred Alvarez   Edmund Blair Bolles
Ludwig Bohler   Irene Boyle

Bob Busha
Daniel Chazin
Karen Daniels
Walt Daniels
David Day
JoAnn and Paul Dolan
Ron Dugger
Ron Dupont, Jr.
Len Frank
Jim Gardineer
Stella Green
Warren Hale
Bob Jonas
Al Kent
Charles Kientzler
Ken Lloyd
Anne Lutkenhouse
Karen Magerlein
Reinhold Martin
Bob Messerschmidt
Robert Moss

William Myles
G. Gail Neffinger
Becky Newman
Laura Newman
Peter Osborne, III
George Perten
Bill and Mary Ann Pruehsner
Peter Rigotti
Robert C. Rooke, Jr.
Ruth Rosenthal
Tom Rupolo
Glenn Scherer
Gene Schweikert
Arch Seamans
Mary Sive
Lisa Tracy-Savoie
Alice Tufel
Phil Tunison
Matt Visco
Richard Warner

'Send your road is clear before you when the old
Spring-fret comes o'er you
And the Red Gods call for you

Kipling: Feet of the Young Men

THE LOOK-OFF

(from the first edition of the *New York Walk Book*, 1923)

oil that was ever *Indian* seems to never lose all of that impress. On the Island of Islands, borne down at one end by the world's biggest burden of steel and stone and pressure of haste and material gain, the primitive sweep of its further free tip, with the forest trees on the stately ledges, still holds the red man's cave, the beached canoe, the air of the Great Spirit. The magic of the moccasin still makes good medicine. Fortunate we are that in civilization lurks the antidote to civilization— that strain in the blood of us, all of us, of cave man and tree man, nomad and seaman, chopper and digger, fisher and trailer, crying out to this call of the earth, to this tug of free foot, up-and-over, to this clamor for out-and-beyond. Happy are we, in our day, harking back to this call, to be part of an ozone revival that fits the growth of our desire, to see the beginning of a break-away into everybody's out-of-doors, and the happy find of a wide, fair wilderness.

The order and fashion of the revival were somewhat in this wise. Our seniors remember the days of swift expansion, when the sole concern was the building site. "Blast the scenery," said the seventies and proceeded to do it. Railroads and roads and money returns from quarries and lumber had full right of way. Into our towns one came through ugly suburbs into uglier urbs. And then, when hope was least, a messenger of the new-old freedom appeared. The bicycle swung us, a generation now gray-haired, round a wide radius of country roads and gave back to us the calves and the leg gear of our patroon saint, Father Knickerbocker, and with the legs two eyes for environs. When the time came for supplanting tandem tires by a rubber quartette, and a touch of the toe leapt past all two legs could do, the motor radius that swept a circle almost infinitely wide gave a new concept of the country. Still attention was focussed on the roadway, and the new driver saw even less over wheel than over handlebar. Next golf arose, and the well-to-do strolled upon greenswards, ever watching a ball. Then scout training arrived to set the young generation

1

on its feet and to teach it to see what it saw and to care for itself in the open. With it came nature study to fill the woods and fields with life and growth. (Our Old-World citizens brought their outing habits with them.) Last of all the war gave us brief glimpses of the happiness of simple living and to marching multitudes of indoor men the sense of hardy well-being. And now the fashion for walking is upon us—walking, with its leisure to observe the detail of beauty; walking, organized and planned, imparting impetus to safeguard and preserve the best of the countryside; walking, the single simple exercise, at once democratic, open-air, wide-eyed, year-round.

It is amusing to watch New York, which is hardly in other ways hesitant, waken by degrees to the idea that as a center for exercise on foot she may claim variety and advantage and adventure surpassed by few cities. You shall choose your walk along the sweep of the beaches of the Atlantic, or the deep hill bays of Long Island, or the rocky coves of Connecticut; over ridges showing fair silhouettes of the citadels and cathedral of commerce—or where beavers build; on the looped, mile-long bridges that span an estuary—or across a canal lock; above precipices overhanging a mighty river and through noble community forests between lonely peaks and little lakes—or just in lovely common country, rolling and wooded, meadowed and elm-dotted, interlaced with chuckling brooks. To and from these multitudinous footways and campsites transportation is provided with an expedition and diversity possible only to a large city. And last of all the chance at all this will be under the variegated stimulus of our particular climate and around the only great capital that is within easy reach of the second color wonder of the world—Indian summer in steep-hill country.

Truly with the "Englysche Bybels" that antedate King James', we may say:
Blessed of the LORDE is *this* land,
> for the sweetnesse of heven, and of the scee vnderliende;
> for the sprynges;
> for the precious thinges off the Sonne;
> for the sweetnesse of the toppes of the oold mounteynes,
>   and for the daynties of the hillis that last foreuer.

TRAILS AND TRAIL DEVELOPMENT

rails were the first paths in America. The routes of the early Native Americans[1] led from villages and campsites to hunting and fishing grounds, often following streams and crossing mountain ranges through the notches and divides of the rugged terrain. The white settlers adopted these routes for hunting, trading, and military expeditions. But unlike the footpaths of Europe, these American paths were marked by ax blazes on trees. Because these early paths often followed the easiest grades, they were natural routes for the highways and railroads to come.

Early Trails and the Search for Open Space

By the early part of the twentieth century, few of the original Native Americans' paths remained. With the advent of railroads, rural areas became more accessible for the city dweller, and people with leisure time sought out the woods and streams for recreation. However, farmers found these fun-seekers to be a nuisance, and so they often posted their property against trespassing. In response, "clubs" of wealthy businessmen from the cities purchased lakes, ponds, and natural areas, and then closed them off to public use.

Barred from access to open space, those who sought exercise and a chance to enjoy nature followed rural roads. Up to about 1900, these roads provided pleasant walking, to be shared with only an occasional, slow-moving

[1]The term "Native American" is used throughout this book when a specific nation is not known.

horse-drawn vehicle. In the first decade of the twentieth century, with the invasion of the automobile, highway surfaces were improved to meet the demands of auto traffic. Secondary routes were asphalted to extend state and county road systems.

Walkers began searching for safer, more pleasurable routes. With the state park system making publicly owned land more available, walkers retreated to long-abandoned paths and eighteenth century woods roads, which offered delightful strolls through second-growth forest. However, because these routes were originally meant to take people someplace, they often missed the scenic areas. So hiking clubs and individuals began to build their own trails over routes that the Native Americans and settlers would never have thought of using. These routes were selected because they offered a vista, a stroll through a stand of silver beech, or access to a place that had previously been inaccessible or unknown. Deer paths often proved useful because they followed natural terrain and were frequently the easiest routes up a mountain or across a valley.

The New York-New Jersey Trail Conference

As trails began to spread throughout the Hudson Highlands and the Wyanokies, it became evident that planned trail systems would be necessary if hiking areas were to be properly utilized and protected. In 1920, Major William A. Welch, general manager of the Palisades Interstate Park, called together representatives of hiking organizations in New York. Their goal was to plan a network of marked trails that would make the Bear Mountain-Harriman State Parks more accessible to the public. The meeting resulted in an informal federation known as the Palisades Interstate Park Trail Conference. Raymond Torrey, Will Monroe, Meade Dobson, Frank Place, J. Ashton Allis, and their friends planned, cut, and marked what are now the major park trails. The first one to be completed was the 20-mile Ramapo-Dunderberg Trail from Jones Point on the Hudson River to Tuxedo. In 1923, the first section of the Appalachian Trail to be finished was constructed in Bear Mountain Park. That same year, the organization changed its name to the New York-New Jersey Trail Conference, uniting under one banner a number of hiking organizations throughout the metropolitan area.

From its founding, the Trail Conference has been an organization of volunteers. In 1998, this not-for-profit federation of over 85 hiking and outdoors clubs and nearly 9,500 individuals maintains a network of over 1,300 miles of marked trails from the Connecticut border to the Delaware Water Gap. With few exceptions, the trails are for foot traffic only. The Trail Conference's veritable corps of trained volunteers has been both repairing eroded and overused trails and building new trails to standards designed to prevent deteriorating conditions. In 1997, 800 volunteers and 65 clubs devoted over 18,000 hours to trail maintenance. But in spite of the Conference's massive efforts, it is estimated that only 2 to 3 percent of the hiking public knows who takes care of the trails.

The Trail Conference also serves as a unified voice for trail concerns and land protection in New York and New Jersey. While not always recognized as an environmental organization, the Trail Conference has, in fact, over many years, been involved in saving open space. When an issue affects trails, the volunteers and staff of the Trail Conference bring their concerns to the attention of organizations that are geared financially and legally to pursue the task. In other instances, the Trail Conference forms a coalition with its affiliated hiking clubs, governmental and law enforcement agencies, other nonprofit groups, and interested citizens to resolve an issue. Partners on various projects have included the Catskill Center, Highlands Coalition, Mohonk Preserve, National Park Service (NPS), New Jersey Department of Environmental Protection (Division of Parks and Forestry), New York-New Jersey Highlands Regional Study, New York Office of Parks, Recreation and Historic Preservation (Taconic Region), New York Department of Environmental Conservation, Open Space Institute, Palisades Interstate Park Commission, Scenic Hudson, United States Forest Service (USFS), and the Sterling Forest Coalition. The Trail Conference's advocacy work also includes generating position papers, conducting public education activities, and raising funds for direct financial support.

Since its founding, Trail Conference volunteers and its member clubs have worked to extend hiking opportunities to the public and to build trails opening new areas. Although much of the land upon which they have built trails is publicly owned, about 25 percent is not. Hikers have enjoyed some areas only through the kindness of landowners on whose property the trails traversed. Unfortunately, the acquisition of public land progressed slowly. As the population grew, public access to some trails was limited when commercial developers and landowners closed trails due to occasional abuses.

Open Space Preservation

In the 1960s, federal, state, and county governments began seriously acquiring land for public use. About the same time, but on a much smaller scale, The Nature Conservancy, the Audubon Society, and numerous local land trusts and conservancies also embarked on efforts to preserve open space. These acquisitions increased opportunities for outdoor recreation.

New York

Preservation of open space in New York is a result of Environmental Quality Bond Acts, budget line items, and private donations. The 1960 and 1972 bond acts added Highland Lakes, Goose Pond Mountain, the Old Croton Aqueduct, the Rockefeller Preserve, Storm King, and Hook Mountain to the state park system and purchased additional acres for Bear Mountain, Rockland Lakes, Fahnestock, and Taconic parks. The 1986 bond act set aside $250 million to acquire, protect, and improve state forest preserves, environmentally sensitive areas, municipal and urban cultural parks, and historic sites. Additions to the Catskill Forest Preserve were a result of both the 1972 and 1986 bond acts. Unfortunately, voters in 1990 defeated a $1.975 billion bond act that would have authorized $800 million for open space preservation.

In 1992, the state adopted the Statewide Comprehensive Plan, which set up a prioritized list for open space acquisitions. The following year the Environmental Protection Act was passed. It included the Environmental Protection Fund, a dedicated revenue stream for environmental programs which included a land acquisition fund.

New Jersey

Started in 1961, New Jersey's Green Acres program has funded the purchase of 340,000 acres of open space and the development of hundreds of recreational facilities throughout the state through eight bond issues totaling $1.1 billion. Federal grants from the Land and Water Conservation Fund supplemented state monies on a 50-50 basis, allowing both the state and counties to acquire acreage. The 1976 Natural Areas System Act has protected some 24,500 acres in the state, including sections of Allamuchy, High Point, Ramapo Mountain, Wawayanda, and Worthington state parks and forests.

Minnewaska

Just before the stunning Storm King victory over Con Edison in 1980 (see

New York Walk Book, chapter 15, "Storm King"), the Trail Conference helped organize yet another massive grass-roots effort, this time to preserve the Shawangunk Ridge. The fight to save Minnewaska, as it became known, was to prevent the Marriott Corporation from constructing a hotel, condominium complex, and championship golf course. In the process, many miles of trails would have been destroyed and Lake Minnewaska would have been polluted (see *New York Walk Book*, chapter 13, "The Shawangunks").

In 1980, the Marriott Corporation submitted a draft of its Environment Impact Statement. Testimony at public hearings pointed out the recreational value of the area and questioned the adequacy of the proposed water supply. The New York State Department of Environmental Conservation gave conditional approval to the environmental impact statement. However, DEC was taken to court, with the case eventually reaching the New York Court of Appeals. By

1985, the Marriott Corporation, exhausted by seven lawsuits, and having spent over a million dollars without ever having broken ground, gave up their plan. Environmental groups pushed for permanent protection, and the property was acquired by the State of New York and absorbed into Minnewaska State Park Preserve.

Sterling Forest

The fight to save Minnewaska was barely over when the next threat reared its ugly head—the planned development of Sterling Forest by its owner, Sterling Forest Corporation. This 20,000-acre corridor connects New York's Harriman Park with the New Jersey Highlands. All previous land preservation efforts paled in comparison with the fight to prevent Sterling Forest from becoming a city of 35,000 people and 8 million square feet of commercial space. As early as 1930, Raymond Torrey recognized the importance of preserving Sterling Forest, with its spectacular views and its accessibility for urban residents in search of nature and open space. His vision was not to be fulfilled in his lifetime. When the Harriman family offered the land to New York State as a park, the state declined the acquisition. At that time, state officials believed that the land had too many wetlands, that there were insufficient funds for management, and that New York had sufficient parklands for the future. Instead, in 1947, City Investing Company purchased the property, and immediately announced plans for development. Fortunately, the several small communities that sprang up in the valley did not impinge on the forests, which stayed intact.

By 1980, Sterling Forest had become the largest undeveloped forested private land remaining in the New York metropolitan area and had been sold several times. A consortium of European investors began actively pursuing development, which would devastate the valley, destroy the Appalachian Trail viewshed in the area, and threaten the water quality of two million New Jersey residents. In 1988, the Trail Conference and the Appalachian Mountain Club founded the Sterling Forest Coalition to press for Sterling Forest preservation. By 1996, 28 hiking and local grass-roots groups were members. In addition, a Public-Private Partnership to Save Sterling Forest was formed by the Palisades Interstate Park Commission, New York-New Jersey Trail Conference, Passaic River Coalition, Environmental Defense Fund, Regional Plan Association, Scenic Hudson, The Nature Conservancy, Sierra Club, and other regional/national organizations. In 1990, Green Acres and Passaic County took the first bold step and condemned 2,100 acres—the New Jersey section of Sterling Forest.

Since the New York section of 17,500 acres included watershed land which would affect New Jersey drinking water and since the Appalachian Trail was threatened, the effort to obtain federal funding toward the acquisition of Sterling Forest resulted in the fight eventually reaching Congress in 1992.

In 1994, New Jersey Governor Christine Todd Whitman signed a bill authorizing $10 million to purchase Sterling Forest land in New York, but only if New York also funded the purchase. Subsequently, New York Governor George Pataki matched New Jersey's support, and the Lila Acheson and DeWitt Wallace Fund for the Hudson Highlands pledged $5 million. Efforts in Congress were bipartisan in 1995 and 1996, but pitted representatives from the eastern states against the western ones. Conservationists presented a united stand and were prepared to sacrifice Sterling Forest if its purchase were contingent on the sale of federal lands in the mid-west or west.

During the Congressional haggling in the spring of 1996, negotiations with Sterling Forest Corporation resulted in their agreeing to sell 15,280 acres for $55 million. The land included in the sale would protect the Appalachian Trail corridor, much of the New Jersey watershed, and the habitat most critical to wildlife. The orchestration of funding sources to complete this sale was extraordinary. Congress finally appropriated $17.5 million, Governor Pataki authorized an additional $6 million, and the Victoria Foundation gave $1 million. Smaller donations from the private sector, including gifts from school children, totaled $500,000. Finally the sale was assured when, in December 1997, the Doris Duke Charitable Foundation donated the remaining $5 million. Sterling Forest Corporation claimed an interest in developing the remaining 2,220 acres, and efforts continue to protect this portion of Sterling Forest.

Trail Development

Interest in trail development is more than a local issue. A nationwide project, Trails for All Americans, seeks to have trail opportunities within 15 minutes of most Americans' homes or places of work. In 1988, the President's Commission on Americans Outdoors called for the creation of a vast network of hiking and jogging trails, bikeways, and bridle paths. The commission envisioned a nationwide system of trails that would tie this country together with threads of green, linking communities and providing access to the natural world.

The New York metropolitan area already has an extensive hiking trail system in place. A perusal of the tables of contents of earlier editions of the *New York Walk Book* attests to the availability of trails in this area for many years past. What was not always evident was the need for linkages between areas, although two major linkages have existed for years. The Long Path begins on the New Jersey Palisades and extends 300 miles northward past the Catskills toward the Adirondacks, linking Harriman with smaller parks and the Catskills. On its way from Georgia to Maine, the Appalachian Trail links the Kittatinnies, the Jersey Highlands, Harriman-Bear Mountain, Hudson Highlands, Fahnestock, and the South Taconics.

Many counties, cities, and towns are connecting their parks with greenways. Existing linkages include the Patriots' Path in New Jersey and the Paumanok Path on Long Island. More linkages are possible as the Highlands Trail wends its way between the Delaware and Hudson Rivers.

Assistance in Developing Trails

The expertise gained in the 1980s when the Appalachian Trail was moved onto protected woodlands helped fuel interest in other trail projects. Although Trail Conference volunteers work with park officials to build new trails, trails connecting protected open space need another type of assistance. The National Park Service Rivers and Trails Assistance Program (later renamed the NPS Rivers, Trails and Conservation Assistance Program) funded portions of the project to extend the Long Path north to the Adirondacks. The Trail Conference's volunteer corps grew to meet the challenge of building 100 miles of trail, and the Trail Conference began building relationships with local residents, municipalities, and private landowners. The 30-mile Shawangunk Ridge Trail also forged similar relationships on a smaller scale.

Another multi-partner trail project—the Highlands Trail—highlights the natural beauty of the New Jersey and New York Highlands region. Begun in 1992 and funded through grants from the NPS Rivers, Trails and Conservation Assistance Program, this trail will run 150 miles along the Highlands Ridge from the Delaware River to the Hudson River. When complete, the Highlands Trail will be a greenway in New York and New Jersey linking publicly owned open spaces. The threat of development in some areas along the route has spurred the project forward. By the end of 1998, 103 miles of trail were built and open to the public.

Threats to Trails and Trail Lands

Even with increased interest in protecting open space and providing more trails, threats that were never before envisioned now endanger both trails and trail lands. Interaction with other special interest or non-traditional user groups has become critical to solving problems.

Fiscal Threats

By the end of the 1980s, increased demands for reduced taxes resulted in massive cuts in state budgets. Monies were no longer available for land purchases, and funds for park management or maintenance were severely curtailed. As a result, not-for-profit organizations have formed partnerships with the state to ensure open space protection and management. For example, since its origin in 1920, the Trail Conference has supplied volunteer trail maintainers. With the budget cuts, state partners have come to rely on these maintainers even more. In New York, Scenic Hudson Land Trust and Open Space Institute own land, that by agreement, the state will manage until it has funds to purchase it. Fishkill Ridge Conservation Area and Hubbard-Perkins Conservation Area are two examples of land managed in this way. These close relationships allow each partner to specialize in what its staff and volunteers do best and to stretch ever-shrinking budgets.

Children's summer camps have also suffered from the recession. They require open space, but the cost of upkeep is sometimes too great for a not-for-profit organization to justify holding on to the property. In 1994, Open Space Institute succeeded in protecting Clear Lake, a Boy Scout property adjacent to Fahnestock State Park. A portion of the property is open to the public for hiking.

Physical Threats

Without proper education, well-meaning outdoor enthusiasts can love a particular trail or scenic place to death. For example, on a holiday weekend in 1994, a nature sanctuary was overrun with visitors because a newspaper article recommended the place. Even when an area can tolerate many visitors, it cannot accommodate the six-pack of beer and the bonfire that some folks consider a necessary part of their outdoor experience.

Non-hiking user groups instinctively use the vast trail network that exists in the New York-New Jersey region, often not realizing that hikers maintain the trails for other hikers. Bicycles, horses, and motorized vehicles cause damage because the soil and trail design are not suited for anything other than foot traffic. Education and signage are important to ensure that correct users are on the trail and to prevent user conflicts.

The illegal use of motorized and other vehicles on park lands destroys trails that volunteers have labored hard to build. Users of all-terrain vehicles (ATVs) often run through sensitive areas, destroying vegetation and damaging the trails by causing siltation, creating pot-holes, and widening the narrow path that has been built to respect and fit into the natural environment. Their noise further degrades the outdoor experience by destroying the natural tranquility that hikers seek.

Public Education

As part of its effort to promote public interest in hiking and to educate people about available resources and the safe, proper use of the trail system, the Trail Conference publishes maps and guidebooks. The maps cover trails in the Catskills, Bear Mountain-Harriman State Parks, North Jersey, West Hudson, East Hudson, Shawangunks, South Taconics, Hudson Palisades, and the Kittatinnies. Besides the *New Jersey Walk Book* and the *New York Walk Book*, the Trail Conference's publications include the *Guide to the Long Path, Health Hints for Hikers, Hiking Guide to the Delaware Water Gap National Recreation Area, Harriman Trails: A Guide and History, Iron Mine Trails, Scenes and Walks in the Northern Shawangunks*, and others. These books complement the *Walk Books*, providing more detailed information.

To join the New York-New Jersey Trail Conference, order publications, or receive more information, contact the New York-New Jersey Trail Conference, G.P.O. Box 2250, New York, NY 10116; (212) 685-9699; visit the Conference's web site, http://www.nynjtc.org; or send e-mail to nynjtc@aol.com.

SUGGESTIONS FOR HIKERS

f you can walk, you can hike; age is no obstacle. Sometimes, you don't even have to be able to walk to enjoy a trail, as a few trails are now accessible to the handicapped. Whatever your goals, the suggestions presented here should provide enough information to help you start hiking.

A good way to become familiar with hiking trails is to meet and learn from experienced hikers, something easily accomplished by hiking with a club, an organized group, or friends who hike regularly. Hiking clubs abound in New Jersey. For a list of them, send your request, with a self-addressed, stamped envelope, to the New York-New Jersey Trail Conference, P.O. Box 2250, New York, NY 10116.

Whether you hike with a formal club or with a group of friends, you will need a knowledge of the area in which you plan to hike if you want to have a safe and enjoyable outing. Maps, guidebooks, park offices, and experienced hikers can give you valuable information. Good trail maps show a trail's location, distance, topographic features, and contour lines. The guidebooks listed under "Further Reading" provide written descriptions of particular trails. Guidebooks and trail maps, including larger versions of the maps in this book, are available for purchase from the New York-New Jersey Trail Conference. Most camping and outdoors stores, as well as many bookstores, carry trail maps and guides. Trail maps for state, county, and local parks are sometimes available at park entrances, but often lack important details.

Planning Your Hike

Planning a hike is easy if you hike with a club. Most hiking clubs publish a regular schedule that lists and describes their planned hikes. Read the description in the club literature or talk to a member, and pick a hike that suits your abilities and interests. Hikes vary by level of difficulty and type, so choose accordingly.

If you cannot or prefer not to hike with a club, and you are a beginning hiker, go with at least two friends. Choose your route from the trails described in this book or in the books listed in "Further Reading," and bring a trail map along.

Level of Hiking Difficulty

Be realistic about your physical condition and any medical limitations you might have; neither you nor your fellow hikers will enjoy the outing if you are frequently stopping to catch your breath along the trail. Once on the trail, pace yourself. If you haven't been physically active for some time, start slowly. If you are in doubt, consult with your doctor before going on a hike.

On smooth, level ground, your pace may be three to four miles an hour. It takes longer to pick your way over a rocky path. As soon as you are going uphill, the speed of walking slows down. To calculate the amount of time needed, allow 20 minutes per mile, not including rest stops. Measure all the ascents and add one minute for every 20 feet of elevation. Downgrades take about the same time as a level trail, unless very rough and steep.

Types of Hikes

The simplest type of hike is *out and back*, which starts at a trailhead, follows the trail (or a network of trails), and returns by the same route. Often, more than one trail begins at a trailhead, so it is possible to go out on one trail and return on another trail, forming a *loop hike*. Hikers can take a *partial loop hike* by retracing their original route for only a portion of the trip. A *shuttle hike* requires planning and, depending upon the number of people hiking, two or more cars. On a shuttle hike, hikers meet at one trailhead in at least two cars. Everyone carpools (or "shuttles") to the other end of the hike—the trailhead where the hike will begin. At least one car is left at the first trailhead, which is the spot where you and your party will finish hiking. Public transportation, if available, may be used to shuttle hikers to the beginning of the hike.

Leading a Hike

Even when experienced hikers are going out with a few friends, one person should assume the role of hike leader, and the other members of the party should understand and respect that role. Like the captain of a ship, a hike leader makes the final decisions but should consider the opinions of the crew.

Every captain needs a first mate. On a hike, that role is fulfilled by the *sweep*, who should be a known strong hiker, who brings up the rear and remains at the back of the group at all times, to make sure that no one is left behind. The leader might assign a different person to be the sweep as various junctions are reached.

If you are leading a hike, consult the appropriate maps and guidebooks before leaving home to determine a place and route consistent with the time available and the interests and strength of the group. Leaders should scout the hike—that is, go on the hike themselves—before leading a group, in order to gain an accurate estimate of driving time to the trailhead, availability of park-ing, and actual hiking time. It is very important to consider the available hours of daylight so that the group will be off the trail before sundown. When estimating hiking time, leaders should consider the hike distance, level of difficulty, and time needed for rest stops (including a lunch break), and perhaps for photography and nature study, and then should allow some additional time (at least an hour) in the event of an unforeseen problem on the trail. A good hike leader plans alternate routes before starting, noting routes that may be used to shorten the hike in case of storm, illness, accident, or an overambitious hike plan.

The size of a hiking group should not exceed 25 people for day hikes. It is difficult for one leader to manage more people than that, and travel is considerably slower with a larger group. If the group has more than 25 people, it is a good idea to find another leader and split into two groups. This second group can hike the route in the opposite direction or start an hour later. In environmentally sensitive areas, such as mountain tops or wet areas, the second group should take an entirely different route.

Before starting the hike, the leader should explain the *rules of the road* (regarding pace, staying with the group, rest stops, smoking, littering, and the like), where the hike is going, and the approximate time of arrival at various junctions. Leaders should also check that the hikers are prepared with enough food and water, rain gear, proper footwear, etc. While on the hike, leaders need to stop frequently enough so that no one lags too far behind. Hike leaders have the responsibility of making sure that the group respects the trail and remains safe. If you plan to lead a hike, take your responsibility seriously!

Safety and Comfort

While the hike leader should look out for the group, individual safety and comfort are primarily the responsibilities of the individual hiker. You can do many things to make sure that your hike proceeds without incident. Begin by making sure that your maps, guidebooks, and equipment are up to date and in good condition.

Hiking Alone

Hiking alone is generally discouraged, especially for those who have not had any trail experience. Even an experienced hiker can have problems, such as an accident. A group of at least three hikers is advisable, because in case of injury, one person can stay with the injured hiker while the third person goes for help.

Whether you are hiking alone or with someone else, always let someone know where you will be hiking and when you plan to return. Remember to check in upon your return. If there is a register book at the trailhead where you begin, make sure to sign your name and starting time. Even experienced hikers have gotten lost on trails that are heavily traveled.

First Aid

For a one-day hike, carry Band-Aids®, an antiseptic for cuts and scratches, moleskin for blisters, and tweezers to remove splinters and ticks. Put the moleskin on irritated spots before a blister forms. Other useful items are an Ace® bandage with clips, gauze pads, an eye cup, antibiotic ointment, adhesive tape, safety pins, and aspirin. Carry these items, plus a pencil and paper, in a lightweight metal box or waterproof case, in your pack.

Learn to recognize the symptoms of hypothermia and heat stroke. These serious problems sneak up on their victims and can be fatal. Hypothermia occurs when the body loses more heat than it can generate, and the body temperature drops. The symptoms of hypothermia include shivering, difficulty using hands, stumbling, odd behavior, losing articles of clothing, speech deficiency, blurred thinking, and amnesia. In the late stages, the shivering is replaced by muscle rigidity, stupor, and drowsiness. In heat stroke, also known as sun stroke, the body temperature rises to over 105 degrees Fahrenheit, and the pulse rate can soar to over 160, possibly followed by convulsions and vomiting. For more details on hypothermia, heat stroke, and other medical emergencies on the trail, refer to books listed in "Further Reading." Even better, take a first aid course. Contact your local Red Cross chapter for information on courses given locally.

Waste Disposal and Sanitation
Carry toilet paper in a plastic bag. Use permanent toilet facilities if they exist in the vicinity where you are hiking. Otherwise, bury waste 6 inches deep, at least 200 feet away from any stream or lake, and at least 50 feet from the trail. Pack out the used toilet paper.

Hunting Season
Since many area parks have hunting season in the late fall, inquire about the dates of the season for any area in which you plan to hike. Park offices can give you hunting schedules, and the *Trail Walker*, published by the New York-New Jersey Trail Conference, prints a hunting schedule in its September/October issue. If you want to hike during hunting season, hike in areas where hunting is prohibited. Wearing blaze orange in areas where hunting is permitted is helpful, but cannot guarantee safety.

Inclement Weather
Inclement weather can be any weather from severe cold to excessive heat, with or without rain or snow, and with or without a thunderstorm—which is dangerous primarily because of lightning. If you are on an exposed ledge or on a mountain peak during a thunderstorm, go to lower, covered ground quickly. If you are on the trail, avoid taking shelter under a lone tree, which will attract lightning.

Wet weather is dangerous to hikers because it can cause hypothermia in the event of exposure. At high altitudes, even during the summer, hikers have lost their lives because they were under-prepared and overexposed. The best way to avoid hypothermia is by carrying the proper clothing in your pack: waterproof rain gear (including a jacket or parka with a hood and rain pants), a wool or pile sweater or shirt, and a polypropylene undergarment for warmth; see the section on "Clothing" (under "Equipment," below).

Winter Hiking
Hiking in winter poses special problems and requires special equipment and clothing, such as crampons or snowshoes. Before you attempt winter hiking, consult some of the books listed under "Further Reading." The first time you

try a winter hike, make sure you are properly equipped, and go with an experienced hiker or, better yet, with an experienced group.

Wild Fruits and Mushrooms
Do not eat any wild plants without positively identifying them. Learn to recognize the common edible berries by hiking with someone who has experience, and by reading some of the publications listed under "Further Reading."

Poison Ivy and Poison Sumac
Poison ivy grows aggressively in all kinds of conditions. On sandy beaches, it is a small shrub, about a foot high. Along stone walls and fences it is a spreading vine, while in the woods it either acts as a ground cover or becomes a climbing vine. It is identified by a group of three green, asymmetrical leaves, which include a short-stemmed middle leaf; often, one edge of a poison ivy leaf is smooth and curved, while the other edge might have one or more serrations. It may bear white or green berries. Avoid contact with all parts of the plant, including the bare vines.

Contact with poison ivy causes a rash which appears from 12 to 48 hours after exposure. The rash is accompanied by intense itching. Secondary infection from contaminated clothing, tools, or animals produces the same reaction. The rash may break out over several days and, contrary to popular opinion, it does not spread, but is the result of the original insult to the skin. Neither your own nor someone else's rash can transmit poison ivy's toxic oil; only exposure to the oil itself will. Over-the-counter medications can help control the itching. If you suspect you have come in contact with poison ivy, wash the affected areas as soon as possible with strong soap, such as laundry detergent or Teknu®.

Poison sumac is a similarly dangerous shrub, found mostly in swampy areas. It has thirteen pointed leaflets, six or more inches in length. It is a rare plant in the east and you will probably not encounter it, especially if you stay on the trail.

Insects
Insect repellent, long sleeves, long pants tucked into your socks, and a hat are the best guards against insects. While DEET (*diethyl M toulamide*) is an effective insect repellent, it can be toxic, especially to infants and children, so it should be used sparingly (30 percent DEET maximum) and only when absolutely necessary.

Ticks are a problem in New Jersey, especially deer ticks, which carry Lyme disease or erlichiosis—serious illnesses. Deer ticks are no bigger than a pinhead, making it difficult to spot them. But the prevalence of ticks in the area should not deter you from hiking if you take proper precautions. Wear long sleeves, tuck long pants into socks, and check for ticks after hiking. As soon as you return home, examine your body thoroughly for ticks, especially in the groin area and armpits. (Ticks gravitate to warm, dark, moist places.) Ticks take several hours to attach themselves. If you are bitten by a tick, take care to remove it slowly with tweezers, so that its mouth part does not remain embedded in the skin. If any part remains in the skin, treat it as a splinter.

If you suspect that you have either Lyme disease or erlichiosis, contact your doctor. Lyme disease symptoms include flu-like symptoms, joint and muscle pain, fatigue, or a bulls-eye rash. Symptoms of erlichiosis include sudden onset of flu-like symptoms, chills, sore throat, high fever, joint and muscle pain, headaches, and low white cell and platelet counts. Both illnesses can be treated with antibiotics, but it is best to catch them as early as possible. Untreated Lyme disease can become a disabling chronic condition. Pamphlets on this disease are available from your doctor or county health department.

Some people are strongly allergic to bee or wasp stings. If you have had a strong reaction in the past, ask your doctor for instructions.

Snakes

Small snakes, such as the garter snake and ribbon snake, are common in New Jersey. The region's two poisonous snakes, the Eastern Timber rattlesnake and the copperhead, are rarely encountered.

A rattlesnake is recognized by the rattle on its tail. Its markings are not uniform, varying in coloration from yellow or tan to nearly black. When suddenly disturbed, a rattlesnake will rattle and attempt to escape rather than attack.

The copperhead is pale brown, with reddish blotches on its body and a coppery tinge on its head. It is not a vicious snake, preferring to escape rather than to attack. But it is slow-moving and quiet, which increases the chance of an unexpected encounter.

When hiking during the snake season (May to October), be alert, particularly when climbing rock ledges and over logs. Look before placing your hand on an overhead ledge for support. If you are bitten, do not panic; note the size and distinguishing marks of the snake. Wrap the bite tightly with a bandage, but not so tightly that you cut off circulation; take aspirin; and proceed at a moderate pace to seek prompt medical attention.

Rabies
In the New York metro area since 1990, rabies has been endemic to wild animals, particularly skunks and raccoons. Do not attempt to feed any wild animal. Stay well clear of any animal acting strangely or a nocturnal animal that is out prowling around in broad daylight. Do not touch any dead animals, as you can contract rabies from a dead animal. Rabies is fatal if not treated promptly. If bitten by any animal, leave the trail and see a doctor immediately.

Bears
While brown bears (grizzlies) are not found in New Jersey's hiking areas, their smaller relative—black bears—have become very prevalent in northern New Jersey. They are more dangerous to your food than to you, and hence are more of a problem for backpackers than for day-hikers. Do not make any attempt to feed them. If you are lucky enough to see one, do not approach the bear. Instead, make lots of noise and move slowly but deliberately in the opposite direction.

Equipment
If you are a new hiker, try using the gear and equipment that you already own as much as possible, until you see what other hikers use, have heard their opinion, and have decided what will suit you best. Appropriate footwear is vital (see below). You might also wish to rent or borrow equipment to help you better determine what you should buy.

The principal hiking equipment is adequate footwear, clothing, a hat, rain gear, safety (first-aid) equipment, insect repellent (in season), food or at least a snack, and at least one quart of water—preferably two—for a day hike. Some hikers like to take a camera, binoculars, or flora/fauna identification books. Still others find that a hiking stick gives them added stability. It is also a good idea to carry cash, a check, or a credit card, in case you need them for an emergency upon leaving the trail. For most hikes that are more than one or two miles long, you will need a pack to carry your gear comfortably. You want to travel light, but not at the cost of being hungry, thirsty, or uncomfortable. Remember, you are supposed to be enjoying yourself.

Equipment
Form personal checklists of equipment that you normally take on various types

of hikes. For example, you may have different lists for different weather, different lengths, or different levels of difficulty. Before leaving on a hike, make sure you have all the items on the list. You will soon determine which pieces of gear you use and which are dead weight. However, do not eliminate safety and first-aid equipment just because you were lucky enough not to need it. Experienced hikers know that it is well worth the effort to carry such equipment all the time, even if you use it only one time out of a hundred, rather than fail to have it with you when you really need it.

Footwear

A good pair of boots is important for hiking. At a minimum, hiking boots should provide water resistance, ankle support, and a non-slip sole. For protection against blisters, wear heavy padded socks (such as wool) over light liner socks that can wick away moisture. Make sure your boots fit properly; your feet should have enough room, but they should neither slide forward in the boot, which can bruise the toes, nor should they have too much heel lift. When purchasing boots, try on several different brands; some will fit your feet noticeably better than others. Remember that if boots are uncomfortable in the store, they will be uncomfortable on the trail.

While many lightweight hiking boots are adequate, you will need insulated leather boots for long, rugged hikes and winter hiking. If you purchase leather boots, make sure to break them in before wearing them for a full day of hiking. Wear them for short intervals at home and then on a few short hikes, making sure they are completely comfortable before you wear them on a longer hike.

Clothing

What you wear depends, of course, on the weather and the time of year. In summer, you can wear a tee-shirt and shorts, or you may want lightweight pants and a long shirt to protect yourself against insects, sun, or scratches from vegetation. A hat with a brim provides protection from the sun. A bandanna is also useful to have in warm weather, to absorb perspiration around the head and neck. For all but the shortest hikes in warm weather, you will also need a warm layer to put on when you stop or as evening approaches; even in the summer, the weather can become severe at high altitudes.

Be prepared for wet weather, whatever the season. Wool and some synthetics, such as polypropylene, provide warmth when wet. Cotton is a poor choice because it retains moisture and takes hours to dry once it becomes wet. Down is also a poor choice in wet weather as it also loses its ability to insulate when wet. If there is any chance of rain or very strong winds, you will want a highly water-resistant, wind-resistant parka or perhaps a poncho.

In cold weather, layering is especially important. Wear your hiking clothes in several thin (rather than fewer heavy) layers. Begin with a light garment next to your skin, such as polypropylene, that will wick away moisture and keep you dry. Add a warm (wool or pile) shirt and/or sweater, depending on the conditions in which you will be hiking. Colder weather may warrant wool pants or long underwear and a long-sleeved wool or synthetic shirt. Do not wear turtlenecks, as they restrict air circulation and increase dampness. Your outer garment should be a waterproof and windproof parka. A hat is essential in cold weather, since you lose most of your body heat through your head. A hat also protects you from the sun (which can be just as dangerous in winter as it is in summer). Other clothing to take in cold weather are wool or synthetic gloves or mittens (mittens retain heat better) and spare dry socks in a water-proof plastic bag.

Do not let your underwear become wet from perspiration. As soon as you feel yourself beginning to perspire, remove a layer (or layers, if needed) of clothing. Put the layer(s) back on when you stop to rest.

Safety Gear
When hiking with a group, share the weight, as not everyone needs everything. Everyone should have a first-aid kit, flashlight, map, and compass. For a compass to be of any use, you must know how to use it. Several books listed under "Further Reading" cover map and compass use. Additional safety items include cigarette lighter, jackknife, personal medications, safety pins, duct tape (wrapped around your water bottle), and a space blanket—an emergency blanket made from aluminized Mylar film, available in camping and outdoors stores.

Food
Take compact, nonperishable, lightweight foods on a hike. A brown-bag lunch might include one or two sandwiches, chips or pretzels, an apple or orange, and a candy bar. Many people fare better snacking continually through the day, rather than having one large meal. Fresh and dried fruit, raw vegetables, trail mix, granola bars, nuts, chocolate, and hard candy are all good snacks. Small children, in particular, run out of energy easily and need frequent refueling.

Water
The importance of taking sufficient water on a hike cannot be overemphasized.

Most people need one or two quarts of water, more in hot weather or on a very long hike. Do not wait until you are thirsty to drink. Make sure you take frequent sips of water as you hike, to prevent dehydration.

For day hikes, bring your own water in a plastic bottle, such as bottled water purchased from a store. Fill a Nalgene® bottle (available from camping supply stores) with tap water from home. Water filters eliminate the need to carry a lot of water, but the good ones are fairly expensive. Do not drink directly from springs, streams, or ponds, as they may be polluted with *Giardia* or coliform bacteria. Do not depend upon finding a reliable water supply at shelters or along the trails.

Pack (Knapsack)

A pack should be large enough to carry your extra garments, lunch, water bottle(s), safety gear, and insect repellent comfortably. A pack that is jammed tight will not be comfortable to carry, and will feel heavier than it actually is.

On the Trail

Hiking is just like walking—you put one foot in front of the other. Most hikers develop a steady rhythm that they can comfortably keep up for the entire hike. Of course, rough terrain can defeat that rhythm. Your speed will vary as the terrain varies and as you change the length of your stride—shorter going uphill or on a rough surface, longer going downhill or on a smooth surface. In rocky areas, be careful about your foot placement, and do not trust a rock or a log to remain still when you put your weight on it, particularly going downhill. A log can easily roll, and lichen or moss on rocks can be deceptively slippery.

Hiking downhill is harder on your knees because of the additional weight dropped on the joint. Do not slam your foot down on the ground; take each step gently and deliberately, with a bent knee, to lessen the pounding on the joint.

Stop and rest periodically—about 5 to 10 minutes each hour. At lunchtime, take off your boots and air out your feet if it is not too cold. Stop at trail junctions if you are traveling in a group and let everyone catch up before proceeding.

Blazes and Cairns

Members of the New York-New Jersey Trail Conference volunteer to be responsible for marking and maintaining over 1,300 miles of trails in the metropolitan area. The trails are marked with either painted blazes or plastic or metal tags.

These blazes communicate various messages. Two blazes, with one painted higher than the other, indicate a change in direction; the top blaze indicates the direction of the turn. Three blazes painted as the three points of a triangle indicate a trail's end or beginning. Each trail is blazed in its own individual color or shape to distinguish it from other trails that it crosses. The trail descriptions in this book indicate the color or shape of each trail's blaze. Where a paint blaze is not practical (for example, above treeline), watch instead for a pile of stones—called a *cairn*—purposely placed to lead you to the next step on the trail.

When you are hiking, you should always be able to see the next blaze in front of you, unless you are on a trail with little chance of making an error.

Lost—You or the Trail?
If you can't find a blaze in front of you, turn around and see if you can spot one going the other way. If you can, use its placement and direction to try and find the next blaze in front of you. If you can't, you should stop, look around, then go back to the last blaze or cairn that you saw. If no blaze or cairn is in sight, look at the ground for a trace of the path. Perhaps you missed a turn in the trail. If no trail is visible, stop and relax. Think about where you have been. Look at your map. Do not wander—you will most likely go in a circle. Three of anything—a shout, whistle, or flash of light—is a call for help. If you are with a group or have recently seen other hikers, signal every few minutes while you wait for your absence to be noted, and for someone to come to your aid.

While waiting for help, begin planning what you will do next. With your map, choose the most direct route out to the nearest road or known trail, based on your best estimation of where you are. Note where north is on the map and correct your bearing for magnetic declination—generally about 12 degrees west of true north in New Jersey. Use your compass to follow the route that you select. In most places, following any stream downhill is a good route. If darkness falls, stay put and keep warm with those extra garments in your pack and possibly with a fire, *but note the following precautions:* build the fire in front of a rock, because its heat will be increased by reflection, having first made sure that you have cleared the ground down to mineral soil. Be careful not to let the fire spread.

Taking Care of the Trails and Woodlands
When you are on the trail, complying with the following hiking practices will be a courtesy to your fellow hikers and lessen your impact on the environment.

Hiker Etiquette

Do not pick flowers or collect rocks or artifacts—leave them there for other hikers to enjoy. Hike quietly! Loud noises disturb the wild animals living near the trails, as well as your fellow hikers, many of whom are on the trail to observe the wildlife and enjoy the tranquility of the woods. Use existing trails, staying in the middle of the path, not on the edge. The trails are frequently placed to protect nearby sensitive or rare vegetation. Shortcutting on switchbacks causes erosion to the area. Not everyone likes dogs, so if you hike with them, keep them under control on a leash. If your dog defecates on or near the trail, bury the waste farther away or pack it out. When hiking with a group, walk single-file except on wide woods roads. Let muddy trails dry out before you use them. If you encounter a wet or muddy spot, walk through it, getting your feet wet, rather than widening the trail at the edges.

Litter

The conscientious hiker's motto is "Leave nothing but footprints." Whatever you carry into the woods, you can carry it out. Do not attempt to burn or bury refuse. Leave the trail, lunch stop, and campsite as if no one had been there. Bring an extra plastic bag along for carrying out your refuse. Help keep the trails the way you would like to find them by picking up litter left by inconsiderate trail users.

Smoking

Leave your cigarettes home when you go hiking, but if you must smoke, do it only when you stop for a break—never when you are moving along the trail. Take along a plastic bag or small metal container to carry out used matches and cigarette butts, and always make sure they are completely out.

Multi-Use Trails

Some trails mentioned in this book are multi-use trails, which means they may be shared with other users such as cyclists, horseback riders, in-line skaters, and, in season, cross-country skiers or snowshoers. People in wheelchairs, even motorized ones, are considered to be on foot. No other type of motorized vehicle, however, should be on a trail. If you encounter an ATV on the trail, take down the license number and report it to the park police.

On trails used by horseback riders, cyclists, and pedestrians, the common practice is for bicycles to yield to pedestrians, and both bicycles and pedestrians to yield to horses. On ski trails, hikers should stay out of the ski track, particularly in areas where there is a machine-set track. The footprint left in the snow by a hiker is dangerous to the skier.

Fires

On day hikes, you should have no need for a fire at all. Backpackers should cook on a backpacker's stove. The only plausible reason for building a fire is for warmth in the event you become lost and cold, and are dealing with emergency bivouac conditions.

Trail Problems

Report trail problems—such as permanent wet spots, missing blazes, and trees blocking the trail—to the New York-New Jersey Trail Conference. Their volunteers maintain most of the trails in the area, and the Trail Conference knows who maintains the remainder of the trails. If you hike often, obtain a supply of trail report cards from the Trail Conference, which you can use to keep a record of trail problems. The sooner you report problems, the sooner they will be fixed.

Do not be a phantom maintainer—that is, do not do the maintainer's work of clearing and blazing the trail. The assigned maintainer will not mind if you pick up small amounts of litter or throw an occasional small branch off the trail, but for more serious problems, make sure to contact the Trail Conference. If you want to maintain a trail, become a Trail Conference member, and let them know of your interest in trail work. A volunteer will assign you to maintain a trail or have a trail crew contact you. Trail crews are Trail Conference members who go out regularly to repair trails in a specific area. By maintaining trails with other hikers, you will learn the correct trail maintenance skills.

Private Property

Hiking trails are not always on public land. They sometimes cross private land, with the owner's permission. When hiking on private property, stay on the trail, leave no litter, and build no fires, so that the landowner will continue to allow the public access.

Park Closings

When the woods are dangerously dry from lack of rain, parks and public areas may be closed to hikers. The New York-New Jersey Trail Conference urges complete cooperation with the public authorities who make these decisions. When the park lands are closed, stay out of the woods, and request others to do likewise.

Overnight Backpacking Trips

Some parks permit overnight backpacking. However, before you go, check with the park concerning their regulations. Adhere to the group size restrictions. Many areas restrict group sizes to ten or fewer, a good rule even if there is no official restriction. If your group is larger, consider staying at two or more distinct campsites in order to lessen the impact on the environment.

PASSAIC FALLS.

THREE

GEOLOGY

ithin a hundred-mile radius of Manhattan, there is as diverse a landscape as can be found anywhere in this country. North from the Battery, staying east of the Hudson through Westchester and on to Connecticut, are the southern reaches of rocky New England terrain. West of the Palisades is the expanse of the Newark Basin. Beyond it lie long, sinuous ridges and valleys running northeast into New York State. Still farther west stretches the Appalachian Plateau, taking in the Poconos and their more steeply eroded cousins to the north, the Catskills. Sandy coastal plains traverse the shores of Long Island and New Jersey. Each of these five distinct physiographic provinces offers its own rewards for hikers.

Distinct though they are, the provinces share a common heritage in the inexorable processes that continue to change the surface of the earth. At the root of all these forces is plate tectonics, which depicts the earth as a hot, somewhat plastic ball with a brittle skin. The interior behaves something like a pot of boiling water, convecting in a rolling motion, and the less dense skin—the continental plates—tends to follow along, floating on the mantle beneath. Where all of this material rises, it breaks up; where it falls, it is compressed or pushed down into the mantle. The junctions of colliding plates are often marked by the formation of mountain ridges, island chains, or deep trenches. These movements take place over virtually incomprehensible eons.

The current general shape of the North American continent dates from the early Cenozoic Era. Most of the locally familiar land forms predate that. The New York region has been subjected to the breakup, collision, and again the breakup of plates, coupled with the unending forces of erosion that make the surface of the earth smoother, in proportion to its size, than an eggshell. The region has also seen volcanism, *orogeny* (mountain building), deposition of sediments, *metamorphism* (heating and compression), and occasional submergence beneath advancing seas. On the surface, immense sheets of ice have periodically bulldozed, scarred, and generally rearranged the land.

Geologists measure time in eras, periods, and epochs. The absolute times, in years, changes as more is learned about fossil and radioactivity dating. Table 1 indicates how many million of years have elapsed since the beginning of each era, period, or epoch as of 1995. For example, earlier editions of the *New York Walk Book* had the Cambrian beginning 600 million years ago versus the 1995 estimate of 570 million years ago.

TABLE 1

Era, Period, or Epoch	Million Years Ago (to 1995)	Era, Period, or Epoch	Million Years Ago (to 1995)
Cenozoic Era		Paleozoic Era	
Pleistocene	1.6	Permian	286
Pliocene	5.3	Pennsylvanian	320
Miocene	23.7	Mississippian	360
Oligocene	36.6	Devonian	408
Eocene	57.8	Silurian	438
Paleocene	66.4	Ordovician	505
		Cambrian	570
Mesozoic Era			
Cretaceous	144	Precambrian Era	4,500
Jurassic	208		
Triassic	245		

The New England Uplands offer hikers rich visual evidence of the forces that have shaped the earth. Two spurs of this complicated, broken terrain extend into the New York area. The Manhattan Prong underlies Westchester, the Bronx, and Manhattan before ending in the northern tip of Staten Island, while the Reading Prong gives the Hudson and New Jersey Highlands their character as it courses southwest into Pennsylvania. Both prongs present evidence of

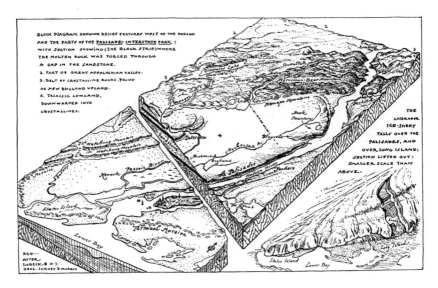

how glaciers, which receded a "mere" ten thousand years ago, left their traces on the oldest rocks visible in the region.

The Highlands are the roots of mountains formed in the middle Proterozoic Epoch of the Precambrian Era, largely from sediments deposited by ancient seas. As they accumulated to a thickness of several miles, they compressed and heated until they metamorphosed into gneiss, marble, and mica-rich schist. These rocks, along with diorite that intruded as magma, are the oldest in the area. Associated with this Highlands Complex is a medium-grained, gray granite, which may be, unlike most, metamorphic in origin. This "Canada Hill granite phase" shows clearly on Anthony's Nose, just east of the Bear Mountain Bridge. Another granite, the igneous rock of Storm King, is highly resistant to erosion and caps the crests of prominent ridges in the Highlands such as Bear Mountain, Dunderberg, and West Mountain.

Even as the mountains rose, during the Grenville Orogeny in the Precambrian Era, erosion gnawed at their flanks, limiting their height to about 15,000 feet and leaving enormous deposits of sediments to the west. By the Cambrian Period, little was left but a flat land of resistant rock. In the late Ordovician Period, the Taconic Orogeny, interpreted as the result of a collision of continental plates, another episode of uplifting and folding began, leaving the Highlands and Taconics in their present position. What was once an eastern

Oscawana Lake : Goose Rocks, glacial boulders wrenched from the surrounding mountains

version of the Rocky Mountains had now become a tortuously folded region with summits no higher than 1,300 feet.

The views from the top of one of these rises is a landscape of rounded knobs and ridges—the result of simple weathering, age upon age of wind and water, freeze and thaw, which reduces the mightiest peaks. Still more of this rounding is the work of waves of Pleistocene glaciers, whose handiwork is visible everywhere in the Highlands. Moving sheets of ice thousands of feet thick scraped their way across the area as they advanced south-southeast. In the process, they abraded north slopes with debris transported from the north, and pried and plucked rocks from south slopes. Called *roches moutonnées* (sheepbacks), these smooth outcrops with rugged south sides are common in the Highlands.

The glaciers also transported large boulders, called *erratics* because they are often of a different composition from the ground upon which they now rest. Sandstone erratics brought 35 miles from Schunemunk Mountain are common in the Highlands. Likewise, chunks of the Highlands appear on the Palisades, and blocks of the Palisades surface in Brooklyn. Finer debris from all these places and points north color the sands of Coney Island. In Harriman Park, erratics dot Hogencamp Mountain, among others. Occasionally, erratics, such as Hippo Rock on Stockbridge Mountain, were propped at odd angles or balanced on smaller rocks and have become popular landmarks for hikers.

Frequently, accumulations of glacial debris, or *drift*, rode to the valley bottoms on torrents of meltwater and piled up in irregular hillocks, or *kames*. The same water settled into shallow glacial lakes throughout the region. Lakes by nature are fleeting phenomena; flowing water tends to down cut their outlets and drain them, turning them into swamps. Patches of valley floor covered in willow are likely the sites of former lakes. Occasionally, the old outlets have been dammed and the lakes re-created, as in the Seven Lakes area of Harriman Park in the 1920s and 1930s.

Subtle footprints of the glaciers exist in the striations and gouges that marked many of the region's exposed rocks as drift ground into them. More pronounced pits and furrows, however, are usually the work of weathering forces. One common feature of the Highlands that is partly glacial in origin is exfoliation, the leaf-like flaking of rock as it uplifts. Much of this uplift has its roots in mountain-building forces, but some is the result of the off-loading of the great ice sheet. Bear Mountain's summit is a good place to see this rounding process at work.

As the majestic Hudson River slices through the Highlands, it illustrates yet another effect of the Pleistocene Era. Ice speeding up as it cut through the narrow Hudson Gorge cut the river channel well below sea level. Thus, the river here is a fjord, the only one on the east coast south of Maine.

The Manhattan Prong of the New England Uplands is a generally younger and less hilly terrain than the Highlands. The oldest rock in the prong, the tough, crystalline Fordham gneiss, dates anywhere from Cambrian to the middle Proterozoic Epoch of the Precambrian Era. Overlying this layer is the glittery mica schist familiar to anyone who has visited Central Park, and the softer Inwood marble. Both date from about the Cambrian–Ordovician boundary. Contact between the two is visible on the Manhattan shore of Spuyten Duyvil. In Westchester and Putnam counties, all three types are complexly folded together.

The Manhattan skyline in the midtown and Wall Street areas reflects in striking profile where the skyscrapers rest on this solid bedrock. In the area in between, which includes Chinatown and Greenwich Village, the bedrock dips too low to anchor the foundations. The tip of the prong continues on to include Clove Lakes Park, LaTourette Park, and other sections traversed by the Staten Island Greenbelt Trail. Prominent here is the greenish serpentinite, visible in Clove Lakes Park and on Forest Avenue. Along with the salt-and-pepper

Harrison diorite of the Bronx and the more northerly Hartland schist, they are the product of the collision of continental plates at the time of the Taconic Orogeny. At that time, an island arc of volcanic origin, analogous to the modern Aleutians, slammed into the East Coast, burying the region that is now the Manhattan Prong, creating igneous intrusions, and metamorphosing some formations. Thus, a portion of the prong is younger rock welded to older types by tectonic forces. Near the tip of the prong, the serpentinite is buried under the terminal Harbor Hill Moraine, the limit of the last advance of the great Wisconsin Ice Sheet. This glacial dumping ground reaches 410 feet above sea level at Todt Hill on Staten Island.

The Ridge and Valley Province constitutes the great Appalachian cordillera (a system of mountain ranges, often with a number of loosely parallel chains) that runs northeast to Newfoundland and southwest to Alabama. In this area, its two prominent features are the Great Valley, extending from the Hudson and Wallkill watersheds to the Shenandoah Valley, and a long, narrow ridge the Lenni Lenape called "Endless Mountain." The latter is now called Shawangunk Mountain in New York, Kittatinny in New Jersey, and Blue and Tuscarora mountains in Pennsylvania.

The Great Valley contains, from the bottom up, layers of sandstone, limestone and dolomite, siltstone, and claystone, all deposited over many millions of years in the Cambrian–Ordovician Period by intruding seas. The bottom layer slightly metamorphosed into quartzite; alongside Kittatinny Mountain, the top layer changed into the largest deposit of gray slate in the country, the Martinsburg formation. Low, steep-sided kames dot the valley.

The rocks of Kittatinny and Shawangunk were deposited atop the valley claystone around the time of the Taconic Orogeny. Their strikingly white quartzite originally consisted of sandstones and conglomerates, which were partially marine sediments and partially the erosional waste of the ancestral Taconics. Called the Queenston Delta, the rubble sloped to the west much in the way the Great Plains now slope to the east from the Rockies, and gradually filled in a shallow western sea that had left limestone deposits. As the mountains wore

down, the rivers that ate at them flowed at a shallower angle, and so were able to carry only finer muds and silts, which formed the darker top layer of the deposits. Orogenic forces during the Acadian Orogeny, in the late Devonian Epoch, folded and faulted the Ridge and Valley Province even as the sediments accumulated. Differential erosion between soft limestones and shales and the more resistant layers created the parallel ridges that mark the region.

One of the best places to observe the features of the province is the Delaware Water Gap, one of the narrowest segments of this mountain system. The gap itself demonstrates the power of the Delaware River as it cut through the gradually uplifting terrain. The cleft was made long before the last ice sheets receded through here about seventeen thousand years ago. Large talus blocks of sandstone and conglomerate on Kittatinny's southeast side overlie Martinsburg slate, which is visible in outcrops along US 46 to the south. East of the gap on I-80, a scenic overlook offers a view of the broad valley and the "endless" mountain.

Two peculiarities of the Ridge and Valley Province are Schunemunk and Bellvale mountains, whose resistant caps of sandstone and conglomerate are more related to the Catskills, at least 20 miles distant, than they are to the surrounding ridges. Though their origin is uncertain, they seem likely to be extensions of the plateau country that lies north and west; whether the plateau once reached even beyond these points is a matter of conjecture.

The Appalachian Plateau itself presents a somewhat less complicated geological history. It was formed from a combination of sediments eroded out of mountains to the east and others deposited by seas to the west in Devonian time. Although at first glance they may seem to be different, the Poconos, Catskills, and much of Central New York are products of the same deposition. The plateau was gently westward-sloping terrain that rose to as much as 4,000 feet above sea level without being radically folded during the ancient mountain-building episodes. Thus, the Poconos and Catskills are not mountains in a strict geological sense. What gave the province the relief it now exhibits was the relentless power of streams carving deep, V-shaped valleys into the plateau.

The Poconos, in particular, retain the aspect of plateau country. From north-bound I-380 or any high overlook, the evenness of the highest elevations becomes apparent. Interspersed with these "mountains" are relatively narrow streambeds. In the Catskills, on the other hand, streams ran their courses through greater thicknesses of sediment; their valleys widened with age and eroded toward the water's source, leaving fractions of the plateau isolated as high peaks. Slide, Thomas Cole, Blackhead, and all the other summits here are what is left of the plateau. A topographical map of the Catskills gives an "aerial view" that makes it easier to understand the extent and direction of these forces.

Glaciation and weathering have helped shape the Catskills into the fabled land of Rip Van Winkle. There is evidence of this in the rounded summits, the talus slopes, the telltale grooves and gouges. Almost any wooded hillside will tell you that subtle changes still occur. Curved tree trunks bending skyward show that in their lifetime the soil has crept downhill, seeking the valley bottom. In ages to come, the plateau will be level again.

After all the orogenic and depositional forces ended, a rifting process—begun when the African continent began to split away from North America, to which it had been welded for over 100 million years—formed the Newark Basin in the Jurassic Period. The floor of the basin is a large block of undeformed sandstones and shales that faulted at its eastern and western edges and tilted slightly downward to the west. Similar fault-block basins are found near Gettysburg, Pennsylvania, and Southbury, Connecticut, and in the Connecticut River Valley. Its northwestern boundary runs roughly from Haverstraw southwest through Suffern and Morristown, and on into Pennsylvania. Called the Ramapo-Canopus Fault, the western side formed a scarp a few thousand feet higher than the eastern expanse; as it eroded, the higher block filled the regions below it with sediments.

As the basin widened, molten rock intruded through cracks in the floor parallel to the Ramapo Fault. The Watchungs and Hook Mountain were formed of fine-grained black basalt that poured out upon the surface. The Palisades—the best known geologic feature in the metropolitan area—intruded in thicknesses up to 1,000 feet, in a line extending from Haverstraw to Staten Island. Unlike the Watchungs, magma never reached the surface while the Palisades were forming. Instead, a subterranean sill cooled and crystallized more slowly into coarser diabase, the columnar rock so prominent in the cliffs along the Hudson. Uplift and weathering then exposed the sill. The freezing and expansion of water seeping into the cliffs has broken the diabase into large blocks that litter the foot of the Palisades. These slopes resemble giant stairs. Deriving its name from *trappa* (Swedish for stairs), traprock has long been quarried in the Palisades, and crushed for industrial uses. The diabase was used extensively in the late nineteenth century as "Belgian bluestone" to pave much of lower Manhattan. The creation of the Palisades Interstate Park Commission helped end quarrying operations that could have left the cliffs extensively scarred. Another basin resource, red sandstone, is still visible in the old brownstone houses of Manhattan and Brooklyn.

Hikers will notice frequent erratics and glacial scarring atop the Palisades. In this province, the Wisconsin Ice Sheet reached as far south as Metuchen and left an arc of terminal moraine that stretched north beyond Morristown before swinging west under what is now I-80. As it receded, the melting ice created Glacial Lake Hackensack, which covered the northern part of the basin west of the Palisades. Today the Meadowlands are its slowly drying vestige.

The Atlantic Coastal Plain, extending from Long Island to Florida, is the youngest of the provinces, having formed out of the unconsolidated sediments of flood plains and river deltas since the late Cretaceous. Abundant plant fossils indicate these nonmarine origins, while sharks' teeth and fragments of marine reptiles suggest periodic invasions of shallow seas. The plain was greatly reduced in width when the sea level rose at the end of the last glacial period. The prepleistocene sediments remain clearly definable throughout the flat expanse of southern New Jersey, where elevations rarely approach 300 feet. Commercial sand and gravel operations, common on the plain, attest to its deltaic origin, and clay deposits figured in a once-thriving pottery industry in New Jersey.

On Long Island, however, much of the original deposition from rivers in New England is buried under two terminal moraines—the Ronkonkoma and the younger Harbor Hill—and the outwash plain created when glacial streams carried sands and silts toward the sea. The island's backbone and eastern forks are all morainal, ending spectacularly in the bluffs of Montauk Point, where rising seas inundated the outwash and brought the surf to the base of the glacial rubble. The same seas invaded a shallow depression that is now Long Island Sound. Many erratics sprinkle the moraine, from huge Shelter Rock in Nassau County to small boulders nestled unobtrusively in quiet corners of the Pine Barrens. Isolated ice blocks left water-filled depressions or kettles such as Lake Ronkonkoma; smaller, dried-out kettles are much less apparent to the eye but are easy to spot on a topographical map of Suffolk County, which will also reveal subtle traces of channels that once bore the ice's runoff seaward.

The coast's numerous barrier beaches and sandspits are the ever-shifting manifestations of littoral drift, the transportation of sand on prevailing ocean currents. So swift is this action that colonial maps of the Jersey Shore and Long Island bear little resemblance to modern ones. Fire Island and Sandy Hook, for instance, have been reshaped considerably by tugging currents and buffeting storms. Indeed, some strands have grown at a rate approaching a mile every quarter century, by geological standards an incredibly swift pace.

The rapid changes wrought in the fragile dunes contrast markedly with the seeming stability of Highlands bedrock. Change governs the landscape. The phrase "to move at a glacial pace" is used to describe a slow procession of events; but in the unfathomable expanses of time involved in shaping the earth, the glaciers were here but yesterday. Their icy breath still chills the hollows and dells they departed ten thousand years ago. The wind atop a Highlands ridge, the surf along the shore, a rushing brook in spring, and the icy talus of the Palisades illustrate the great forces still at work. We can contemplate with awe the hundreds of millions of years of history beneath our feet as we walk in solitude in this, our speck of time in an ever-old, ever-new world.

FOUR

THE PALISADES

ome unknown early voyager up the Hudson named the cliffs of the lower river the Palisades, probably because the giant pillars of traprock bore a likeness to the palisaded villages of the Native Americans. This unique geological formation begins at the Rahway River in New Jersey, crosses the western edge of Staten Island, continues north along the river into Rockland County, New York, turns inland at Haverstraw Bay, and then ends abruptly at Mount Ivy. The cliffs are most prominent from Edgewater, New Jersey, to Haverstraw, New York, with a brief detour inland at Nyack. The Long Path traverses most of the ridgetop. When combined with the numerous intersecting or nearby trails and byways, it offers many opportunities for circular routes encompassing not only woods and meadows but history and interesting architecture. See the *New York Walk Book* chapter 17, "The Palisades," for information about the New York Palisades.

History

Well-documented Palisades events began on September 13, 1609, when Henry Hudson, sailing on the *Half Moon,* made his second anchorage of the day opposite the present location of Fort Lee, New Jersey. Hudson sailed north on the river as far as the present site of Albany in search of the Northwest Passage, and returned on finding no outlet up the river.

The narrow strip of land between the river and the cliffs from Fort Lee to Alpine was known as "Under the Mountain." It had more inhabitants than all of northern New Jersey save Hackensack. Within this large community of

Ruckmans, where the cliff is 520 feet above the river and 280 feet sheer drop. A slid pillar Dobbs Ferry; the country back of Tarrytown. Sleepy Hollow and Irving's country. Below Forest View Basin terraced farms, there were densely settled areas with names like "Pear Tree," "Pickletown," and "Undercliff." At the beginning of the twentieth century, descendants of the original settlers were still tilling the ground and gathering French pears from tall and ancient trees. These families became rich, thanks to the shallows of the river and the rocks on the shore. The river swarmed with shad in season. The swamp-edged island of Manhattan required docks and bulkheads, and the Palisades offered up the needed building materials in hard blocks of stone ready-shaped for erecting walls, as well as soft stone for constructing houses.

In the days when river steamers burned wood, it was cut on top of the Palisades and pitched down where the water was deep inshore, hence High Gutter Point at the state line. When fireplaces heated houses, wealthy New Yorkers bought sections of land on top of the plateau, each with a convenient spot for throwing down wood. These pitching points had to have a smooth or small-stone slope with a fair landing place below or a cliff edge overhanging the river. If there were huge rocks, logs would wedge or smash; consequently, a wooden chute was built to slide the timbers to shore. One of these spots was at Allison Point.

The Palisades played an integral role during the American Revolution. In 1776, General Hugh Mercer of the Continental Army built Fort Lee so he could retain control of the river. On top of the cliff, a redoubt guarded the sunken ships and chained logs stretching across to Jeffries Hook on the Manhattan side, where the little red lighthouse now stands under the George Washington Bridge. In November 1776, after General George Washington retreated from the Battle of White Plains, he watched from the west shore the British attack on Fort Washington in Manhattan and the subsequent surrender. As General Charles Cornwallis crossed the Hudson River to Alpine with six thousand men, Washington had to order his troops to abandon Fort Lee and all its stores of war material in such haste that the British found kettles on the fires when they arrived.

Geology

The contrast between the red sandstone, in horizontal strata at the bottom of the cliffs, and the gray vertical columns above it, may intrigue the hiker in the Palisades. The bedrock of the Palisades section of the Palisades Interstate Park is of two kinds: sedimentary sandstones and shales, and igneous intrusive basalt. Both were formed during the late Triassic and early Jurassic periods. At that time, as dinosaurs began to dominate the land mass, the Atlantic Ocean basin started to open. Down-dropped fault blocks formed. For some millions of years, sand and mud washed down from surrounding highlands and spread out over wide areas in sedimentary layers thousands of feet thick. Consolidated by pressure and by the deposition of mineral matter that penetrated the porous mass and cemented particles together, these deposits are today the reddish-brown horizontal strata known to geologists as the Newark Series.

After these sedimentary strata were laid down, molten rock was forced upward through rifts and then between sedimentary layers to form a single, prominent sill, the Palisades, about 1,000 feet thick for some 40 miles along the Hudson. As the molten mass cooled underground, contraction fissures broke the sheet into crude vertical columns, often hexagonal or pentagonal in outline. The gradual erosion of the sandstone exposed these contraction joints to the elements. Repeated freezing and thawing caused huge blocks to be pried off and create the talus slopes at the base.

Newark sandstone forms the walls of most of the old Dutch farmhouses in northern New Jersey and Rockland County, as well as the brownstone fronts of many older private homes in Manhattan. The reddish ledges of Newark sandstone are exposed in many places along the Shore Trail. The rock occurs near the river level, but is often hidden behind the talus.

Natural History

Along the narrow strip between the river shore and the cliffs, there are a surprising variety of trees, shrubs, and flowering plants. Up to 1895, there were also 11,000 acres of unbroken forest on the top of the Palisades, providing some of the finest timber in New Jersey. The red oak, which is the state tree of New Jersey, is the most common and fastest-growing species. Other common trees are the black birch, white oak, tulip tree, black oak, chestnut oak, sweet gum, and sugar maple, the state tree of New York. A common understory tree is the flowering dogwood. A fast-growing weed tree from China, tree of heaven (*ailanthus altissima*), grows along the shore in sunny spots.

History of the Palisades Interstate Park

The beginning of the Palisades Interstate Park dates from the time when New York City was slowly aroused to the devastations of the quarrymen blasting along the cliffs for traprock. About the middle of the nineteenth century, much of the loose and easily accessible talus was pushed down to be used as ships'

ballast. The real menace to the Palisades came with the demand for more con-
crete to build skyscrapers and roads. Quarries were opened from Weehawken
to Verdrietige Hook above Nyack. To check this activity, New York and New
Jersey jointly created the Palisades Interstate Park Commission (PIPC) in 1900.
Enabling legislation was pushed in New Jersey by the New Jersey Federation of
Women's Clubs. In New York, Andrew H. Green, founder of the American
Scenic and Historic Preservation Society, worked for the necessary legislation
with the support of Governor Theodore Roosevelt and other conservation-
minded officials. Land was acquired and developed as parkland with all needed
facilities.

In the early days, most of this development was accomplished through
money donated by the commissioners and other interested individuals, with
most of the early protection occurring in New Jersey. Eventually, it was the two
states which provided funds for development projects. Of the many individuals
who contributed generously of time, talents, and money in creating the system
of parks, special recognition must be given to George W. Perkins, Sr., who was
the Commission's first president and the organizing genius of its development.
The story of his leadership should be coupled with the generosity of J. Pierpont
Morgan at a critical time, and other notable gifts of land and funds, both
private and public. As a result, quarrying of the river faces of many mountains
in Rockland County was stopped. Later, the Commission was also charged
with preserving the natural beauty of the lands lying in New York State on the
west side of the Hudson, including the Ramapo Mountains as well as state
park lands in Rockland and Orange counties and those in Sullivan and Ulster
counties outside the Catskill Forest Preserve.

In 1933, John D. Rockefeller, Jr., offered to PIPC certain parcels of land on
top of the Palisades that he had been assembling for some time. He wanted to
preserve the land lying along the top of the Palisades from uses that were in-
consistent with PIPC's ownership and to protect the Palisades themselves. He
also hoped that an adequately wide strip of the land might ultimately be developed as a parkway. At the time, there seemed little likelihood of finding funds
for a parkway, but various lines were explored. In 1935, legislation was passed
that enabled the Commission to accept the deeds to the land offered. Additional properties were donated by the Twombleys and by the trustees of the
estate of W. O. Allison. The parkway, completed to Bear Mountain in 1958, is
a tree-lined, limited-access drive for noncommercial traffic only. Since 1937,
both the New York and New Jersey sections of the Palisades Interstate Park

have been administered by the Palisades Interstate Park Commission under a compact that legally cemented a uniquely successful tradition of cooperation between two states.

PALISADES INTERSTATE PARK

The Palisades Interstate Park encompasses 2,472 acres along the Hudson River from Fort Lee to the New York-New Jersey state line. It is a long narrow park, averaging less than an eighth of a mile wide between the cliff-top and the water; the maximum elevation at the face is 530 feet.

Fishing and crabbing are allowed in the stretch between Ross Dock and Englewood, and from the shore at Alpine. Swimming is prohibited. The park is easily accessible by public transportation. The Red & Tan Lines' 9 and 9A buses run hourly along US 9W to and from the bus terminal at the George Washington Bridge.

Trails in Palisades Interstate Park

Two main trails traverse the length of the Jersey Palisades, the Shore Trail and the Long Path. In addition, at State Line Lookout there are numerous old bridle paths, built in the 1930s, that crisscross that area between the cliffs and the parkway. These paths are now used for walking and, given the proper snow conditions, cross-country skiing. They all intersect the old US 9W roadbed, now serving as the access road to the Lookout and continuing northward to the state line. Several footpaths connect the Shore Trail and the Long Path, and at Englewood and Alpine roads descend to the river, where there is parking. These paths are connected midway by the Henry Hudson Drive, built in 1909, which is closed to walkers.

Long Path   *Length: 12.7 miles Blaze: turquoise*
This major trail runs along the top of the cliffs as it begins its journey to the Mohawk River. See chapter 14, "Long Distance Trails," or the *Guide to the Long Path* for a complete description of the 12.7 miles.

Shore Trail   *Length: 13.5 miles Blaze: white*
With consummate landscape art, the Shore Trail wanders past high monoliths and giant stone staircases from one view to another on a course that is on a par

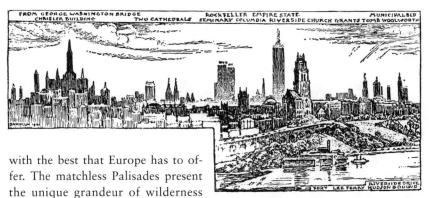

FROM GEORGE WASHINGTON BRIDGE   ROCKEFELLER EMPIRE STATE   MUNICIPALBLD
CHRISLER BUILDING   TWO CATHEDRALS   SEMINARY COLUMBIA RIVERSIDE CHURCH GRANTS TOMB WOOLWORTH

RIVERSIDE DRIVE
FORT LEE FERRY HUDSON BOULVD

with the best that Europe has to offer. The matchless Palisades present the unique grandeur of wilderness within sight of one of the biggest cities in the world. The Shore Trail is mostly a broad and level path, but at Forest View, about 10.5 miles from the start, its character becomes rugged as it weaves up and down among the talus, finally ascending to the cliff-top near the state line.

The trail can be reached via foot or bus across the George Washington Bridge to Bridge Plaza in Fort Lee. From the bus stop, a walk south to the first cross street and a left turn toward the river leads to Hudson Terrace. Here, the hiker should turn right. Soon, the entrance to the Fort Lee Historic Park is on the left. Footpaths lead to views of Manhattan, the Statue of Liberty, and Staten Island. The earthworks of 1776, on the southern tip (Bluff Point), have been recreated. This redoubt guarded the barriers placed in the river to prevent passage by the British. There is a museum on the grounds, whose exhibits explain these historical events. An asphalt path takes interested walkers to the location of the batteries and a close-up view of the bridge. Picnic tables are located nearby, and parking is available.

Returning to the street, the hiker turns left and follows Hudson Terrace downhill to the park entrance and the beginning of the Palisades Shore Trail. It follows the shore with occasional white blazes. Steps lead down to the shore, where hikers can walk north to the boat launching ramp under the bridge. Passing former Hazard and Carpenter beaches, hikers will note the absence of talus at the base of the cliff, the result of the quarrying done here. Carpenters Trail, at 2.0 miles from the Bridge Plaza, is the first of five connectors between the Shore Trail (white) and the Long Path (turquoise). The middle section of the Shore Trail presents some of the finest cliff faces on the Palisades. Just north of the Carpenters Trail, the Shore Trail reaches Ross Dock, where water is available seasonally.

Cleft above Bombay Hook

For more than a mile north above Ross Dock, open groves are arranged as picnic places. Just beyond, at the southern end of the Englewood Boat Basin, where the Englewood Approach Road reaches the shore, the second connector trail to the top leaves to the left. It follows a cascading stream for part of the way, and also is routed along the sidewalk of the access road.

Parking is available at the Englewood Boat Basin, which makes it an ideal starting point for those who come by car. As the path continues north, it crosses picnic grounds at Bloomers Dock, passes Franks Rock, a huge boulder hanging between path and shore, and winds by Undercliff Dock, with its large, well-shaded picnic area on an upper terrace. This whole stretch was the settlement known as "Under the Mountain" in the days before the park was established. Scattered between the small farms were quarries, fishing shacks, and manure and bone factories. South of Undercliff, on the upper level, is a cemetery, a relic of this settlement. The point above is High Tom.

Picnic tables fashioned from fallen rock are found along the way north at Canoe Beach, 1.5 miles north of the boat basin. Just beyond is Powder Dock, with Clinton Point looming above between the trees. After crossing Lost Brook, which flows under the talus, the trail arrives at Lambiers Dock. From the tip of the dock, there is a profile of several headlands as far as Man-in-the-Rock, the northern column of Bombay Hook.

The trail reaches Greenbrook Falls, a trickle in August and an ice mass in January, but impressive when seen from the riverbank after the spring rains. There is much loosened rock here, but the columnar structure is evident south of the brook. About four miles from Englewood, the Shore Trail reaches Huylers Dock, an important transfer point for goods and passengers between the interior of New Jersey and New York City. The third connector trail, the Huylers Landing Trail (red), follows the old road (said to be used by the British under Cornwallis to ascend the cliffs in 1776) up to the Long Path on top.

For the remaining mile to the Alpine Boat Basin, the path wanders up and down the washouts along the river's edge. Beyond a fine growth of laurel is a big boulder called *HayKeePook* (his body). Legend has it that a lovelorn Native American committed suicide here. When the trail reaches the grassy level, the slender pinnacle of Bombay Hook is visible to the north. This highest, most isolated, and most conspicuous pillar of rock along the Palisades curves up 70 feet between two mighty slides.

The Shore Trail soon reaches the Alpine Boat Basin, with parking and picnic facilities. Just beyond is the Blackledge-Kearney House. Originally it was a farm house, then a nineteenth century tavern, and eventually the first park headquarters. In the summer, it is open as a museum. Behind the Blackledge-Kearney House is the fourth connector path, which joins the Long Path at the present Park Headquarters, formerly the Oltman House.

Northward from Alpine, about 9 miles from the start, a wide path goes past hemlocks, a brook, and then Cape Flyaway, where Native American artifacts have been found. Beyond is a fork. Bearing left, the upland path traverses a former picnic ground before returning to the Shore Trail just south of Bombay Hook. The fork to the right leads to Excelsior Dock and on to the grassy expanse at Twombleys Landing, named for the former owner who gave the grounds to the park. Because of the layers of oyster shells found here, this area is presumed to have been a site of permanent Native American camps.

A half-mile farther, beyond the point at which the upland trail rejoins the Shore Trail and near a stand of white birch, hikers have a view of the two vast bastions called Ruckman Point. A little farther north is Indian Head; from here, the best-rendered view of this natural stone sculpture becomes apparent—not a Native American or a patroon, but a Yankee pioneer. Near the former lawn of Forest View Landing, the last connector path, Forest View Trail (blue and white), ascends to the top of the cliff. The upper part has steep steps with high risers. At the top, a left turn on the Long Path brings hikers to a stone castle commemorating the work of the New Jersey Federation of Women's Clubs in securing the first lands of the park. The trail continues west on a footbridge over the parkway to the Alpine Scout Camp and a bus stop on US 9W. Turning right at the top on the Long Path leads to State Line Lookout, with parking.

Forest View is 11.5 miles from Fort Lee. The final two miles of the Shore

Trail contain its most striking scenery—the 500-foot cliffs of Indian Head, the rough talus of the Giant Stairs, and princess trees clinging to the talus. Heading north and upward, hikers will observe some immense blocks of stone shed from the cliffs. The caves and cavities created by these rock masses are homes for raccoons, foxes, rodents, and snakes. The Shore Trail soon reaches the Giant Stairs, a series of traverses over mixed scree and talus alternating with wooded segments. This stretch of rock scrambling is slow and difficult for even the agile hiker.

The Giant Stairs north of Forrest View, opposite Hastings, in the Autumn

Giant Stairs is a mile from Forest View. Descending the "stairs" to the shore, the trail ultimately passes a swampy section that marks the state line. The trail, in addition to the white blaze, has now acquired a lazy crescent one. Double blazes of both types mark the fork where the Shore Trail veers left and begins a switchback ascent to intersect the Long Path (turquoise) just north of High Gutter Point. A left turn on the Long Path leads to State Line Lookout one mile away, while a right turn on the Long Path leads, in half a mile, to US 9W just north of the state line at the entrance to Lamont-Doherty Earth Observatory of Columbia University.

An indistinct path continues straight ahead along the shore and leads to the Italian Garden, with the ruins of colonnades, at the foot of Peanut Leap Falls. Once part of the Lamont estate, it is now a nature preserve. To return to the Long Path directly from the garden, the hiker ascends a path that starts northward from a small patio on the north side of the waterfall. This path parallels the streambed, joining the Long Path just beyond where it fords the stream. Turning left on the Long Path leads past the northern trailhead of the Shore Trail and on to State Line Lookout in 1.2 miles. A right turn leads to US 9W at the state line.

OTHER AREAS NEAR THE PALISADES

Set back from the Palisades are other areas of interest to hikers who enjoy short walks. These areas are large enough to need a few hours to explore, yet small enough to offer a short respite from the bustle of urban life. The diverse habitats and a chance to observe wildlife tempt visitors to return and savor the centers in different seasons.

Flat Rock Brook Nature Center

The 150-acre Flat Rock Brook Nature Center is nestled in a bustling urban area. It was founded in 1973 to protect open space in Englewood and provide environmental education for both children and adults. The 3.5 miles of marked trails take visitors through a stream, wetlands, ponds, wildflower meadows, quarry cliffs, and woodlands. An 800-foot boardwalk loop trail is accessible to the handicapped.

To reach Flat Rock Brook Nature Center, take Route 4 to the Jones Road exit in Englewood. Make a right at the top of the ramp, and continue to the first stop sign. Turn right onto Van Nostrand Avenue, and proceed to the top of the hill, where the visitor center and parking area are located. For more information, contact Flat Rock Brook Nature Center, 443 Van Nostrand Avenue, Englewood, NJ 07631; (201)567-1265.

Lost Brook Preserve and Tenafly Nature Center

Although Lost Brook Preserve and the Tenafly Nature Center are contiguous and share a trail system, they are separate entities. Since they are on an important migratory flyway, there are many opportunities to observe or photograph species that live there or pass through. The Lost Brook Preserve is owned and maintained by the borough of Tenafly. Five miles of trails wind throughout the 330-acre preserve. The Tenafly Nature Center Association operates the Tenafly Nature Center, leasing the land from the borough. There are two miles of trails in 50 acres of woodland.

Public transportation is available to the park via the Red and Tan Lines 9 and 9A buses. From US 9W in Tenafly, go west on East Clinton Avenue. At the next traffic light, turn right onto Engle Street and then turn right onto Hudson Avenue. For more information, contact the Tenafly Nature Center, 313 Hudson Avenue, Tenafly, NJ 07670; (201) 568-6093.

FIVE

EASTERN JERSEY HIGHLANDS

he New Jersey Highlands are rich in both history and scenic beauty. Strategically placed among the thirteen colonies, New Jersey was the focal point of considerable activity during the American Revolution. Located both on the coast and in a direct line between Boston and Philadelphia, New Jersey offered something else besides its strategic location—the iron-laden Highlands. No longer mined in the second half of the twentieth century, the hills now offer other treasures to hikers. Pink and white mountain laurel shimmer on the Wyanokies' sunlit slopes in June. Tiny wildflowers grow among shards of iron, remnants of the area's once-thriving iron industry. Winter snows cling to the hemlocks, firs, and unadorned laurel to create fairytale-like forests. Erratics, evidence of glaciers long receded, are scattered on the hillsides.

Thanks to forward-thinking citizens, the estates of bygone eras have become state and county parks with trail networks. As the acreage of preserved open space has grown, so has number of hiking trails, thus providing greater access to a region that hikers have long treasured.

Geology

The Highlands are shaped by several ranges. The most easterly of these is the Ramapo Mountain Range, which anchors its northeastern section at Tomkins

Cove, New York, on the Hudson River, and crosses into New Jersey at Mahwah, just below Suffern.

As it heads southwest, the range defines a distinctly different geologic province from the Newark Basin farther east. The Ramapo River channels along the Great Border Fault (Ramapo) that separates the metamorphic rock complex of the Ramapos from the Triassic sandstone and shale of the lowlands, out of which rise the diabase intrusions that form the Palisades and the basalt extrusions that form the Watchungs. In general, the Precambrian crystalline rocks of the Ramapos are sharply distinguishable, both by topography and by composition, from those in the Newark Basin. Glaciation of the peaks and lake sediments in the eroded sedimentary blocks have created a terrain in the Ramapos of rugged ridges and gentle valleys.

Most of the area known as the New Jersey Highlands lies beyond the Wanaque River's western shore. Although the Ramapo Mountains to the east also are considered part of the Highlands, the two sections differ geologically as much from one another as the Ramapos do from the Newark Basin.

History

Iron mining and smelting in the Ringwood area began around 1740 with the formation of the Ringwood Company, named after a town in the New Forest of England. The company was organized by colonists of New York City and Newark, who subsequently sold their interests to an English group, the American Iron Company. It was this group that in 1765 brought over Peter Hasenclever, a German, but with English iron-mining and smelting experience. Hasenclever became one of the foremost ironmasters in this country and is credited as the founder of a major industrial enterprise in the Highlands. He brought hundreds of iron miners, charcoal burners, and other specialists from Germany. His operations were extended to Long Pond as well as into the Hudson Highlands and the Mohawk Valley.

Hasenclever introduced the newest English and German methods and greatly improved output at Ringwood. He built a dam on Long Pond to form Greenwood Lake in order to supply blast power for operating the furnaces in that area, which remained in operation from 1766 to 1882. He also dammed Tuxedo Lake so that its outlet, Summit Brook, could flow into Ringwood River to increase the supply of water power for the furnaces at Ringwood Manor.

Difficulties caused by overextension of his business, failure to receive payment from England for his iron, and the general disturbance of international

trade as unrest grew in the colonies led Hasenclever to suffer one of the biggest economic crashes of the time. He was dismissed by his English employers, whom he then sued—but by the time his suit obtained a judgment against them, he had died.

In 1771, Hasenclever's former employers brought over Robert Erskine, a Scottish engineer, to straighten out the iron business at Ringwood and elsewhere. Operating the mines there, Erskine sided with his adopted country when the colonies revolted, and Ringwood as well as Long Pond Ironworks became among the chief munitions works for the Americans. In fact, much of Washington's maneuvering in northern New Jersey after the fall of New York was designed to defend Ringwood and keep it hidden in the forests. The second of the great iron chains across the Hudson, at West Point, was made of metal from the Long Mine near Sterling Lake.

In 1777, Erskine was appointed Surveyor General to the American Army by General Washington and made the first good maps of the Highlands of northern New Jersey and southern New York. He died in 1780, and his remains were placed in a stone vault on the Manor property in a graveyard where more than 150 soldiers of the Revolution are reported to have been buried. George Washington, who was present at the Manor the day Erskine died, returned in 1782 to plant a tree at Erskine's grave. The grave may still be seen on the west shore of Sally's Pond, but the tree was destroyed by lightning in 1912.

Following the Revolution, the Ringwood Ironworks were inactive until 1807 when Martin Ryerson purchased them and operated them successfully. Because of the high grade ore in the mines, the works were purchased in 1853 by Peter Cooper, owner of the Trenton Ironworks, inventor, philanthropist, and founder of Cooper Union for the Advancement of Science in New York City. Abram Stevens Hewitt, Cooper's partner and later son-in law, managed the business and eventually became America's foremost ironmaster of the nineteenth century.

During the Civil War years, the Trenton Ironworks, using Ringwood and Long Pond iron, supplied the Union Army. Following the war, as Cooper, Hewitt & Company, the two men expanded their business interests and, by 1870, purchased other ironworks. Hewitt was involved in politics, serving in Congress for several terms and as mayor of New York City.

Cooper became one of the largest single landowners in New Jersey, with the Ringwood properties consisting of nearly 100,000 acres. Upon Cooper's death in 1884, title to Ringwood Manor passed to his son-in-law, Hewitt.

History of the Parks

In 1936, Abram Hewitt's son Erskine deeded the Ringwood Manor House and 95 surrounding acres to the state of New Jersey. His nephew, Norvin Hewitt Green, gave additional property, bringing the total to 579 acres. He also donated 1,000 acres in the Wyanokies which became the Norvin Green State Forest. The Abram S. Hewitt State Forest, another gift, is west of Greenwood Lake and south of the New York state line.

State, federal, and Bergen County funding has allowed numerous additions to be made to the publicly owned acreage in the Ramapos. In 1964, a 541-acre tract including Shepherd Lake was added. In 1966, a 1,000-acre tract containing Skylands Manor was purchased from Shelton College, and in 1972 the Bear Swamp Lake section was acquired from a vacation home club. In 1976, the estate of the late Clifford F. MacEvoy became Ramapo Mountain State Forest. Next, in 1978, came the purchase of the Green Engineering Camp of Cooper Union, which contained several trails laid out by the former Cooper

Union Hiking Club. The 1981 acquisition of the 540-acre Muscarelle Tract closed the gap between Ringwood State Park and Ramapo Mountain State Forest.

Public enjoyment of the Ramapos was further broadened by state- and county-funded expansion of the Ramapo Valley County Reservation, whose trails provide access to the Ramapos from the east. The 1993 purchase of the Ramapo Land Company property created an almost solid expanse of public land in the Ramapos along the New York border. Boy Scout properties in the area also are instrumental in retaining open space.

Natural History

The forests of the Ramapos are regarded by many naturalists as an intermediate zone between the central hardwood forests, as exemplified by the mixed oak forests of the nearby Palisades to the south and east, and the northern hardwood forests of upstate New York and New England. The Ramapos contain elements of both. On dry, sunny hillsides and ridges, the mixed oak forest predominates, characterized by five species of oak (red, white, black, scarlet, and chestnut) and two hickories (mockernut and pignut). Flowering dogwood flourishes in the understory, and the shrub layer is composed of maple-leaf viburnum, blueberry, huckleberry, mountain laurel, and pink azalea. On the most open, exposed summits, red cedar and pitch pine grow from the cracks in the granite and gneiss.

White pine

In the valleys and on the cooler, more shaded slopes of the Ramapos, however, a more northern type of forest takes over. Sugar maple, beech, hemlock, yellow and black birch, and some white pine form the climax forest here. Yellow birch and white pine are rare on the Palisades, as is the small striped maple, whose green-and-white-striped trunks are so common in the understory of the Ramapo valleys. On the other hand, the huge, straight tulip trees that are seen on the slopes below the Palisades are not nearly as common in the

Ramapos, and the sweetgum, one of the dominant trees in Palisades wet woods, is absent altogether, since it reaches its northern limit on the Palisades. Red maple is the most common tree in the Ramapo lowland swamps and along its stream banks, along with shagbark hickory, elm, ash, tupelo, and big sycamores. Spicebush, sweet pepperbush, swamp azalea, highbush blueberry, and elderberry make up the dense shrub layer in Ramapo wetlands.

Since the forests of the Ramapos are more extensive and less disturbed than those of the Palisades, the hiker can expect to see a greater diversity of animal life. Deer are common, beavers (or at least their lodges and dams) are seen occasionally in the ponds, and sometimes a porcupine or mink is reported. Black bears have reestablished themselves. Copperhead and black snakes (both racers and rat snakes) are sometimes encountered. The rocky, more rugged sections represent one of the last strongholds of the timber rattlesnake in New Jersey. They are very rarely encountered by hikers and need not be feared, if left alone. Ruffed grouse, broad-winged hawks, great horned owls, pileated woodpeckers, brown creepers, hooded warblers, ovenbirds, scarlet tanagers, and towhees are just a few of the more unusual birds that nest in the forests of the Ramapos, and over two hundred other species use these woods throughout the year.

Mountain Biking in New Jersey

The increased use of mountain bikes on trails in New Jersey has created conflicts between user groups. In 1998, these issues are far from settled, as the dialogue continues. Some trails, specified below on a park-by-park basis, have been designated for multiple-use, but these designations may change over time. New Jersey state law provides for positive signing. If the signs don't explicitly say that bikes are permitted, then they are forbidden. The same rule applies to horse usage. Hiking is always allowed on marked and unmarked paths without explicit signs. An aggressive campaign to install signs at trailheads and trail crossings was begun in 1997 and will continue. The signs are primarily brown flexible fiberglass wands about 3-4 feet high with decals showing the permitted uses in international symbols. With the low state budgets of recent years, there is very little money to enforce the laws. It is the responsibility of both hikers and bikers to educate their user groups about the signing law and to tell violators they meet on the trails about the law.

CAMPGAW COUNTY RESERVATION

Located in Mahwah and under the jurisdiction of the Bergen County Parks Department, the 1,300-acre Campgaw County Reservation primarily offers hiking, skiing, archery, picnicking, and camping (by permit only). Bicycles are not allowed on the trails. Fees charged vary for county residents and nonresidents. The reservation is bounded on the east by Campgaw Road (off Darlington Avenue, 0.3 mile from US 202), where there is access, and on the west by US 202. The entrance road crosses I-287 (with the nearest exits at Suffern and Franklin Lakes).

The main parking lot is 0.6 mile from Campgaw Road, or some 250 feet past the gated entrance to the ski area. Another parking lot is at the end of the camp road another 0.5 mile farther. This road may be closed in winter.

For more information, contact the Bergen County Parks Department at (201) 646-2680, or its office in Darlington at (201) 327-3500. The telephone number for Campgaw's offices is (201) 327-7800, and maps may be requested by calling (201) 327-3500.

Trails in Campgaw County Reservation

There are seven marked trails totaling five miles on Campgaw Mountain as well as five miles of unmarked trails.

Beeches Trail   *Length: 0.3 mile Blaze: green*
The Beeches Trail connects the Indian Trail (yellow) with the Old Cedar Trail (red). It begins on the Old Cedar Trail, 0.2 mile from the trailhead, crosses two old toboggan runs, and ends at the Indian Trail, downhill from the cross-country ski trails.

Dogwood Lane Trail   *Length: 0.3 mile Blaze: white*
This trail connects the Hemlock (orange) and Grey Birches (pink) trails. It starts on the Grey Birches Trail, 0.5 mile from the main parking lot. The Dogwood Lane Trail makes a sharp left turn in less than 0.1 mile, crosses the ski road, and reaches the Hemlock Trail (orange) 0.3 mile from its junction with a service road.

Grey Birches Trail   *Length: 0.8 mile Blaze: pink*
This connection to the main entrance road for the Campgaw County Reservation first travels east on a service road from the first parking lot and, in less

than 0.1 mile, bears left into the woods on an old dirt road. The Grey Birches Trail crosses a power line, then the main park road, and at 0.5 mile turns right just before the terminus of the Dogwood Lane Trail (white). It crosses two stone walls before ending at the main road, 0.2 mile from Campgaw Road.

Hemlock Trail *Length: 0.8 mile Blaze: orange*
The Hemlock Trail circles the lake which serves the snowmaking operations for the ski area and is seen from the ski access road. It intersects the Dogwood Lane (white) and Indian (yellow) trails soon after they leave the parking lot, and reaches the lake in 0.1 mile on the left. It bears left at the ski road and again at a spring. At 0.5 mile, it joins a service road and soon thereafter joins the Indian Trail (yellow), bears left with it, and returns to the Dogwood Lane Trail (white).

Indian Trail *Length: 0.5 mile Blaze: yellow*
The beginning of the Indian Trail, one of three leading to the top of the ski slope (the other two are the Old Cedar and the Rocky Ridge trails), is reached by following the Hemlock Trail (orange) 0.7 mile to a service road. The Indian Trail bears right and heads up some steps, soon crossing the Beeches Trail (green). At about 0.3 mile from its start, the Indian Trail merges with a cross-country ski trail and continues uphill. A pipeline is soon crossed, and the trail ends 0.1 mile later.

Old Cedar Trail *Length: 1.1 miles Blaze: red*
This trail to the top of the ski slope begins just before the camp road cul-de-sac, where it bears right (north). It crosses a power line after about 0.1 mile, and soon after turns left at the terminus of the Beeches Trail (green). After crossing an old rock wall and an intermittent stream, and meeting the Rocky Ridge Trail (blue), the Old Cedar Trail again bears left. The trail descends slightly, then climbs again before crossing a pipeline and reaching the top, where it ends.

Rocky Ridge Trail *Length: 0.9 mile Blaze: blue*
Another trail leading to the top of the ski slope, the Rocky Ridge Trail heads west from the second parking lot past the pavilion. It proceeds uphill, crossing the Beeches Trail (green) at 0.3 mile. A steep climb begins at 0.4 mile, and the trail bears right when it meets the Old Cedar Trail (red). After another 0.2 mile, it crosses a pipeline and shortly thereafter reaches the top of the ski slope, where it ends.

LAKE LAGRANDE, or ROTTEN POND

RAMAPO MOUNTAIN STATE FOREST

A rugged 2,264-acre area, Ramapo Mountain State Forest has elevations ranging from 200 to 1,100 feet. It includes the wild lands of Oakland, Pompton Lakes, Wanaque, and Ringwood. The centerpiece of the park is Ramapo Lake, formerly called Rotten Pond (or Lake LeGrande), a name more than likely derived from Dutch settlers who called it Rote (Rat) Pond for the muskrats they trapped there. Fishing is permitted, but swimming is not. Several private holdings at the southern end of the state forest are served by one-lane access roads, which are closed to the public. Public access is by foot only. Other estate roads have been allowed to deteriorate, and some are marked in places as hiking trails. Some also serve as ski-touring trails. One patrol road encircles the lake. The northern part of the forest is wild and open to hunters as well as hikers. No fires or camping are permitted.

Hikers arriving by car have four access points near I-287, Exit 57 (Skyline Drive.) The first access point is a short distance north on Skyline Drive on the left, signed Ramapo Mountain State Forest. Referred to as the upper parking area, the second access point is one mile north on Skyline Drive on the left. The third parking area is about 1.1 miles south of the interchange on West Oakland Avenue at Pool Hollow Road, on the right, just short of the railroad tracks. The fourth access point is reached by turning right onto Schuyler Avenue, some 2.1 miles south of the Skyline Drive intersection, and then right onto Barbara Drive. There is parking for several cars near the end of this road.

Public transportation to the area is provided by NJ Transit bus lines 75 from Newark, 191/193, 194/195, and 196/197 from New York, and 746 from Ridgewood. For more information, contact Ramapo Mountain State Forest, Box 1304, Ringwood, NJ 07456; (973) 962-7031.

Trails in Ramapo Mountain State Forest

More than 20 miles of trails have been laid out since the state purchased the Ramapo Mountain State Forest. Units of the Youth Conservation Corps cleared those routes in 1977 and 1978. The trails provide gradual ascents to viewpoints on rock ledges from which the land may drop off sharply. Two thrutrails traverse the state forest: the Hoeferlin Memorial Trail honoring William Hoeferlin, a noted trailblazer and mapmaker, and the historic Cannonball Road, which originated at Pompton Lakes, formerly the site of an iron furnace. All trails east of Skyline Drive are hiking only, as is the Hoeferlin Memorial Trail from Pool Hollow Road.

Cannonball Trail   *Length: 7.0 miles Blaze: white C on red*
In *Vanishing Ironworks of the Ramapos* (Rutgers University Press, 1966, out of print), James M. Ransom defines the Cannonball Road, after which this trail is named, as part historic, part legendary. His historical evidence about the Pompton Furnace reveals that cannonballs were cast here in great quantity during the American Revolution. The furnace was located adjacent to the northern end of the natural basalt rock dam of Pompton Lakes. A portion of the support for the charging bridge from the hillside to the top of the furnace is all that remains.

From here, the obvious valley route to the Hudson would have followed the Ramapo River to Stony Point, the present route of US 202. Because the Loyalists might have warned the British, it seems reasonable to believe that a hidden route was laid out through the Ramapos. This route had to have easy grades over the ridge for heavily laden oxen-drawn wagons. In the 1970s, the old route was uncovered using old maps and Ransom's book.

To reach the southern trailhead in Pompton Lakes, hikers should take I-287 to Exit 57 (Skyline Drive), and proceed south on West Oakland Avenue, which becomes Colfax Avenue. In 2.1 miles, turn right on Schuyler Avenue, cross the railroad tracks, and then turn right onto Barbara Drive. Parking is available on the left side of the street just before it ends in a cul-de-sac.

The Cannonball Trail begins at the cul-de-sac, where it enters the woods to the left. It immediately turns right and crosses a railroad siding leading into the former duPont plant. The trail then skirts a ballfield and bears left, climbing steeply into the woods and entering Ramapo Mountain State Forest. At the top of the steep rise, the trail turns sharply left and continues to run above and parallel to a fence. Soon it crosses a woods road, the historic Cannonball Road. At 0.3 mile, after crossing a stream on logs, it turns right and follows along the road. As the trail approaches I-287, the sound of traffic gradually increases. After crossing a bridge over a stream, the Cannonball Trail bears left at a Y junction and, at 0.9 mile, joins the Hoeferlin Memorial Trail (yellow), which enters from the right. Both trails cross I-287 on a pedestrian bridge and then continue ahead on a woods road, passing a large boulder on the right. At 1.1 miles, the Hoeferlin Memorial Trail turns right onto a footpath, while the Cannonball Trail continues straight ahead on the woods road.

At 1.3 miles, the Cannonball Trail bears right at a Y junction and ascends a rocky, eroded section of the historic road. It crosses a woods road at 1.4 miles, turns right on a former estate road, and turns left at a Y junction. Following a gravel road which runs along the western edge of Ramapo Lake, it passes a caretaker's house. At 2.2 miles, another gravel road joins from the left, and the trail follows the road over a causeway across a corner of the lake. A short distance beyond the causeway, the Cannonball Trail turns left onto an intersecting gravel road. It continues on this road for 450 feet and then turns right on a footpath along with the MacEvoy Trail (blue) that joins from the road ahead.

The footpath reaches another estate road at 2.6 miles. Here, the MacEvoy Trail turns right, while the Cannonball Trail turns left, following the estate road uphill. At a sharp bend in the road, the Castle Point Trail (white), which leads uphill to the ruins of a former mansion, begins to the left. At the top of the hill, where the road bears sharp left, the Cannonball Trail continues straight ahead on a footpath into the woods. It crosses a stream and begins to ascend, steeply in places, to the height of the ridge. The trail briefly follows a paved road at 3.0 miles, detours to the right on a footpath, then rejoins the road, passing a private home on the right. At 3.3 miles, it again goes into the woods, paralleling the road, and finally rejoins the road. At 3.6 miles, after passing the northern trailhead of the Castle Point Trail to the left, it reaches Skyline Drive.

The Cannonball Trail crosses Skyline Drive and continues north on a wide woods road. At 3.7 miles, it rejoins the Hoeferlin Memorial Trail (yellow), which comes in from the right, and the two trails stay together for the next 1.6 miles. The joint trails continue northward, parallel to and just east of Skyline Drive. At 4.3 miles, they emerge again onto Skyline Drive where a pipeline crosses the road. Limited parking is available here. After passing a small building, the trails bear right and reenter the woods. At 4.7 miles, the trails turn left on an access road leading to a radio tower. They turn right, leaving the road, and continue on a footpath. At this point, a red-blazed side trail leads left to Matapan Rock, a viewpoint overlooking the Wanaque Reservoir. After passing abandoned cars on the right, the Hoeferlin and Cannonball trails bear left and ascend the ridge.

At 5.3 miles, the Cannonball Trail departs to the right and begins to descend, while the Hoeferlin Memorial Trail continues ahead along the ridge. The Cannonball Trail skirts a large swamp and crosses its outlet. With minor ups and downs, it joins, at 6.1 miles, the original Cannonball Road, proceeding north through Camp Yaw Paw, a charcoal production site in the 1850s. It then enters Ringwood State Park, passing the terminus of the Crossover Trail (white) at 6.6 miles. The Cannonball Trail then descends and, at 7.0 miles, it ends at the dam at the south end of Bear Swamp Lake.

Castle Point Trail   *Length: 1.0 mile Blaze: white*
The highlight of this trail is a burned-out fieldstone mansion, which looks out over a panorama of lake and mountain. Foxcroft, as the mansion was called, was built around 1910 by William Porter, a stockbroker. His widow occupied it until her death in 1940. It fell into ruin in the late 1950s.

From the upper parking area on Skyline Drive, the trailhead for the Castle Point Trail is reached via an 0.2-mile walk north on Skyline Drive to a blacktop road on the left. The Castle Point Trail starts shortly off this road on the right and soon reaches a rock ledge with views west. The trail zigzags down a steep slope to a logging road, then breaks out to a grass-covered pipeline, which it follows left around a wide bend. At the foot of the steep slope, the trail turns left, goes onto a woods road, then heads south uphill to a spot offering wide views west to Wanaque Reservoir. The trail passes a stone tower on the way to the burned-out shell of the mansion. The trail climbs over the rock wall and drops down the point, ending at a gravel driveway a few yards from the Cannonball Trail.

Hoeferlin Memorial Trail   *Length: 9.0 miles Blaze: yellow*
Not to be confused with the blue-blazed Hoeferlin Trail in Wawayanda State

Park, the yellow-blazed Hoeferlin Memorial Trail honors the same man, William Hoeferlin, a dedicated hiker. The Hoeferlin Memorial Trail runs along the ridge of the Ramapo Mountains from Pompton Lakes to the north end of Bear Swamp Lake. To reach the southern trailhead, take Exit 57 (Skyline Drive) from I-287 and proceed south on West Oakland Avenue for 1.1 miles. Turn right onto Pool Hollow Road, where there is room to park several cars on the north side, just west of the intersection with West Oakland Avenue.

The Hoeferlin Memorial Trail begins at Pool Hollow Road and proceeds west. It crosses the tracks of the active New York, Susquehanna and Western Railroad, and passes a pond to the right. In 0.2 mile, it reaches a gate and continues ahead, ascending gradually on an old estate road. The trail comes quite close to I-287, with the sound of traffic becoming audible. At 0.5 mile, it passes a grassy road going off to the right which was the former route of the trail, cut off when I-287 was constructed. The Hoeferlin Memorial Trail continues ahead on the estate road and, at 0.7 mile, it turns right, joining the Cannonball Trail (white C on red). Both trails cross I-287 on a pedestrian bridge.

The trails continue ahead on a woods road, passing a large boulder on the right. At 0.9 mile, the Hoeferlin Memorial Trail turns right on a footpath, leaving the Cannonball Trail. It soon begins to ascend steeply, and passes a large boulder on the left. At 1.2 miles, the Hoeferlin Memorial Trail makes a right turn onto an old estate road, with the original pavement now almost completely eroded. In another 450 feet, it bears left onto an intersecting woods road. Fifty feet beyond this point, another woods road branches off to the right, leading to an overlook over I-287 and beyond, and then rejoining the main woods road. Soon, the Hoeferlin Memorial Trail bears left, leaving the road. It briefly joins an old woods road, and then it descends to cross a stream at 1.4 miles.

The Hoeferlin Memorial Trail now begins a steady ascent and reaches a rock ledge with a view to the southeast of High Mountain of the Watchung Range. The trail passes another viewpoint at 1.7 miles, and soon begins to ascend more steeply. At the top of the steep climb, it reaches the Lookout Trail (red) and bears left, joining one branch of the Lookout Trail, while the other branch of the Lookout Trail continues straight ahead. The two trails reach a viewpoint at 1.9 miles, with Ramapo Lake visible to the right, and a quarry in the distance on the left. After passing a swampy area, the two trails reach, at 2.2 miles, another viewpoint with an panoramic view over Ramapo Lake. The trails now descend steadily and, at 2.4 miles, come out on the dirt road that encircles Ramapo Lake. The Lookout Trail (red) ends here, while the Hoeferlin Memorial Trail turns right and follows the road along the lakeshore. In 350 feet, it passes the other end of the Lookout Trail (red) on the right, and then it crosses the dam.

At 2.6 miles, the dam ends, and the Hoeferlin Memorial Trail bears right and goes up a paved road. At a bend in the road, the trail leaves to the right and re-enters the woods on a footpath. It crosses several streams and eventually joins a dirt road as it winds upwards, twice coming close to the paved road. At 3.6 miles, the Hoeferlin Memorial Trail again turns right on the paved road, and at 3.8 miles it reaches the upper parking area on Skyline Drive.

The trail crosses the highway and turns left, passing the entrance road to Camp Tamarack. It then turns right, reentering the woods, and climbs steeply to a rock ledge at 3.9 miles. After descending, first steeply and then more moderately, it reaches another junction with the Cannonball Trail (white C on red). Here, at 4.2 miles, the Hoeferlin Memorial Trail turns right, rejoining the Cannonball Trail on a wide woods road, and the two trails stay together for the next 1.6 miles. The joint trails continue northward, parallel to and just east of Skyline Drive. At 4.8 miles, they emerge again onto Skyline Drive where a pipeline crosses the road. Limited parking is available here. After passing a small building, the trails bear right and reenter the woods. At 5.2 miles, the trails turn left on an access road leading to a radio tower. In 50 feet, they turn right, leaving the road, and continue on a footpath. At this point, a red-blazed side trail leads left to Matapan Rock, a viewpoint overlooking the Wanaque Reservoir. The joint Hoeferlin and Cannonball trails pass some abandoned cars to the right, bear left, and ascend the ridge.

At 5.8 miles, the Cannonball Trail (white C on red) departs to the right, while the Hoeferlin Memorial Trail continues ahead along the ridge. Then, at 6.2 miles, the Ringwood-Ramapo Trail (red) goes off to the left. Shortly thereafter, the Hoeferlin Memorial Trail leaves the state forest and enters Boy Scout property, the North Quad of Camp Glen Gray. It once more passes through the state forest, and then enters Camp Yaw Paw, where it climbs to reach Erskine Lookout at 7.3 miles, with views to the west over the Wanaque Reservoir.

Proceeding northeast from Erskine Lookout, the Hoeferlin Memorial Trail borders state land to the right, and soon crosses a faintly-blazed blue trail from Camp Yaw Paw. It enters Ringwood State Park, and climbs to Ilgenstein Rock, which it reaches at 7.9 miles. Here a rock ledge provides a view east over Bear Swamp Lake and beyond. Just before the viewpoint, the Crossover Trail (white) comes up from the lake and joins the Hoeferlin Memorial Trail. At 8.3 miles, the Crossover Trail leaves to the left, bound for Skylands Manor. The Hoeferlin Memorial Trail continues north, passes the pre-Civil War Butler Mine diggings on the left, and then descends the ridge to a tricky brook crossing. It ends, at 9.0 miles, at its junction with the Shore Trail (blue) at the shore of Bear Swamp Lake.

Lookout Trail   *Length: 1.8 miles Blaze: red*
Access to this trail is via the MacEvoy Trail and then a road around Ramapo Lake. Several yards past the south end of Ramapo Lake dam, the Lookout Trail leaves the shore road on the left, rising and then dropping to the edge of a wetland before leading up to the top of the ridge. The trail goes left around the rim of a wide cirque and up two short pitches, one around a knob, another around a cliff, to join the Hoeferlin Memorial Trail (yellow) at the top, 1.2 miles from the trailhead. From the viewpoint at an open rock ledge, the two trails go north, passing a second rocky viewpoint amid scrub pine, which gives views across Ramapo Lake and the mountains of Norvin Green State Forest. From the lookout, the combined trails drop down to the gravel road at the lakeshore, where the Lookout Trail ends. Including the access trail from the lower parking area, the round trip is 3.5 miles.

MacEvoy Trail   *Length: 2.2 miles Blaze: blue*
Named for Clifford MacEvoy, a contractor for large public works whose estate became Ramapo Mountain State Forest, the MacEvoy Trail provides access to the north shore of Ramapo Lake. From the south end of the Skyline Drive lower parking area, the trail climbs to the lake in 0.6 mile, passing the Todd Trail (white) on the right, 500 feet short of the dam. The MacEvoy Trail follows the gravel road along the north shore, going right at a Y junction and heading uphill through gateposts. At the second curve at 1.1 miles, the trail joins the Cannonball Trail (white C on red) and turns left into the woods. Both trails turn left at the southern terminus of the Castle Point Trail (white). Upon reaching a grass-covered road, the Cannonball Trail turns left, while the MacEvoy Trail goes right, leading in 0.2 mile to a pipeline. The MacEvoy Trail jogs right and left along the pipeline before turning left close to a woods road. After approximately 0.5 mile, it goes downhill to Wolfe Drive at its dead end in a housing development in Wanaque, where there is parking for two cars. From here, it is 1.8 miles via Wolfe Drive, Cannonball Road, and Conklintown Road to Ringwood Avenue (County 511), which is served by NJ Transit bus 196/197.

Todd Trail   *Length: 2.0 miles Blaze: white*
Starting at the upper parking area on Skyline Drive, the trail traverses land east of Skyline Drive, taking in a wide viewpoint. From the road, the Todd Trail heads east downhill with ups and downs around ravines and reaches a gravel road joining Camp Tamarack with the former Camp Todd. In sight of the former ranger's cabin, the trail diverts right, uphill, to wide views east from grassy Todd Hill, before traversing a side slope. It then descends, using pieces of an abandoned camp road, before turning left off the road and crossing a hill to Skyline Drive. On the west side, it traverses lowlands before ascending a ridge and then descends to a stream valley, wet at times. A short ascent brings the Todd Trail out to its junction with the MacEvoy Trail (blue), 500 feet east of Ramapo Lake.

Yellow Trail   *Length: 4.1 miles Blaze: yellow*
The Yellow Trail provides a link from Skyline Drive to Camp Yaw Paw. It follows a more easterly route than the Cannonball Trail (white C on red), and may be combined with it to make an 8-mile loop.

To reach the southern trailhead of the Yellow Trail, take the Todd Trail (white) east from the upper parking area on Skyline Drive. After about half a mile, the Todd Trail goes right on a woods road, then immediately turns left on another road. The Yellow Trail begins on the left, about 250 feet beyond this point. It soon reaches the shore of Lake Todd and, bending to the left, follows along the western shore of the lake, passing a rock which offers views of the lake. The trail then bears right, leaving the lake, and ascends a knoll, then descends steadily. After passing a small waterfall on a stream to the left, it crosses the stream at 0.7 mile and continues along an eroded woods road, ascending gradually for about half a mile. It goes through the intersection of several stone walls, passes a stone foundation to the left, and begins a steady descent. After crossing a blue-blazed line (marking the boundary of Boy Scout Camp Glen Gray) and joining a Boy Scout trail, the Yellow Trail reaches a paved road (which leads into Camp Glen Gray) at 1.5 miles, and turns right, following the road to the east.

In 0.2 mile, the Yellow Trail reaches the camp entrance and turns left onto Midvale Mountain Road. It continues along this road for a quarter of a mile, passing several large homes. Where the paved road bends to the right, the Yellow Trail continues straight ahead on a woods road, passing two locked gates. It soon turns left, crossing a brook on a wooden bridge, then turns right and runs along the brook. At 2.4 miles, the Yellow Trail turns left and begins a gradual ascent on switchbacks, as the Yellow-Silver Trail continues straight ahead. In another 0.3 mile, after passing a rusted metal frame to the right, the Yellow Trail turns right, leaving the woods road it has been following, and begins a steeper ascent. It reaches the height of land (996 feet) at 2.9 miles, with views to the east. From here, on a clear day, the Manhattan skyline is visible.

The Yellow Trail now begins to descend, soon briefly joining a Boy Scout trail marked with an X on a yellow background. Be careful to follow the plain yellow blazes, as the two trails soon diverge. At 3.4 miles, the Yellow Trail turns left on a woods road, soon crossing a stream and then the route of a buried gas pipeline. After crossing a swampy area on puncheon, the trail passes in front of the Dogwood Cabin of Boy Scout Camp Yaw Paw. It soon bears left, and ends at 4.1 miles at the Cannonball Trail (white C on red), with a small lean-to on the right. To return to the start, turn left on the Cannonball Trail and follow it south for 3.1 miles, then bear left and continue for 0.5 mile on the Hoeferlin Memorial Trail (yellow) to the upper parking area on Skyline Drive.

RAMAPO VALLEY COUNTY RESERVATION

European immigrants first settled what is now Ramapo Valley County Reservation around 1720. Rock walls from the farms that sprang up are still present, and the reservation once boasted gristmills and sawmills, as well as a bronze foundry. The land was ultimately purchased by A. B. Darling, whose country estate gave the name Darlington to the area. The foundation of his manor house, near the entrance to the park, is still visible.

In 1972, money from the Green Acres program and the federal government created the 2,145-acre Ramapo Valley County Reservation. Left in its natural wild state by the Bergen County Park Commission, which administers the area, the reservation is mostly hilly, forming the eastern tier of the Ramapos. No open fires are allowed in the park without a permit. Tent camping, which also requires a permit, is allowed only in designated areas near Scarlet Oak Pond and the Ramapo River. The Park Commission has instituted a carry-in–carry-out policy for trash at this location. Bicycles are not allowed on any of the trails in the Reservation.

Access to the reservation is from a parking area on Ramapo Valley Road (US 202) in Mahwah. There is access for the disabled. For more information, contact the reservation at (201) 825-1388 or the Bergen County Parks Department at (201) 646-2680.

Trails in Ramapo Valley County Reservation

Ramapo Valley County Reservation provides the opportunity for both rugged day-long hiking and pleasant afternoon strolling, as well as offering access to state lands on its western flank. A wildlife sanctuary, it includes among its features the Ramapo River, Scarlet Oak Pond, Macmillan Reservoir, and Hawk Rock.

Halifax Trail   *Length: 2.6 miles Blaze: green on white*

The Halifax Trail starts on the north side of Scarlet Oak Pond off the unmarked shore path circling the pond. It climbs to Hawk Rock, a popular overlook, at 0.4 mile, then continues up the mountain to cross a pipeline and head

down into Havemeyer Hollow. Following a woods road north, it passes the Havemeyer Trail (blue on white) on the left at 0.7 mile,

and almost immediately arrives at a stream crossing. Continuing on the woods road another 0.4 mile, the trail turns left into the woods and at 1.6 miles crosses another pipeline, finally arriving at a junction of woods roads and the pipeline near Bear Swamp Lake.

The trail crosses the pipeline along a gravel service road and makes a right turn down to the inlet at the north end of the lake. Less than 100 feet beyond the inlet, the trail turns right (north), leaving the reservation property to enter the Skylands section of Ringwood State Park. The remaining 2.9 miles of this trail are described in the section on Ringwood State Park.

Havemeyer Trail   *Length: 0.8 mile Blaze: blue on white*

This trail connects the Halifax Trail (green) with the Ridge Trail (blue). Starting at the Halifax Trail end, the trail goes southwest, steeply uphill with a gain of 500 feet. Going right on a woods road at 0.4 mile, it reaches the White Trail at 0.5 mile at the top of the ridge. It turns left to follow the White Trail for 400 feet before turning off to the right. It then crosses a gas pipeline before reaching its end at the Ridge Trail.

Marsh Loop Trail   *Length: 0.3 mile Blaze: red*
A level connector trail between the Silver and Yellow-Silver trails, the Marsh Loop leaves the Silver Trail 0.2 mile from the terminus of the Yellow-Silver Trail and loops back in a generally southerly direction, skirting a marshy area.

Red-Silver Trail   *Length: 0.7 mile Blaze: red/silver*
Skirting Rocky Mountain, this trail connects the Silver Trail (silver) with the Shore Trail (blue) at Bear Swamp Lake. Generally rocky, the trail passes some rock outcrops, skirts the edge of a marsh, and crosses a pipeline before reaching the lake.

Ridge Trail   *Length: 2.0 miles Blaze: blue*
The Ridge and Silver trails form a loop hike wholly within the reservation. Starting from the Silver Trail 0.7 mile from its beginning, the Ridge Trail climbs moderately as a wide rocky path. At 0.5 mile, there is a 140-yard side trail to the left to a rock ledge lookout over the Ramapo Valley and the Manhattan skyline beyond. The White Trail continues straight ahead on the woods road at 0.6 mile, while the Ridge Trail bears left and climbs briefly, following an old stone wall. At 1.2 miles, the Ridge Trail intersects the Havemeyer Trail (blue on white), which goes off to the right, while the Ridge Trail bears left on a woods road. The remains of the Nickel Mine are located here. The trail descends and makes a gentle 90-degree turn to the left. It continues downhill to its end at the Silver Trail at 2.0 miles.

River Trail   *Length: 0.7 mile Blaze: red on white*
Also known as the Swamp Loop Trail, the River Trail is accessible from the rear of the first picnic site on the left of the Silver Trail, near the start of Scarlet Oak Pond. This level and sometimes wet trail parallels the Ramapo River for much of its length and returns to its starting point.

Shore Trail   *Length: 1.0 mile Blaze: blue*
This trail begins at the south end of Bear Swamp Lake, where the Cannonball Trail (white C on red) ends, and follows the lake's west shore. Proceeding north and passing the ruins of cottages, the trail hugs the lake for 0.5 mile to the northern terminus of the Hoeferlin Memorial Trail (yellow) on the left, then continues to a bridge crossing the inlet at the lake's northern end. Turning south, the trail follows the shore for 0.2 mile to the gravel perimeter road leading south to the dam and returns to its beginning, completely circling the lake.

Silver Trail   *Length: 2.7 miles Blaze: silver disk*
Of the reservation's many trails, the Silver Trail is the primary feeder trail.
Starting at the parking area, the trail crosses the Ramapo River and follows the
northwest shore of Scarlet Oak Pond, which is reached in 800 feet. An unmarked shore path loops around the pond in open fields. As the trail leaves the
end of the pond at 0.4 mile, the Waterfall Trail (yellow) branches off to the left.
The lower leg of the Ridge Trail (blue) goes off to the right at 0.7 mile, while
the Silver Trail follows the reservation service road uphill. After a stream crossing 700 feet farther on, the Silver Trail passes the terminus of the Waterfall
Trail (yellow) and proceeds uphill toward Macmillan Reservoir. After a second
stream crossing, an unmarked trail, leading to the eastern shore of the Reservoir, splits off on the right. Macmillan Reservoir is reached at 1.0 mile.

The Silver Trail continues to climb. At 1.1 miles, the Yellow-Silver Trail
starts on the left. As the trail grade begins to descend at 1.4 miles, the Marsh
Loop Trail (red) leaves, also to the left. In 700 feet, the upper leg of the Ridge
Trail (blue) diverts right. At 1.7 miles, at a not too obvious turn and just prior
to an intermittent stream, the Red-Silver Trail goes straight ahead, while the
Silver Trail turns left. The Silver Trail ends at Bear Swamp Road at 2.7 miles.

Waterfall Trail   *Length: 0.5 mile Blaze: yellow on white*
A loop off the Silver Trail, beginning opposite Scarlet Oak Pond, the Waterfall
Trail starts as a wide, flat, sandy path and eventually becomes a narrow, rocky,
hilly trail after it crosses a stream near the ruins of an old foundation. As it
proceeds uphill, it passes the waterfall for which it is named and ends at the
Silver Trail on the service road at 0.5 mile.

White Trail   *Length: 1.2 miles Blaze: white*
The White Trail diverges from the Ridge Trail (blue) approximately 1.3 miles
from the parking area. Within 0.1 mile, it passes an unmarked woods road on
the right. After a slight incline, the trail descends on a wide rocky path and
crosses, at 0.2 mile, the Tenneco gas pipeline, which it roughly parallels for the
rest of its length. The trail reaches an old rock wall at 0.4 mile, and soon joins
the Havemeyer Trail (blue on white), which splits off to the left. In 400 feet, the
Havemeyer Trail descends steeply to the right, while the White Trail continues
straight ahead, soon noticeably narrower. It parallels old rock walls and the
pipeline on its left. The White Trail ends at the Algonquin gas pipeline.

To reach Drag Hill where there are views in both directions along the pipeline and to the hills beyond, follow the pipeline 400 feet uphill to the left to the noisy junction of the Algonquin and Tenneco gas pipelines, with their microwave control tower. Continue another 360 yards to the top of Drag Hill.

Yellow-Silver Trail   *Length: 2.2 miles Blaze: yellow/silver*
Starting from the Silver Trail, this trail passes through the southern portion of the reservation. It skirts Matty Price Hill and crosses Bear Swamp Brook on the Bear Swamp Road bridge, about 1.2 miles from the trailhead. It continues southwest to a switchback woods road leading into Camp Glen Gray and ends at the Yellow Trail, described above in the Ramapo Mountain State Forest section.

RINGWOOD STATE PARK

Bordering New York State, Ringwood State Park features both wild and cultivated land. The park originally centered around Ringwood Manor, a rambling old mansion containing a priceless collection of relics from the iron-making days, as well as the furnishings of the Coopers and Hewitts from about 1810 to 1930. For more information about Ringwood Manor, see the history section above.

Also contained in the park are Shepherd Lake, with picnicking, swimming, and boating facilities, and Skylands Manor. The 44-room Tudor mansion of native granite was competed in 1929 by Clarence McKenzie Lewis, who had purchased the land from Francis Lynde Stetson. Stetson had hired Samuel Parson, Jr., founder of the American Society of Landscape Architects, protege of Frederick Law Olmstead and at one time New York City parks commissioner, to design the grounds. Lewis, like Stetson, was a trustee of the New York Botanical Garden. He set out to make the property a botanical showplace featuring symmetry, color, texture, form, and fragrance. Skylands Gardens was the first property purchased under the Green Acres program. In March 1984, the 96 acres surrounding the manor house were designated the New Jersey State Botanical Garden. Volunteers help maintain the plantings. Skylands Manor is open for tours at least one Sunday per month from March to December. For more information, contact Skylands Manor at (973) 962-7527.

Access to this area by car from the northeast is from NY 17 just south of Sloatsburg, New York. Sterling Mine Road (County 72) becomes Sloatsburg Road when it crosses into New Jersey. There are two major parking areas, first, Ringwood Manor on the right and, then, Skylands Manor on the left. The Skylands Manor entrance is also the access to Shepherd Lake. These three areas can also be approached from the south via Skyline Drive and Greenwood Lake Turnpike (County 511), with a turnoff on Sloatsburg Road. There is a seasonal entrance fee.

Hikers may also reach the area via New Jersey Transit bus 196/197 from New York City. There is a stop at the Cupsaw Lake entrance at Skylands Road along Greenwood Lake Turnpike and another at the Ringwood Municipal Building. From the Cupsaw Lake stop, follow Skylands Road 0.8 mile to Cupsaw Avenue and continue straight ahead another 0.4 mile to the park entrance gate. Turn right at the T junction.

Hunting is permitted in designated areas of the park, subject to New Jersey's fish, game, and wildlife laws. For more information about the park and Skylands, contact Ringwood State Park, Box 1304, Ringwood, NJ 07456; (973) 962-7031.

🥾 Trails in Ringwood State Park

More than 27 miles of trails in the park wind their way through a variety of habitats. Trails frequently intersect each other as they meander through the woods, providing hikers with a variety of choices. Cross-country skiing is permitted when conditions are favorable. Mountain bikes are permitted on some trails which have been marked with signs, but they are not allowed on any trails that do not have a sign with the international bicycle symbol. The trails listed below are all hiking only, except for parts of the Crossover Trail near Ringwood Manor. Many woods roads, especially in the Brushwood Section, are multiple-use and, as of 1998, there are a few new bicycle trails.

Cooper Union Trail   *Length: 4.9 miles Blaze: yellow*
Accessible from Sloatsburg Road, just short of the New York state line, the Cooper Union Trail enters the woods on a woods road and, at 0.1 mile, reaches the northern terminus of the Cupsaw Brook Trail (blue) at a Y junction. The Cooper Union Trail bears right and goes up Cupsaw Mountain alternately on and off woods roads. Near the summit and 150 feet from a shelter, the trail leaves the woods road and turns right on the Ringwood-Ramapo Trail (red) at 0.5 mile. The two trails separate after 200 feet, with the Cooper Union Trail going left and the Ringwood-Ramapo Trail continuing straight ahead to descend the mountain. At 1.1 miles, the Cooper Union Trail meets the southern terminus of the Cupsaw Brook Trail (blue), which approaches from the left. In another few hundred feet it meets the Crossover Trail (white).

A quarter of a mile later, the Cooper Union Trail crosses Morris Avenue and soon joins a gas pipeline, which it follows west before turning left into the woods at 2.0 miles. The trail meets a well-worn woods road and follows it due south. Turning to the east, the trail crosses Carltondale Road at 3.0 miles.

At 3.2 miles, the trail crosses a small bridge and immediately becomes a woods road. The Cooper Union Trail, at 3.3 miles, begins a lollipop loop over Governor Mountain. The trail follows the woods road straight ahead and reaches the summit at 4.0 miles, where there are views to the west. The view south and west over the Wanaque Reservoir is 100 yards farther at Suicide Ledge. To complete the loop, the hiker should take the trail left from the ledge over a shoulder, dropping down to a wet spot and then traversing up a rocky ridge heading north. Turning west, the trail rejoins the path up the mountain 4.9 miles from the beginning of the trail and 1.9 miles from Carltondale Road. The round trip from Carltondale Road to the views is 2.2 miles.

Crossover Trail   *Length: 6.2 miles Blaze: white*
This trail connects Ringwood Manor with Bear Swamp Lake in Ramapo Valley County Reservation. Its western terminus can be reached by following the Ringwood-Ramapo Trail (red) from the Ringwood Manor picnic area, where parking is available, east across Sloatsburg Road. Just east of the road, the Crossover Trail turns right to contour Cupsaw Mountain. In 0.8 mile, it crosses the Cooper Union Trail (yellow), then emerges onto Morris Avenue at 1.3 miles. The trail turns left onto the road, crosses a bridge over Cupsaw Brook, and then follows the road up the hill to a pipeline, where it turns right. Skirting a sewage plant by following the pipeline a short distance, the trail turns left into dense woods and continues up the hill to Skylands Manor.

The trail follows the main entrance road between two stone eagles. A parking lot is on the left, and the manor house and New Jersey Botanical Gardens are ahead to the right. At the end of the parking lot, the trail turns left onto a driveway, passing through the manor grounds before turning left again onto a woods road. Shortly afterward, at 2.7 miles, the Halifax Trail (green) starts off to the left up Mount Defiance.

For the next several miles, the Crossover Trail makes use of estate carriage roads. It crosses the Ringwood-Ramapo Trail (red) at 3.5 miles at the top of the southern shoulder of Mount Defiance, then continues down a rocky stretch to cross Glasmere Ponds Road. Here the trail bends to the right, then to the left, crossing two other woods roads. Below Gatum Pond, it turns right for a short distance. The path ascends to Gatum Pond, with a waterfall on the right. Rejoining the road, the Crossover Trail skirts the pond, then passes a field that is reserved for use by a model airplane club. Ascending Pierson Ridge, the trail leaves the carriage road about 100 yards past a hairpin turn and heads uphill in a southeasterly direction, gradually narrowing until it meets the Hoeferlin Memorial Trail (yellow) at 5.6 miles from the trailhead. Turning right, it joins the Hoeferlin Memorial Trail south to Ilgenstein Rock, with a panoramic view east to Bear Swamp Lake just below and the Manhattan skyline in the distance. Here at 6.0 miles, the Crossover Trail leaves the Hoeferlin Memorial Trail and descends sharply to end at the Cannonball Trail (white C on red), which can be followed north to Bear Swamp Lake.

Cupsaw Brook Trail   *Length: 1.4 miles Blaze: blue*
Both ends of the Cupsaw Brook Trail connect to the Cooper Union Trail (yellow), enabling hikers to make a loop hike or avoid a climb over Cupsaw Mountain. The trail, accessible from the Cooper Union Trail 0.1 mile or 1.1 miles from Sloatsburg Road, is off and on woods roads.

From the southern intersection with the Cooper Union Trail, the Cupsaw Brook Trail follows the base of Cupsaw Mountain. At 0.3 mile, the Ringwood-Ramapo Trail (red) joins from the left, and the two trails cross a stream on stepping stones. They separate at a Y junction, with the Cupsaw Brook Trail going left. Following along first one stream and then another, the trail reaches a T junction at 1.1 miles and bears left. Ascending, it crosses a gas pipeline and then heads downhill, paralleling the state line. It ends at the Cooper Union Trail (yellow), 0.1 mile from Sloatsburg Road, where there is parking.

Halifax Trail   *Length: 2.9 miles Blaze: green*
The western terminus of the Halifax Trail is on the Crossover Trail (white), approximately 0.3 mile from Parking Lot A at Skylands Manor. The Halifax Trail ascends Mount Defiance on a series of switchbacks. Near the top, on a short unmarked spur to the left, a viewpoint offers vistas to the northwest over Ringwood, West Milford, and Sterling Forest, with Bearfort Ridge in the distance. The trail continues east, skirting a rock formation on the left, and at 0.5 mile crosses the Ringwood-Ramapo Trail (red) before descending on switchbacks to a woods road at Glasmere Ponds. The trail turns left onto the road, then quickly turns right onto another woods road that passes between the two ponds. Veering off to the left into woods and gradually ascending to a third woods road, the

Halifax Trail cuts across a hairpin turn in the road. After crossing another woods road and a pipeline, the trail reaches a small summit on Pierson Ridge.

From the summit, the Halifax Trail descends a short distance to cross Pierson Ridge Road at 1.6 miles. Continuing to descend, it passes a swamp on the right and crosses yet another woods road. It again crosses the pipeline and descends through the woods to Bear Swamp Lake. See page 68 on the Ramapo Valley County Reservation for a description of the rest of this trail.

Manor Trail   *Length: 2.2 miles Blaze: blue*

This loop trail through the woods west of Ringwood Manor is an easy hike for beginners and families with children. From the parking lot at Ringwood Manor, proceed past the rear of the manor house and then turn right up the stone steps. A left turn onto a dirt road at the top of the steps leads to the beginning of the trail in about 300 feet.

To the right, the trail follows a woods road to its junction with the White Trail at 0.3 mile. The Manor Trail turns left and crosses two streams at 0.5 and 0.8 mile, respectively, and emerges from the woods on a pipeline at 1.1 miles. After crossing the pipeline, the trail goes through the woods for about 20 feet and turns left onto a woods road. At the bottom of the hill at 1.5 miles, the trail follows the woods road to the left while another woods road, blocked by boulders, leads off to the right to Margaret King Avenue. The trail continues past a residence on the right and an old water tower on the left. At 1.8 miles, there is a gate on the right, with the road to the Ringwood Municipal Building and the bus stop beyond it. Just past the gate, the trail turns left, still following a dirt road. On the right is Sally's Pond and a view of the manor house. Slightly farther ahead on the right is a cemetery containing the graves of the Hewitts, Erskines, and Morrises, among others. The trail continues back to the starting point at the parking lot.

Ringwood-Ramapo Trail   *Length: 8.6 miles Blaze: red*

From the Ringwood Manor picnic area, where parking is available, the Ringwood-Ramapo Trail crosses Ringwood River on a sturdy bridge, then crosses Sloatsburg Road before heading uphill over Cupsaw Mountain. At 0.3 mile, the Cooper Union Trail (yellow) comes in from the right, only to separate 200 feet later at a T junction with a woods road. The Ringwood-Ramapo Trail turns right, passes a shelter, and then descends. At 0.6 mile, it turns left to join the Cupsaw Brook Trail (blue) for 200 feet. Together, the trails cross Cupsaw Brook and then separate, with the Cupsaw Brook Trail (blue) going left. The Ringwood-Ramapo Trail follows the brook and then climbs to Shepherd Lake at 2.0 miles. The trail follows the south shore of the lake, passing the beach, boat launch, and boat rental docks. It joins an estate road through a large hemlock grove along the south shore, then makes a right turn uphill. After crossing a gas pipeline at 2.4 miles, the Ringwood-Ramapo Trail begins a steep ascent up the northern shoulder of Mount Defiance. Near the 1,040-foot summit there is a view to the northwest, with Bearfort Ridge in the distance. Heading south, the trail descends slightly from the top of the ridge and parallels a large rock formation on the right. It crosses the Halifax Trail (green) at 2.9 miles, with a lookout 250 yards to the right over Skylands Manor. The trail continues south, joining an estate carriage road before intersecting the Crossover Trail (white) at 3.8 miles at the top of the shoulder.

Directly ahead, the Ringwood-Ramapo Trail continues south to a rock ledge called Warm Puppy Rock, with a view to the south, then drops down the ridge to cross a road leading north to Glasmere Pond at 4.3 miles. After descending to a brook, which it crosses on a stone slab, the trail travels through a meadow to a fire road. Making a left turn, it follows the road south, then turns right into woods. It meets a faint woods road and follows it uphill through a low pass to a broader woods road. A left turn leads to the south end of Catnest Swamp. The trail follows the woods road to the right, soon coming to a T junction with another woods road, which leads to the Brushwood section to the left and the Cooper Hill Park housing development to the right.

At the T junction, the Ringwood-Ramapo Trail plunges into the woods. It curves to the right, ascends a small hill, then descends to the left and parallels

High Mountain Brook for 0.75 mile, including a short section on a faint woods road. Opposite a cleft rock on the right, the trail turns left and crosses the brook. It resumes its southerly course, gradually ascending High Mountain at an angle. During the ascent, rock fields alternate with smoother ground. The trail levels off, with rock formations on the left, after which there is a short pitch through a rock pile before the trail levels off again. It follows the state property line south, past a viewpoint to the west. The Ringwood-Ramapo Trail ends at the Hoeferlin Memorial Trail (yellow), some 2.4 trail miles from the upper parking area on Skyline Drive in Ramapo Mountain State Forest.

White Trail   *Length: 1.0 mile Blaze: white*
A connector between the Ringwood Manor picnic area and the Manor Trail (blue), this trail has its western terminus 0.3 mile from the beginning of the Manor Trail. It ends near the brook along which the picnic area is situated and connects there with the Ringwood-Ramapo Trail (red).

WYANOKIES

The 34-square-mile area of the Wyanokie Highlands, which includes the 3,907-acre Norvin Green State Forest, has one of the largest concentrations of trails in the state. Wyanokie is a variant of the Native American word Winaki, commonly rendered Wanaque, meaning "Land of Sassafras." Norvin Hewitt Green, nephew of Ringwood Manor owner Abram S. Hewitt, donated this land, which is now Norvin Green State Forest, to the State of New Jersey in 1946. Elevations here range from 400 to 1,300 feet, and the hiker, though within sight of the Manhattan skyline, can find peace and beauty aplenty in the area's streams, waterfalls, and scenic vistas. Also featured are several abandoned iron mines, one of which may be entered. In 1998, the trails are all hiking only, as there are no signs designating other uses.

Primary access to the area is at the Weis Ecology Center, affiliated with the New Jersey Audubon Society. It is located on Snake Den Road East, uphill from West Brook Road. Groups planning to park a number of cars should call the Weis Ecology Center in advance at (973) 835-2160. This central starting point is approached from County 511, north of Midvale, over a causeway across Wanaque Reservoir.

The reservoir property, which the Wyanokie area borders, is patrolled by uniformed guards of the North Jersey District Water Supply Commission. Hikers are warned not to cross boundary lines into watershed property.

Norvin Green State Forest is administered by Ringwood State Park. For more information, contact Ringwood State Park, P.O. Box 1304, Ringwood, NJ 07456; (973) 962-7031.

Trails in the Wyanokies

The original trails in Norvin Green State Forest were laid out in the early 1920s by Dr. Will S. Monroe of Montclair and his co-workers in the Green Mountain Club. When he retired, the property and trail maintenance were taken over by the Nature Friends, who named the area Camp Midvale. Their former camp is now the Weis Ecology Center, a non-profit environmental education organization. The trails outside of the state forest traverse private lands. Hikers are asked to respect private property and stay on the trails. Failure to do so could jeopardize the largess of the owners in allowing the public to hike.

Burnt Meadow Trail *Length: 1.5 miles Blaze: yellow*
The Burnt Meadow Trail begins on top of Horse Pond Mountain, reached by following the Hewitt-Butler Trail (blue) 0.9 mile from its northern trailhead on County 511 and continuing south on the Horse Pond Mountain Trail (white) for 1.0 mile. After descending to Burnt Meadow Road at 0.7 mile, the trail follows the road for fifty feet, then reenters the woods to ascend Long Mountain and to reach its terminus at the Hewitt-Butler Trail (blue) at 1.5 miles.

Carris Hill Trail *Length: 1.0 mile Blaze: yellow*
The Carris Hill Trail connects the Lower Trail (white) with the Hewitt-Butler Trail (blue). It begins on the Lower Trail (white) 1.2 miles from its northern terminus at the Wyanokie Circular Trail (red on white), which in turn is 1.0 mile south of Snake Den Road East. The trail ascends steeply to a view of the Wanaque Reservoir and the surrounding mountains, followed by another view as it reaches Carris Hill and the Hewitt-Butler Trail (blue).

Hewitt-Butler Trail (northern section) *Length: 7.1 miles Blaze: blue*
Featuring multiple views, the Hewitt-Butler Trail extends from Hewitt to Bloomingdale. Parking for its northern terminus is on County 511, across from the junction with East Shore Road. The section ends at West Brook Road where there is limited parking to the right on the south side of the road. Public trans-

portation is available to the northern trailhead on NJ Transit bus 197. Beginning in 1998, the section between West Brook Road and the Weis Ecology Center was closed. For more information about the status of this section, contact the New York-New Jersey Trail Conference at (212) 685-9699.

The Hewitt-Butler Trail starts at a brook crossing just south of the parking area. It goes uphill to join a woods road and, almost immediately, leaves to the right. The trail continues straight down toward the Monksville Reservoir. Crossing a low, wet area, it climbs a bank to an abandoned railbed, turning left and following it above the reservoir for 0.2 mile. Approximately 100 yards after crossing a pipeline, the trail leaves the railbed to the right and winds uphill through the woods. After crossing a small stream, it climbs a short rocky slope, and, at 0.9 mile, passes the northern end of the Horse Pond Mountain Trail (white), which the Highlands Trail follows to the left.

At 1.2 miles, the Hewitt-Butler Trail joins the joint Highlands and Horse Pond Mountain trails until, at 1.4 miles, the Hewitt-Butler reaches a power line and turns right on the right-of-way, leaving the other two trails. Crossing Burnt Meadow Road, the Hewitt-Butler Trail continues to follow the power line until it turns left into the woods at 1.8 miles. It ascends, with some ups and downs, to a ridge with a view of Long Hill ahead and another view, southeast, of the Ramapos and Garrett Mountain in the Watchungs. The trail continues to a clearing just before reaching the end of the Burnt Meadow Trail (yellow) at 2.3 miles. The Hewitt-Butler Trail climbs to the Long Hill ridge, reaching, at 2.9 miles, a view from northeast to southeast which includes the Manhattan skyline.

Starting at 3.5 miles, the trail follows a power line along the Long Hill ridge until, at 4.5 miles, it reaches a view to the southwest. As the trail bears generally to the southeast, over the next mile, Kitchell Lake may occasionally be seen to the southwest in the leaf-off season. There are several views to the south at 5.7 miles. The trail circles a house at the top of a hill and arrives at Manaticut Point with a view to the east and south at 6.6 miles. It zigzags very steeply down the mountain to cross West Brook and reach West Brook Road 7.1 miles from the trailhead. The Highlands Trail (teal diamond) is co-aligned with the Hewitt-Butler Trail in several places.

Hewitt-Butler Trail (southern section)   *Length: 6.8 miles Blaze: blue*
The southern section of the Hewitt-Butler Trail begins at the Weis Ecology Center and ends at Camp Vacamus, which is reached from Exit 53 on I-287 by taking Hamburg Turnpike west through Butler. At 1.4 miles, Hamburg Turn-

pike turns right where County 511 turns left. Continue on Hamburg Turnpike for 1.2 miles to Macopin Road and turn right. There are signs for Camp Vacamus on the right in a little over a mile. There is also parking at the Glenwild Avenue crossing, which can be reached from I-287 by taking Exit 53 west to Bloomingdale. Take County 694 (Main Street) 1.4 miles through Bloomingdale, bear right as it becomes Hamburg Turnpike, and shortly turn right at the Y junction onto Glenwild Avenue toward West Milford. The parking is on the right after 3.2 miles along Glenwild Avenue. Beginning in 1998, the section between West Brook Road and the Weis Ecology Center was closed. For more information about this section's status, contact the New York-New Jersey Trail Conference at (212) 685-9699.

This section of the Hewitt-Butler Trail begins on Snake Den Road, which should be followed west from Weis Ecology Center. The blazing begins 200 feet before the road becomes unpaved, and in another 400 feet, the Hewitt-Butler Trail turns left off unpaved Snake Den Road East to join the Mine Trail (yellow on white) on its ascent of Carris Hill. The two trails separate at 0.3 mile, with the Mine Trail going to the left. The Hewitt-Butler Trail passes the terminus of the Macopin Trail (white) at 0.6 mile, and just below the top of Wyanokie High Point, it joins the Wyanokie Circular Trail (red on white) at 0.8 mile. The two trails soon separate, with the Hewitt-Butler going right. The trail ascends to Yoo-Hoo Point at 1.3 miles and reaches the Carris Hill Trail (yellow), at 1.8 miles, on Carris Hill, with views in many directions. Descending, the trail passes the end of Post Brook Trail (white) at 2.5 miles and turns right. After crossing a brook and then paralleling Post Brook, the trail joins the Wyanokie Crest Trail (yellow on white) as it comes in from the left at 2.8 miles and leaves to the right at 2.9 miles. The Hewitt-Butler Trail bears left at 3.6 miles at the end of the Otter Hole Trail (green). Crossing Post Brook, the Hewitt-Butler Trail ascends to and crosses Glenwild Avenue at 3.7 miles.

Entering the woods, it passes the Torne Trail (red) at 3.8 miles and makes a steep ascent of Torne Mountain. (The Torne Trail is a bypass around the peak.) The summit offers views of the surrounding valley and mountains. Continuing past the other end of the Torne Trail (red) at 4.4 miles, the Hewitt-Butler Trail reaches the views on Osio Rock. Descending west, it reaches a valley floor and turns south to cross a brook at 5.0 miles. After slowly ascending, leveling off, and then gradually descending, the trail crosses a small brook and a woods road. It then climbs a small rise before finally dropping down to reach a parking area at 6.8 miles at the entrance to Camp Vacamus, at Henion Pond (also

known as Lake Larriwien). This small parking area is made available to hikers through the courtesy of the camp's directors. Hikers are asked not to overcrowd the area, but to leave spaces for camp vehicles and, if necessary, to park outside the camp's property. The camp grounds are private, and the pond is not open to the public for swimming or fishing.

The Highlands Trail (teal diamond) is co-aligned with the Hewitt-Butler in several places in the Norvin Green State Forest.

Highlands Trail *Length: 13.0 miles Blaze: teal diamond*
Within the Wyanokies, the Highlands Trail is co-aligned on portions of Hewitt-Butler (blue), Horse Pond Mountain (white), Stonetown Circular (red), Wyanokie Circular (red), Mine (yellow on white), Wyanokie Crest (yellow on white), and Otter Hole (green) trails. See chapter 14, "Long Distance Trails," for a complete description of the exact route.

Horse Pond Mountain Trail *Length: 2.0 miles Blaze: white*
The Horse Pond Mountain Trail connects the Hewitt-Butler Trail (blue) in Long Pond Ironworks State Park with the Stonetown Circular Trail (red triangle on white) on Harrison Mountain. Access to the north end is via the Hewitt-Butler Trail (blue) 0.9 mile from its trailhead. Access to the south end requires taking the Stonetown Circular Trail from its crossing of Stonetown Road at Lake Rickonda Road. The trail traverses the length of Horse Pond Mountain, with views of the Monksville Reservoir, and then climbs Harrison Mountain to the south. Here, it ends at the Stonetown Circular Trail. A short walk on the Stonetown Circular Trail to a power line crossing provides a nearly 360-degree view of both Wanaque and Monksville reservoirs and the mountains beyond. The entire trail is co-aligned with the Highlands Trail (teal diamond).

Lower Trail *Length: 1.4 miles Blaze: white*
The Lower Trail extends between the Wyanokie Circular Trail (red on white) east of High Point and the Post Brook Trail (white) east of Chikahoki Falls. Its northern terminus is reached by following the Wyanokie Circular Trail south 1.0 mile from Snake Den Road East. It borders the Wanaque Reservoir property line and, near its southern end, passes the Carris Hill Trail (yellow).

Macopin Trail *Length: 0.5 mile Blaze: white*
The Macopin Trail traverses the flanks of Wyanokie High Point to provide a connection between the Otter Hole Trail (green) and the Hewitt-Butler Trail (blue) for hikers who want to avoid climbing over Wyanokie High Point. Its western terminus is 1.8 miles north of Glenwild Avenue along the Otter Hole Trail.

Mine Trail (eastern section) *Length: 2.9 miles Blaze: yellow on white*
The Mine Trail, which takes the hiker to a mine that can be entered, begins on Snake Den Road East, 50 yards from the eastern end of the Weis Ecology Center first parking lot. It ends at the junction with the Otter Hole Trail (green).

Initially passing through private land, the trail runs jointly with the Wyanokie Circular Trail (red on white), but branches off to the right at 0.2 mile. Descending steeply, the Mine Trail crosses a brook before reaching Wyanokie Falls at 0.5 mile. After crossing the Wyanokie Circular Trail at 0.7 mile, the Mine Trail, at 0.8 mile, ascends to the viewpoint on Ball Mountain, named for two large ball-shaped rock outcrops.

The trail continues along the ridge to a viewpoint before descending to Roomy Mine at 1.2 miles. This mine, which was opened about 1840 and worked until 1857, extends nearly 100 feet into the hillside and may be entered. In a short distance, the Mine Trail again joins the Wyanokie Circular Trail to pass the flooded Blue Mine at 1.6 miles. After crossing a brook, the Mine Trail leaves the Wyanokie Circular Trail at 1.8 miles. It follows a low route to join the Hewitt-Butler Trail (blue) at 2.5 miles, and together they reach Snake Den Road East (unpaved) at 2.6 miles. Here, the Hewitt-Butler Trail turns right, while the Mine Trail turns left and passes the abandoned Winfield Farm before reaching the end of the Otter Hole Trail (green) at 2.9 miles. Beginning in 1998, the section between the Otter Hole Trail and Boy Scout Lake is closed. For more information about the status of this section, contact the New York-New Jersey Trail Conference at (212) 685-9699.

Mine Trail (western section)   *Length: 1.2 miles Blaze: yellow on white*
The Mine Trail resumes at the dam at Boy Scout Lake. Just across the dam, the Mine Trail turns north (right) to follow the outlet of the lake to West Brook Road, where it ends at 1.2 miles. Parking is available 0.3 mile west on West Brook Road.

Monks Trail   *Length: 1.7 miles Blaze: white*
Although a short loop, the Monks Trail in Long Pond Iron Works State Park offers hikers a pleasant jaunt through varied terrain, including a view over the Monksville Reservoir. Adding the 0.1-mile round trip to the viewpoint and the walk on the service road and through the parking lot results in a hike of 2.3 miles. The viewpoint is approximately halfway through the hike. The route is suitable for cross-country skiing, conditions permitting. The Monks Trail is accessible from the boat launch parking area for the Wanaque Reservoir located 0.5 mile north of the intersection of Margaret King Avenue and County 511. For those hikers wishing a shorter hike, access to the viewpoint is possible via an unmarked side trail from the boat launch parking area located 0.4 mile south

of the intersection of Margaret King Avenue and County 511.

From the northern boat launch parking area, walk towards the entrance. The trailhead is 0.1 mile from the entrance on the right-hand side of road, just after the NO PARKING signs. The Monks Trail enters the woods up a short flight of wooden steps, and begins a gradual climb. At 0.1 mile, it turns right onto a woods road and passes through a hardwood forest with boulders littering the ground. It crosses under a power line at 0.4 mile and then crosses a gas line. Turning right off the woods road at 0.5 mile, the trail crosses a seasonal stream and then follows a narrow ridge. The trail then passes an unmarked side trail which leads to the southern boat launch parking area, off of County 511.

The trail continues to climb and reaches an unmarked side trail to a viewpoint over the Monksville Reservoir. The Monks Trail descends, sometimes steeply, passing a rock face covered with lichen and a bed of ferns. It reaches the power line again, and turns left towards the utility road, where it ends at 1.7 miles. The boat launch parking lot is 0.5 mile to the right.

Otter Hole Trail   *Length: 2.0 miles Blaze: green*
The Otter Hole Trail connects the Hewitt-Butler Trail (blue) at the Otter Hole and the Mine Trail (yellow on white). The southern terminus of the Otter Hole Trail is on the Hewitt-Butler Trail less than 0.1 mile across a brook north of where the Hewitt-Butler Trail crosses Glenwild Avenue. Proceeding north along an old farm road, the Otter Hole Trail, at 0.5 mile, crosses the Wyanokie Crest Trail (yellow) and descends gradually to meet the Wyanokie Circular Trail (red on white) at 1.2 miles. It passes the end of the Macopin Trail (white) on the right in 1.6 miles. Leaving the farm road, it ascends, traverses the base of Assiniwikam Mountain, and ends at the Mine Trail (yellow on white). The Highlands Trail (teal diamond) is co-aligned with 0.5 mile of the southern part of the trail. Parking is available where the Hewitt-Butler Trail crosses Glenwild Avenue.

Outlaw Trail   *Length: 0.3 mile Blaze: orange*
Connecting the Wyanokie Circular (red on white) and Wyanokie Crest (yellow) trails, the Outlaw Trail is a level shortcut that takes hikers through mountain laurel.

Post Brook Trail   *Length: 3.0 miles Blaze: white*
Parking for the Post Brook Trail is at the junction of County 511 and Doty

Road in Haskell. The trail follows Doty Road one mile west before entering the woods to the right and passing between hills to a rhododendron grove. After crossing two more roads, it zigzags around boulders through a ravine of hemlocks. It crosses Post Brook twice, then parallels it, passes the southern terminus of the Lower Trail (white), then Chikahoki Falls, and ends at the Hewitt-Butler Trail (blue).

Stonetown Circular Trail   *Length: 9.6 miles Blaze: red triangle on white*
The Stonetown Circular Trail completes a circuit on both sides of Stonetown Road west of the Wanaque Reservoir. Much of its route is through predominantly oak forest. It crosses and follows roads three times and has four places where hikers can park cars. Since there is steep climbing on either side, and the trail is fairly long, some hikers do only one side at a time. Ample parking is available at the lower ballfield parking lot on Mary Roth Drive (0.5 mile north of West Brook Road), at Lake Rickonda Road, at the end of White Road, and at a gate to watershed property.

From the ballfield parking lot, the Stonetown Circular Trail turns left onto Stonetown Road, and passes the fire house. At 0.3 mile, the trail turns left on Magee Road, crosses a bridge at 0.5 mile, and turns right onto a woods road. It leaves the woods road at 0.8 mile, only to return briefly before ascending to reach a seasonal view to the south at 1.1 miles. Following the ridge, the trail reaches Signal Rock at 1.3 miles, with a view of Windbeam Mountain. Descending past boulders and alternating between woods roads and footpaths, the trail turns and winds along a rocky path to reach the base of Tory Rocks at 1.9 miles. The tumbled boulders offer some shelter beneath them and are reported to have been hideouts of Tory soldiers during the American Revolution. The Stonetown Circular Trail makes a short steep climb to a 270-degree view on the top of Tory Rocks and then descends. After two left turns onto woods roads, the trail reaches,

Rhododendron

at 2.4 miles, unpaved Burnt Meadow Road and turns right onto the road. At 2.8 miles, the trail crosses a bridge and leaves the road to the right.

The Stonetown Circular Trail follows woods roads over the next 0.4 mile. After turning right, the trail climbs Harrison Mountain and, at 3.3 miles, reaches the ridge. Following the ridge on woods roads, the trail crosses a power line at 3.9 miles. At 4.1 miles, it passes the terminus of Horse Pond Mountain Trail (white) on the left, where the Highlands Trail (teal diamond) also joins. The Highlands Trail and the Stonetown Circular Trail are co-aligned for the remaining 5.3 miles on the eastern portion of the loop.

The two trails descend to cross the power line service road at 4.2 miles. Directly under the power line, they reach a nearly 360-degree view of both Wanaque and Monksville reservoirs and the mountains beyond. To the southeast are Board, Bear, and Windbeam mountains that the Stonetown Circular Trail will traverse to complete the loop. The trail descends from the lookout on a narrow path through a laurel grove. After crossing a stream, it reaches the end of Lake Rickonda Road at 4.7 miles, where parking is available.

The trail follows Lake Rickonda Road, reaches Stonetown Road at 4.9 miles, and turns left. After following the road for 0.3 mile, the trail turns right onto White Road. At 5.6 miles, at the end of White Road (where there is parking), the trail turns left and almost immediately turns right, to enter the woods. After crossing a large slab of rock, the trail descends to reach, at 5.8 miles, the first of three stream crossings. After crossing the third stream at 6.1 miles, the trail ascends Board Mountain. At 6.3 miles, there is a view to the north of the Monksville Reservoir dam. The trail goes over to the top of Board Mountain and, at 6.5 miles, begins a steep descent. After crossing a woods road at 6.8 miles, the trail ascends Bear Mountain with views at 7.2 miles, mainly to the west. Immediately after a view south of the Wanaque Reservoir, the trail picks its way down a rocky crag. It jogs first right onto a woods road and then off to the left to begin a long ascent of Windbeam Mountain. After reaching the top at 8.3 miles, the trail descends briefly into a saddle, ascends to a view to the north, and then descends into a second saddle. At the top of the next rise, at 8.9 miles, there is a view to the west and, almost immediately, a view to the east over the reservoir. A long, steep descent on a treadway with sidehill construction and steps culminates on Stonetown Road at 9.4 miles where the Highlands Trail (teal diamond) departs to the left and the Stonetown Circular Trail turns right. One or two cars may be left off the road at a watershed gate but not blocking it, a few yards up Stonetown Road. The trail follows the road to return to Mary Roth Drive at 9.6 miles, completing the loop.

Torne Trail
Length: 0.5 mile Blaze: red

Beginning on the Hewitt-Butler Trail (blue) just south of Glenwild Avenue, the Torne Trail bypasses the Hewitt-Butler's ascent to the peak of Torne Mountain, rejoining the Hewitt-Butler at a point southeast of the mountain. Parking is available at Glenwild Avenue.

W Trail
Length: 1.1 miles Blaze: W on white square

The W Trail is entirely on the Weis Ecology Center property and is used for nature walks. It also provides a prettier alternative to walking along paved Snake Den Road to reach the Hewitt-Butler and Mine trails. It is a lollypop-shaped trail—a long handle with a loop at the end. The trail begins and ends at the red signboard at the west end of the field containing the Nature Center. After crossing several wooden bridges, it reaches and turns right onto Snake Den Road East (unpaved) at the point where a bridge is missing. It leaves the road in 200 feet, going left along a stream. At 0.5 mile, it turns right, away from the stream, and passes through the former Winfield Farm before turning right on the Mine Trail (yellow) on unpaved Snake Den Road East, completing the loop at 0.7 mile. At the missing bridge (above), it turns left to return to the beginning at 1.1 miles.

Wyanokie Circular Trail
Length: 4.4 miles Blaze: red on white

Hikers on the Wyanokie Circular Trail should pay attention at trail junctions, as, over its course, the trail crosses, leaves or joins seven different trails, some of them more than once. Because there are so many trail crossings, a wide variety of hikes are possible through the mostly open, hardwood forest.

Beginning on Snake Den Road East, 50 yards from the eastern end of the Weis Ecology Center first parking lot, the Wyanokie Circular Trail, along with the Mine Trail (yellow on white), passes between houses and enters the woods. At 0.2 mile, the Wyanokie Circular Trail continues straight ahead as the Mine Trail (yellow on white) leaves to the right. The trails cross at 0.3 mile, and then, at 0.6 mile, join again. At a T junction, they turn right and cross Blue Mine Brook on a wooden footbridge, with the water-filled Blue Mine straight ahead on the left. At 1.0 mile, the Mine Trail veers off to the right. In 100 yards, after crossing another stream, the Wyanokie Circular Trail passes the end of the Lower Trail (white) on the left.

The trail begins a steep ascent and reaches open views to the south at 1.7 miles, and then comes to a view to the east. At 1.8 miles, it reaches Wyanokie High Point, with a panoramic view, including the Manhattan skyline on the horizon. At the base of a short, steep descent, it meets the Hewitt-Butler Trail (blue), which comes in from the right. At 2.0 miles, the trails split at a Y junction, where the Hewitt-Butler leaves to the left. Passing through a laurel thicket, the Wyanokie Circular Trail crosses a woods road and enters a tunnel of mountain laurel at 2.7 miles.

Pitch pine

After passing the end of the Outlaw Trail (orange) at 2.9 miles, the Wyanokie Circular Trail crosses the Otter Hole Trail (green) at 3.1 miles. Weaving through a forest of glacial erratics, the Wyanokie Circular Trail crosses a gravel road at 3.4 miles. It climbs steeply up the sides of a ravine before crossing the Wyanokie Crest Trail (yellow) at 3.6 miles near the top of Assiniwikam Mountain. Gradually descending, the trail crosses a tributary of Boy Scout Lake, and then at 4.1 miles meets a woods road which becomes Snake Den Road West. There are NO PARKING signs posted in the area. The road continues on the west shore of Boy Scout Lake (owned by the Borough of West Caldwell) and at the end of the lake, the trail turns right. It crosses a dam and intersects the Mine Trail (yellow) at 4.4 miles.

Beginning in 1998, the section between Boy Scout Lake and the Weis Ecology Center was closed. For more information about this section, contact the New York-New Jersey Trail Conference at (212) 685-9699. The Highlands Trail (teal diamond) is co-aligned in several sections.

Wyanokie Crest Trail   *Length: 4.7 miles Blaze: yellow*
The Wyanokie Crest Trail traverses the two highest summits in the Wyanokies, Buck and Assiniwikam mountains. Its southern terminus is on Glenwild Avenue, 0.7 mile south of Otter Hole and just north of Lake Kampfe. Parking is available at the trailhead. See the Hewitt-Butler Trail (southern section) above

for driving instructions to Glenwild Avenue.

The trail heads north, following a tributary of Lake Kampfe, crossing it twice as it meanders through a glacial wetland. It proceeds over a series of small hills and crosses Post Brook to turn right onto the Hewitt-Butler Trail (blue) at 0.6 mile. Leaving the Hewitt-Butler Trail at 0.7 mile, the Wyanokie Crest Trail swings north, descending gently to a feeder of Post Brook at 0.9 mile.

The next mile is perhaps one of the wildest areas in all of Norvin Green State Forest. The trail closely follows the stream, with its many roaring cascades, uphill, with occasional rough footing. This section is particularly scenic during high water. Leaving the stream at 1.3 miles, the trail skirts a swampy area before ascending steeply to an open outcropping with seasonal views. Meandering up and down and through boulders, the trail rises west to its high point on the ridge. Continuing on this ridge, the trail emerges, at 1.9 miles, at a viewpoint with steep ledges which overlooks Buck Mountain. The trail descends, tunneling through laurel and crossing a brook and the Otter Hole Trail (green) at 2.3 miles, where the Highlands Trail joins it. After descending to a hollow, the trail makes an abrupt climb of 200 feet to the ledges of Buck Mountain, with its panoramic view, at 2.5 miles. The trail soon reaches a second view, this time of the Otter Hole area, Torne Mountain, and hills to the west and south.

Continuing north through laurel, the Highlands Trail (teal diamond) departs to the left, and then the Wyanokie Crest Trail ascends to a rockface. Unfortunately, at 1,290 feet, the highest point in the Wyanokies has no view. Descending, the Wyanokie Crest Trail attains a secondary summit before reaching another viewpoint, which offers its best vistas in winter. From here, the rounded summit of Assiniwikam Mountain is visible.

Descending gradually from Buck Mountain at 3.2 miles, the trail reaches a series of brooks, which it follows closely, and then crosses a woods road. It then ascends the slopes of Assiniwikam Mountain, intersecting, at 4.6 miles, the Wyanokie Circular Trail (red on white). This mountain, with its glacially-smoothed bedrock, has several false summits, and the footing is occasionally difficult. In winter there are views west just off the trail atop the first main summit at 4.7 miles.

Beginning in 1998, the section between Assiniwikam Mountain and the Hewitt-Butler Trail was closed. For more information about this section, contact the New York-New Jersey Trail Conference at (212) 685-9699. The Highlands Trail (teal diamond) is co-aligned briefly in two places.

SIX

GREENWOOD LAKE AREA

he long sliver of water that re-
sulted when Peter Hasenclever built a dam at Long Pond to provide power for
his ironworks downstream is now known as Greenwood Lake. The ironworks
site is still in evidence, and hikers on the Sterling Ridge Trail can see the old
furnace and giant waterwheels—one of them rebuilt—just south of a
hemlock-laced section of the Wanaque River. The Monksville Reservoir in West
Milford and Ringwood, created by damming the Wanaque River north of the
Wanaque Reservoir, was completed in 1987. The ironworks site, now Long
Pond Ironworks State Park, was protected, though much beautiful land was
submerged. Most of the area east of the lake and not in New Jersey is within
the formerly privately owned Sterling Forest. See chapter 1, "Trails and Trail
Development, " for more details about the history of the fight to save Sterling
Forest from development.

Bearfort Ridge, consisting of Paleozoic sandstone and quartz conglomerate, is the southern continuation of Schunemunk Mountain in New York. Greenwood Lake is a shale and limestone valley. This down-faulted wedge is sand-
wiched between the Wawayanda and Wyanokie plateaus.

BOUNDARY WALKS

For someone highly skilled in the use of compass and topographic map, trac-
ing the New York-New Jersey boundary can be an excellent exercise and a true
challenge. The southern boundary of Rockland and Orange counties runs for

many miles through the deep woods of the Highlands. At the end of every mile, measured from the Hudson River, there is a small, inconspicuous stone marker. All the other boundaries of New Jersey are natural shorelines or river courses.

The northeastern boundary was first defined in 1664, when James, Duke of York, sold the province of New Jersey to Berkeley and Carteret. The terminal points were defined as the mouth of "the northernmost branch of the said bay or river Delaware, which is 41° 40' of latitude [there is no such point], and the intersection of latitude 41° with Hudson's River." The actual positions of the terminal points were not agreed on until 1769. In 1770, a joint Colonial boundary commission tried to locate the line, but was discomfited by a show of weapons and other evidence of unfriendliness on the part of residents of the coastal plain section. Consequently they took to the woods to do what they could toward defining the boundary there. The cause of all this hostility, one may surmise, was local satisfaction with a state of affairs that made it difficult for either colony to collect taxes. The job was finally completed, however, and mile markers were set in 1774. Many of them can still be found down among the leaves and bushes, with their antiquated and amateurishly carved lettering.

A more precise survey was made just one hundred years later, in 1874, and was followed by a joint state resurvey in 1882, when new markers were set alongside the old stones. The new ones are of granite, with dressed tops 6 inches square projecting 6 inches out of the ground. Even these are difficult to find, particularly under a heavy snow.

The 1874 and 1882 surveys, made with reference to astronomically fixed positions, revealed that the boundary of 1774 had the general shape of a dog's hind leg, for a reason unsuspected by the pioneers. The 1774 survey was done with the magnetic compass and, since the Highlands are full of magnetic iron ore, the compass line rambles accordingly. At Greenwood Lake the marker was 2,415 feet, or nearly half a mile, southwest of the straight line between the termini. Since the land in the Highlands was of little value, the commissioners, being practical men, left well enough alone and did not disturb the mileposts of 1774. New York State thus retained, through magnetic attraction, a good many acres that the Duke of York intended to convey to the proprietors of New Jersey.

An interesting series of walks begins with Stone Number 15 in Suffern and continues approximately northwest for 33.5 miles to Stone Number 49, near Port Jervis. Number 21 is about a tenth of a mile east of the woods road leading north from Ringwood Manor and the White Trail, which starts there. Number 23

GREENWOOD LAKE *seen from near* TERRACE POND

is about a tenth of a mile northwest of the woods road that leads southwest from the vicinity of the former Sterling Furnace, and it can be reached by a woods road leaving the Sterling Ridge Trail (blue on white) about a mile north of Hewitt. Number 26 is on the northwest shore of Greenwood Lake, and the State Line Trail (blue dot on white square) has its start there. The distance between Numbers 22 and 23 is just under 0.9 mile; evidently, someone accidentally dropped ten chains (660 feet) from his count in 1774. In some sections the boundary is hazily indicated by dim dark-red blazes on the trees, deviating from the true course as if marking surveyors' gores.

The best time to follow the boundary is in the beginning of winter after the lakes and swamps are frozen, but before the snow has become too deep to permit finding the markers.

ABRAM S. HEWITT STATE FOREST

Immediately west of Greenwood Lake lies the Bearfort Mountain area, almost wholly within the Abram S. Hewitt State Forest, which is administered by Wawayanda State Park. It includes Surprise Lake and offers many viewpoints. Access to the trails is from a parking area on Warwick Turnpike about a mile west of the southern end of Greenwood Lake. For more information about Hewitt State Forest, contact Wawayanda State Park, P.O. Box 198, Highland Lakes, NJ 07422; (973) 553-4462.

93

Trails in Abram S. Hewitt State Forest

All trails within Abram S. Hewitt State Forest are designated hiking only. Greenwood Lake extends across the state line, with portions of its shoreline densely settled, particularly on the west side of the lake. The hiking trails are along the ridge and offer views over the lake.

Appalachian Trail　　　　　　　　　*Length: 0.8 mile Blaze: white*

A section of this long-distance trail provides an 0.3-mile connection between the State Line Trail (blue dot on white square) and the Ernest Walter Trail (yellow). The southbound trail continues west of that trail junction for half a mile before leaving the park. See chapter 14, "Long Distance Trails," for more details, or the *Appalachian Trail Guide to New York-New Jersey* for a complete description of the trail.

Bearfort Ridge Trail　　　　　　　*Length: 2.4 miles Blaze: white*

This trail, accessible via NJ Transit buses 196 and 197, starts near a concrete bridge, where parking is available, on the north side of Warwick Turnpike, less than a mile west of the intersection with Lakeside Road (County 511). From the eastern end of the bridge, the trail ascends through a hemlock grove to a woods road, but soon turns left as the Quail Trail (orange) continues straight ahead. The Bearfort Ridge Trail passes two small streams, and then climbs steeply to the top of the ridge, where there are open views to the south and west. It continues at basically the same elevation, about 1,300 feet, except for short descents into stream channels. For over a mile, the trail follows ridges comprised of deep-red Silurian puddingstone (Shawangunk Conglomerate) in a summit forest of pitch pine and scrub oak. Just before its northern end at the Ernest Walter Trail (yellow), there are several viewpoints, including a view of Surprise Lake to the north.

Ernest Walter Trail　　　　　　　*Length: 2.1 miles Blaze: yellow*

This interior trail, accessible from other trails, is named for a dedicated hiker and trail worker. It encircles Surprise Lake and West Pond. Its eastern terminus is 0.6 mile from the trailhead for the State Line Trail. At 0.2 mile from the beginning of the trail, a large, glacially-smoothed projection of conglomerate provides views to the east of Greenwood Lake and Sterling Ridge. Crossing west, the trail passes Surprise Lake and a rhododendron grove, ascending to the Bearfort Ridge Trail (white). The trail continues cross-ridge, with many abrupt and rocky ups and downs. Turning north, with continued rocky footing, the trail eventually ends at the Appalachian Trail.

Quail Trail *Length: 2.2 miles Blaze: orange*
This trail leaves the Bearfort Ridge Trail (white) 0.1 mile from Warwick Turnpike and follows woods roads uphill most of the way to its end at the junction with the Ernest Walter Trail (yellow) at Surprise Lake. It provides a more gradual ascent than the Bearfort Ridge Trail (white) but is somewhat wetter, particularly in spring. Several swampy sections must be negotiated after crossing Cooley Brook at 1.4 miles.

State Line Trail *Length: 1.2 miles Blaze: blue dot on white square*
The trail begins about seventy feet south of the New York-New Jersey state line on County 511, on the north side of a stream that passes under the road. Unfortunately, parking is difficult near the trailhead. Public transportation via NJ Transit buses 196 and 197 is available. From the trailhead, the trail soon crosses a brook and after about a quarter of a mile begins a climb through an oak forest, following a rocky streambed. Near the top of the ridge, at 0.6 mile, the Ernest Walter Trail (yellow) veers off to the left while the State Line Trail continues over a series of rocky ridges until it terminates at its junction with the Appalachian Trail (white) on the main ridge.

STERLING FOREST

The area that is now known as Sterling Forest played an important role in the history of early mining and the smelting industry and contains remains of over twenty old mines and several furnaces. Several of the mine shafts have been filled in and closed. Sterling Mine, one of those that no longer can be seen, opened in 1750. Its shaft sloped nearly 1,000 feet under Sterling Lake. It was the principal iron producer from 1900 to 1921, when it closed down along with the other Sterling workings. Southwest ridges are faced on the west by steep rugged cliffs, hidden in dense forest and invisible from any outside point, but striking to encounter in this little-visited region.

The New Jersey portions of Sterling Forest are protected as parts of the Wanaque Wildlife Management Area, Long Pond Ironworks State Park, and

Passaic County Park, while the New York portion is Sterling Forest State Park, part of the Palisades Interstate Park. As of 1998, the Palisades Interstate Park Commission has not developed a management plan for the state park.

Users of Sterling Forest should obtain the Greenwood Lake and Sloatsburg USGS topographic quadrangle maps. For more information about Wanaque Wildlife Management Area, contact New Jersey DEP, Division of Fish, Game and Wildlife, 501 East State Street, P.O. Box 400, Trenton, NJ 08625; (609) 292-2965. For more information about Sterling Forest State Park, contact the Palisades Interstate Park, Administration Building, Bear Mountain, NY 10911; (914) 786-2701.

Trails in Sterling Forest

The network of trails within Sterling Forest ignores not only park boundaries but also the state line. Rather than separate the trail descriptions according to who manages the property, the trails are listed as if they were managed by one entity and the land manager so noted.

Allis Trail   *Length: 2.5 miles Blaze: blue*

The Allis Trail, which serves as an access point to the Appalachian Trail (white), was named for J. Ashton Allis, a pioneer hiker and trail builder in the metropolitan area, and for many years president of the Fresh Air Club. It is part of Sterling Forest State Park.

Parking is on NY 17A. If coming from the east, it is 1.4 miles west of the traffic light at Sterling Forest Ski Area. If coming from the west, the parking is on the north side of the road just after a sharp right turn, 1.5 miles from the Sterling Ridge Trail parking and 3.3 miles from the junction of NY 210 and NY 17A in Greenwood Lake village. The trailhead is on NY 17A, 80 yards east of the parking, but it is safer to follow the pipeline east from the back of the parking area to the top of a rise.

Almost immediately after leaving its southern terminus on NY 17A, the trail crosses a pipeline and a power line before reaching Sterling Mountain, where there is a view of Schunemunk Mountain. From here, it descends to the Appalachian Trail west of Mombasha High Point. The Highlands Trail (teal diamond) is co-aligned for the entire length.

Highlands Trail *Length: 8.6 miles Blaze: teal diamond*
The Highlands Trail is co-aligned with the Sterling Ridge Trail (blue on white);
see below for a brief description.

Jennings Hollow Trail *Length: 3.0 miles Blaze: yellow*
Starting less than a mile from the southern terminus of the Sterling Ridge Trail
(blue on white), this old road follows a brook for the first 1.5 miles, passing
the stone walls and foundations of former farms. It crosses the brook at the
base of a mountain, where the brook tumbles down over rocks through a hemlock ravine near the New Jersey-New York state line. Here the trail turns west
and south on another woods road, and ends on the East Shore Road at a
wooden bridge. About a quarter mile before the southern terminus, an alternate route recrosses the brook and returns to the Jennings Hollow Trail about
one mile from its start at the Sterling Ridge Trail. The Jennings Hollow Trail is
in the Wanaque Wildlife Management Area, which is managed for hunting
deer, wild turkey, and grouse, and for fishing trout, bass, and chain pickerel.

Sterling Ridge Trail *Length: 8.6 miles Blaze: blue on white*
 The Sterling Ridge Trail traverses the Tuxedo Mountains between Hewitt

Waterwheels of the Long Pond Ironworks

in New Jersey and NY 17A in New York. After starting in New Jersey as part of the Long Pond Ironworks State Park, the trail enters the Wanaque Wildlife Management Area and then crosses the state line into Sterling Forest State Park. Since the wildlife management area and Sterling Forest State Park permit hunting, hikers are cautioned to wear blaze orange or limit their hiking in New Jersey to Sundays during hunting season. Parking is available on County 511 across from the junction with East Shore Road. Public transportation is available to the northern trailhead on NJ Transit bus 197.

Near the southern end of the Sterling Ridge Trail are the ruins of Peter Hasenclever's Long Pond Ironworks. Founded in 1766 and in operation until 1882, the ironworks once supported a thriving community.

The trail begins in New Jersey at the guard rail blocking the old main street of what was the village of Hewitt. It is lined with remnants of the sawmill and other village buildings in the form of foundations and crumbling walls. The road intersects with another old road at the site of what was the company store. The trail proceeds to the furnace site as it angles across the road.

The ironworks site is officially closed to the public, and hikers are requested to remain on the trail. The complex contains the remains of the old furnace, which dates back to the eighteenth century, and in the past has been the object of vandalism. The ruins of the Hasenclever furnace were discovered in a mound covered with leaves in 1956 and were excavated in 1967. Two original 25-foot waterwheels burned in 1957. One has been stabilized in its ruined condition; the other was reconstructed on its original hub in 1994 with a grant from the New Jersey Historic Trust and Green Acres funds. The Friends of the Long Pond Ironworks is spearheading restoration efforts and is offering public tours and programs; for information, contact them at (973) 839-0128.

From the furnace site, the Sterling Ridge Trail, at 0.4 mile, crosses the river on a suspension bridge to follow an old road, which veers away from the river and follows a tributary. At 1.1 miles, the trail passes the beginning of the Jennings Hollow Trail (yellow). The Sterling Ridge Trail ascends Big Beech Mountain, levels off, and ascends more steeply. The false summit, at 2.0 miles, has views to the southwest and the summit, at 2.2 miles, has views of Bearfort Mountain and the Wyanokies. The Sterling Ridge Trail begins a steep descent and reaches the New York-New Jersey state line at 2.6 miles.

After crossing several woods roads, the trail ascends to reach, at 3.1 miles, a high point with views to the south and then, at 3.4 miles, descends to a view to the west. At 3.9 miles, the trail makes a right turn followed by a steep ascent and then level ridge walking. At 5.0 miles, the trail makes a sharp left turn and ascends to reach a fire tower with 360-degree views of Sterling Forest. Over the next 2.1 miles, the Sterling Ridge Trail has many ups and downs with viewpoints along the way, including views of Sterling Lake at 5.9 miles and 6.4 miles. The trail crosses a power line at 7.5 miles and enters the woods. At 8.6 miles, it reaches NY 17A where it ends. The trailhead is 1.8 miles east of the junction of NY 210 and NY 17A in Greenwood Lake village. A wide spot on the south side of the road accommodates parking for a few cars. The Highlands Trail (teal diamond) is co-aligned for the entire length.

WAWAYANDA STATE PARK

Wawayanda State Park embraces almost 15,000 acres of forests and waters in the rough, hilly country of the New Jersey Highlands. The name, pronounced *Wa-wa-yanda*, is the phonetic rendition of the Lenape name, said to mean "winding, winding water." The name was first applied, around 1700, to the meadowlands in the valley below. Wawayanda Lake, one of the focal points of the park, is 1.5 miles long, has 5.5 miles of wooded shoreline, and covers 255 acres.

Ten-acre Laurel Pond, east of Wawayanda Lake is mostly spring-fed and fairly deep. At the southeast end of the pond, on a steep slope, is a stand of hemlock, possibly the only virgin timber on the mountain. Toward the eastern part of the Wawayanda "Plateau" (it is not a plateau in the geological sense), on which the park is situated, various old woods roads and paths lead southward and penetrate one of the finest jungles of this kind in New Jersey. The extensive stand of southern white cedar is far away from and above its usual stands along the seacoast marshes.

The section of park located to the east of Clinton Road and including the Terrace Pond area was designated a natural area in 1978. The pond, a popular hiking destination since the 1930s, lies at an altitude of 1,380 feet and is surrounded by high cliffs of pudding-stone conglomerate, massive rhododendron, and blueberry swamps.

Wawayanda State Park also includes High Breeze Farm National Historic District. Located on Barrett Road, the 160-acre farm is one of the last intact nineteenth-century farmsteads in the North Jersey Highlands. Owned by the Barrett family from 1860 to 1983, it was acquired by the state's Department of Environmental Protection (DEP) to buffer the Appalachian Trail. The farm was declared a National Historic District in 1989. The DEP is pursuing plans to develop it as a living history museum, but as of 1998, it is closed to the public.

The main entrance to the park is off Warwick Turnpike, about 3 miles north of Upper Greenwood Lake. For more information, contact Wawayanda State Park, P.O. Box 198, Highland Lakes, NJ 07422; (973) 853-4462.

History

Wawayanda Lake, once called Double Pond, was originally two bodies of water separated by a narrow strip of land that is still partly visible on the west side of Barker Island, in the center of the present lake. In 1846, the Thomas Iron Company rebuilt the earthen dam at the northeastern end of the lake. A wing dam also was constructed on the eastern shore, over which the waters spill to help feed Laurel Pond. These dams raised the lake level about 7½ feet.

Three hundred feet beyond the northeast end of Wawayanda Lake, along Wawayanda Road, are the remains of a charcoal blast furnace where iron was produced. Oliver Ames and his sons William, Oakes, and Oliver, Jr. constructed the furnace in 1845–46. William supervised the work. His initials, "W.L.A.," and the date "1846" are still visible on a lintel in the main arch of the old furnace, which operated from 1846 to 1866. The iron produced here went to make shovels and wheels for railroad cars. During the Civil War, the Ames factories filled government orders for shovels and swords.

The Wawayanda iron mine, now covered, was first opened in 1776. It was located 2.5 miles northeast of the iron furnace along the east side of Wawayanda Road and consisted of five openings or shafts. The largest was 100 feet in depth and traveled along a vein of ore 12 to 15 feet wide. Men and mules worked in shifts in the mines, hauling the ore and tailings to the surface. The mule barn was directly opposite the most southeasterly shaft, across a small creek on the west side of Wawayanda Road. The foundation of the barn still exists. Tradition has it that several men and one or more mules were buried in a tunnel cave-in.

Recognized as a recreational resource since the 1850s, Wawayanda Lake and its environs were only secured for permanent public use beginning in 1963. A developer was eyeing the property then owned by the New Jersey Zinc Company, which was in financial distress, with the intent of turning it into a subdivision. The Green Acres bond program made the acquisition of Lake Wawayanda one of its top priorities, and the purchase of the first 4,000 acres took place in 1963. Eleven adjacent tracts, totaling 3,200 acres, were added in 1966, with subsequent purchases bringing it up to its present size.

The first YMCA camp in the United States was at Wawayanda Lake. Camp

Wawayanda operated here first in 1888, and continuously from 1903 to 1917, when it moved to Lake Aeroflex, as it is known today, in Andover (now Kittatinny Valley State Park). By the late 1950s, the camp moved to its current location at Frost Valley in the Catskills.

Trails in Wawayanda State Park

The trail system currently totals almost sixty miles of hiking trails and woods roads, some of which are marked as trails. Park trail maps are available from the ranger's office at the address above. Most of the woods roads are fairly level and are excellent for cross-country skiing when conditions are favorable. Snow cover accumulates earlier and lasts longer here than in other areas because of the higher elevation, heavy foliage, and numerous evergreens. The trails listed below are among the most scenic in the park.

Appalachian Trail   *Length: 5.5 miles Blaze: white*
This major trail traverses the park. See chapter 14, "Long Distance Trails," for a brief description, or the *Appalachian Trail Guide to New York-New Jersey* for a complete description of the 5.5 miles.

Banker Trail   *Length: 1.5 miles Blaze: yellow*
The Banker Trail begins at the end of Banker Road, where there is limited parking. It parallels a fence marking private property, and then crosses a stream through a wet and muddy section at 0.1 mile. The trail rises to drier ground through mixed deciduous and hemlock woods and passes the end of the Cedar Swamp Trail (blue) on the right at 1.2 miles. The Banker Trail ends at Cherry Ridge Road (unmarked), where limited parking is also available.

Black Eagle Trail   *Length: 0.7 mile Blaze: green on white*
A multi-use trail beginning in the middle of the Hoeferlin Trail (blue), the Black Eagle Trail travels through a high canopy forest, as well as a cool, quiet pine forest. The Black Eagle Trail is popular with families and cross-country skiers because it has a mild, gentle grade and a few small hills. The trail crosses the park entrance road before ending at Wawayanda Road.

Cedar Swamp Trail

Length: 1.3 miles Blaze: blue

Passing through some of the most spectacular foliage in the park, Cedar Swamp Trail's northern terminus is on the Double Pond Trail (yellow), 0.8 mile from Banker Road or 1.3 miles from the Wawayanda Lake parking area. Passing first through an open deciduous forest for 0.5 mile, the trail then descends slightly to cross approximately 700 feet of cedar swamp on a boardwalk through extensive rhododendron growth. Continuing through drier sections of mixed hardwoods and evergreens, it ends at the Banker Trail (yellow). Parking is available on Banker Road, 0.7 mile off Warwick Turnpike at Upper Greenwood Lake, and on Cherry Ridge Road, near the southern end of the Banker Trail, off Clinton Road.

Double Pond Trail

Length: 1.7 miles Blaze: yellow

Formerly Double Pond Road, this multi-use trail, with only a few visible blazes, starts at Banker Road 0.7 mile off Warwick Turnpike near Upper Greenwood Lake. It passes the Hoeferlin Trail (blue) in 0.5 mile, and then the Cedar Swamp (blue) and Red Dot (red) trails at 0.8 and 1.5 miles, respectively. Before reaching the furnace and Wawayanda Lake area, the Double Pond Trail crosses Cedar Swamp, which may be muddy in wet weather. Parking is available on Banker Road and at Wawayanda Lake.

Hoeferlin Trail

Length: 1.8 miles Blaze: blue

Though named for William Hoeferlin, this trail bears no other relation to the Hoeferlin Memorial Trail (yellow) in the Ramapos. Parking is available at the park office.

Starting from the Appalachian Trail, 0.6 mile north of the park office, the Hoeferlin Trail continues south on a wide level lane, often used by cross-country skiers. At the park office, it crosses the main park entrance road. After a gentle climb, the corridor is lined with mountain laurel, which hides an active frog pond to the right. A short distance ahead, the trail passes one end of the Black Eagle Trail (green). Gradually, the trail begins to narrow, with a long gentle slope downward, which in places resembles a rocky stream bed. About halfway down the trail, on the right, is a field of ferns shaded by a high canopy of hardwoods. The ever-increasing rocky nature of the trail is interspersed with a soft carpeting from the abundant conifers. Increasingly the trail is lined with rhododendrons until they form an intimate tunnel. The trail ends at the Double Pond Trail (yellow), which can be followed to the left for 0.5 mile to parking on Banker Road.

Laurel Pond Trail   *Length: 1.5 miles Blaze: yellow*

A former road, this multi-use trail begins near the remains of the furnace at the northeast end of Wawayanda Lake. It passes Laurel Pond, then climbs gradually to a high point just east of the lake. Partial views of the area are found from the summit of this rise just off the trail. The Laurel Pond Trail then heads gradually downhill through deep woods to its junction with Cherry Ridge Road, closed at this point to motor traffic. Parking is available at Wawayanda Lake.

Lookout Trail   *Length: 1.3 miles Blaze: white*

Beginning on Cherry Ridge Road (unmarked) about 150 yards west of the end of the Laurel Pond Trail (yellow), the Lookout Trail heads south through a stand of mature hemlocks and then hardwood trees. The ridge to the west is Cherry Ridge. The trail drops steeply past large boulders and reaches Lake Lookout at 0.9 mile. The grassy area on the shore of the lake is a pleasant lunch place. The Lookout Trail ends at the Old Coal Trail (red).

Old Coal Trail   *Length: 2.2 miles Blaze: red*

The Old Coal Trail starts on Clinton Road at a gated woods road about 100 yards south of parking area P7 for the Terrace Pond South trailhead. Almost immediately it passes a wet, marshy section of Bearfort Waters and then passes a camping facility (Wildcat Mountain Wilderness Center, Project of U.S.E.). The woods road proceeds gradually uphill through hardwood forest and, at 0.4 mile, passes the start of the Bearfort Waters/Clinton Trail (yellow). The trail goes through sections of dense mountain laurel, passes a large stone wall, and reaches a gas line at 1.3 miles. After crossing a wet area, the trail reaches the Lookout Trail (white) on the left at 1.7 miles. The Old Coal Trail ends at Cherry Ridge Road (unmarked), which leads 2.1 miles to Clinton Road.

Red Dot Trail   *Length: 1.1 miles Blaze: red dot on white*

This circular multi-use trail leaves the Double Pond Trail (yellow) 1.5 miles from Banker Road. Approximately 0.1 mile from the start, the trail divides to form a circular path through primarily deciduous forest, with an interesting ridge on the western side of the loop. About halfway around the loop (at the southern end), an unmarked trail leads south to meet Cherry Ridge Road.

Spring North Trail   *Length: 2.0 miles Blaze: blue*

The Spring North Trail is a hiking-only trail. It starts on Stephens Road, about

0.5 mile off Union Valley Road (County 513), where parking is available. The trailhead is close to the northeast terminus of the Hanks East Trail (white). Beginning on a woods road, the trail passes first through a frequently wet area and then an old furnace site. In about 1.4 miles, it gently climbs the eastern slope of Bearfort Mountain. As it crosses over the ridge, the trail swings west along an old pipeline to the Terrace Pond Red Trail, where it ends.

Terrace Pond Circular

Length: 0.7 mile Blaze: white

This scenic trail around Terrace Pond intersects four trails: Terrace Pond North, Terrace Pond South, Terrace Pond Red, and Yellow Dot. Hikers to the pond will find good lunch spots overlooking the pond on the trail's western side, although the proximity of the area to Clinton Road sometimes makes these spots a bit too populated for the hiker seeking solitude. Parking is available on Clinton Road, approximately 7.8 miles north of NJ 23.

Terrace Pond North Trail

Length: 4.5 miles Blaze: blue

This trail leaves the Terrace Pond South Trail (yellow) a few yards in from Clinton Road. It bears left through the woods for 0.5 mile to a pipeline, which it follows for another 0.5 mile before turning right into the woods and then up and down over rocky ridges to reach the pond. There are views to the west along the way. At Terrace Pond, it intersects with the White Trail, circling the pond, and continues past the north end of the pond to rejoin the pipeline for another 0.5 mile before turning left to end on Warwick Turnpike. This section of the trail is rugged, with several steep

TERRACE POND
conglomerate, reddish with white markings
covered with lickens. base fluted.

ups and downs and some viewpoints. Parking is available on Clinton Road, approximately 7.8 miles north of NJ 23, and at the trailhead on Warwick Turnpike.

Terrace Pond Red Trail
Length: 1.7 miles Blaze: red

A hiking-only trail in the Bearfort Natural Area, the Terrace Pond Red Trail starts from parking area P8 on Stephens Road, approximately 0.8 mile off Union Valley Road (County 513), and near the gate for the Fire Tower West Trail (yellow). Heading northeast, it gently climbs at first and then passes interesting rock formations and goes through rich forests. It ends at the Terrace Pond Circular (white), which provides access to the Terrace Pond area.

Terrace Pond South Trail
Length: 1.4 miles Blaze: yellow

The Terrace Pond South Trail, a hiking-only trail in the Bearfort Natural Area, provides access to stands of rhododendron and blueberry bushes. It leads circuitously east and south then swings north again toward Terrace Pond. Along this northerly leg, views of the nearby Bearfort Mountain can be seen to the east. The Terrace Pond Red Trail crosses just south of Terrace Pond. The Terrace Pond South Trail ends at the white-blazed trail circling the pond. Parking is available on Clinton Road, approximately 7.8 miles north of NJ 23.

Wingdam Trail
Length: 1.2 miles Blaze: blue

The Wingdam Trail starts on a gravel road leading from the parking lot at the north end of Wawayanda Lake. To reach the trailhead, cross the stone dam at the end of lake and pass through the barrier of large boulders. Following a wide gravel woods road, the Wingdam Trail reaches a wooden bridge and the wing dam on the right at 0.4 mile. The water spilling under the bridge feeds Laurel Pond, which may be seen through the trees on the left after leaving the bridge. After passing several woods roads, the trail narrows and then climbs steeply to a hilltop with a rocky grassy area at 0.9 mile. The Wingdam Trail descends and then ends at the Laurel Pond Trail (yellow).

Yellow Dot Trail
Length: 2.0 miles Blaze: yellow

The northern terminus for the hiking-only Yellow Dot Trail is on the Terrace Pond Circular (white), approximately midway on the east side of Terrace Pond. From here the Yellow Dot travels briefly east, then turns right downhill, meeting the Terrace Pond Red Trail in about 0.5 mile and ending at the Terrace Pond South Trail (yellow) at a Y junction. The last portion of the trail is on a woods road. Parking is available on Clinton Road, approximately 7.8 miles north of NJ 23.

SEVEN

NORTHWESTERN JERSEY

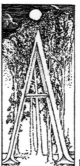

lthough New Jersey is thought of as highly industrialized, the northwestern part of the state is still largely rural and rugged, with farmlands and forests. In just Sussex County alone, there are over 80,000 acres of protected open space, including mountains, woodlands, wetlands, and farms. Warren County has immense water resources—reservoirs, rivers, lakes, and streams. Remnants of former railroads are throughout the area, some of which have been converted to rail trails, while others lie neglected with ties and ballast still intact.

In the nineteenth century, as the economy began shifting from agricultural to industrial with the iron industry as its center, villages developed around iron working centers, water power, or rapid routes of communication. Yet as one industry died or changed, these villages survived because they also served the surrounding agricultural communities. In the 1990s, since both I-78 and I-80 provide rapid access to the area, some towns have changed once again and become bedroom communities. Still others have become part of the tourist industry for hunters, fishermen, golfers, and others who enjoy the outdoors.

The Highlands Trail will eventually span the area from Mahlon Dickerson Reservation in Morris County to Phillipsburg on the Delaware River. Volunteers from the New York-New Jersey Trail Conference have been working with local parks and private landowners to connect open space but, as of 1998, there are several gaps. When the trail crosses private property, hikers should stay on the trail so that the landowners will continue to allow public access.

Lenni Lenape

Long before the white man arrived in North American, present-day New Jersey was home to the Lenni Lenape, which means "original people." The Munsees lived in the area north of the Delaware Water Gap as far as Kingston. The Unamis lived south of the Raritan River. Although the two main groups had language differences, they shared similar lifestyles. They were peaceful people, and for the most part formed friendly contacts with the white settlers.

Unfortunately, not much remains of the Lenape culture, but they left their imprint in place names. Anyone visiting the western part of the state will notice the plethora of place names ending in "ong". This suffix in the Munsee dialect meant "in," "in the," "on," "out of," or "place where there is," with the last meaning likely to be the more accurate. Prior to the arrival of the European settlers, the Munsee did not attach a name to an individual stream. When asked, they usually used a term that referred to an important event in the area or locally pursued economic activity.

Land-Use Practices

During early European settlement, several types of land use evolved. Estate owners purchased large tracts which frequently contained the most valuable parcels of land. Because these wealthy landowners financed surveys, they were able to locate the water power sites, valuable mineral deposits, and fertile soils. Their land management consisted, in part, of leasing the land to tenants. When these farmers cut wood to sell to the local charcoal industry, a common practice was to clear cut the wood lots. Later, small landowners appeared. Known as freeholders, they owned small tracts which included farm fields and wood lots. They were concerned with maintaining the woodlands but, like tenant farmers, did not always observe sound agricultural practices. In time a fourth group evolved, and often used the land to ruin. With land plentiful,

squatters cultivated the land and illegally harvested wood to sell to the charcoal industry. With no ties to the land, they moved on when they exhausted the supplies. The effects of the above land-use practices are evident in the 1990s landscapes, with second- and third-growth forests and farming in the valleys.

Geology

The northwest portion of New Jersey falls within the valley portion of the Ridge and Valley physiographic province. Twelve miles wide and forty miles long, it runs from the Delaware River to the Hudson River. The rocks, mostly sandstone, shale, or limestone, have been folded and faulted even though the valley landscape is relatively flat.

The area is geologically interesting, as there is an abundance of mineral wealth, with over 300 different kinds of minerals, many of which are fluorescent. Franklin in Sussex County is considered the fluorescent mineral capital of the world, with thirty types of minerals found nowhere else in the world. Here, the New Jersey Zinc Company mined 500,000 tons of zinc ore annually until 1954, when the ore finally ran out.

Franklin has a rich history of mining, particularly of iron and zinc. Two commercial operations have displays of rocks and on the history of mining in the region. For more information, contact the Franklin Mineral Museum, P.O. Box 54, Evans Street, Franklin, NJ 07416; (973) 827-3481, or the Sterling Hill Mine & Museum, 30 Plant Street, Ogdensburg, NJ 07439; (973) 209-7212.

ALLAMUCHY MOUNTAIN & STEPHENS STATE PARKS

Embracing most of the Allamuchy Mountain upland between County 517 and the Musconetcong River, and bisected by I-80, Allamuchy Mountain and Stephens State Parks comprise 9,200 acres. Allamuchy Mountain State Park is undeveloped and offers hunting and fishing opportunities, as well as both marked and unmarked hiking trails. In contrast, Stephens State Park has camping, fishing, and picnic facilities and Waterloo Village, a restoration of Andover Forge, once a busy port along the Morris Canal. Earlier, it produced cannonballs for the colonists.

Allamuchy Mountain State Park presents a blend of forest, northern marshlands, and overgrown pastures, a mixture that supports an abundance of wildlife. The former pastures along the access road have their acreage and estimated age of abandonment posted on signs, allowing one to see clearly the effects of plant succession. The 15 miles of marked trails and 10 miles of unmarked trails shown on the park map include the yellow-blazed trail (2.4 miles), the red-blazed trail (0.3 mile), the red-dot-blazed trail (0.8 mile), the blue-blazed trail (2.0 miles), and the white-blazed trail (4.0 miles). A segment of the Highlands Trail (teal diamond) is in Stephens State Park.

As of 1998, the Allamuchy Natural Area around Deer Park Pond, south of I-80, is the most accessible section. To reach the Deer Park section of Allamuchy Mountain State Park from I-80 (Exit 19), take County 517 south for two miles and turn left onto Deer Park Road at a small brick house on the northeast corner of the intersection. Reach the state land and the main parking area after about a mile on this narrow dirt road. Two other parking areas are located farther along the road at approximately one-mile intervals.

By parking at the second area, one can hike due north on a woods road for about one and a half miles to the overlook of the rest area on I-80 eastbound. This overlook is to the left of the trail and can be reached by following a short side path. Bearing right from this point, and swinging around to a southerly direction, the hiker can return to the parking area via a different trail that leads to Deer Park Pond. The park access road leads back to the parking area.

An alternate entrance to the hiking trails is via two rest areas on eastbound I-80. The one closest to County 517 is designated "Scenic Area." From that scenic area, a yellow trail leads to the white trail. From parking lot at the second rest area, a pink-blazed trail extends to the blue-blazed trail. Hikers can use this trail to access the other park trails, avoiding the rough road access from County 517. Users of Allamuchy State Park who wish to explore the area further should obtain the Tranquility and Stanhope topographic quadrangle maps. For more information on both parks or a park map, contact Stephens State Park, 800 Willow Grove Street, Hackettstown, NJ 07840; (908) 852-3790.

HAMBURG MOUNTAIN
WILDLIFE MANAGEMENT AREA

This 2,442-acre tract is for those hikers who enjoy the challenge of bushwhacking or following unmarked woods roads and want to be away from crowds; however, Hamburg Mountain Wildlife Management Area is not the place to hike during hunting season. Elevations range from 700 to 1,495 feet. The upland mixed hardwood forest, with a blueberry understory, has pockets of hemlock, rhododendron, and laurel. Wetlands are found in the narrow valleys.

Access to Hamburg Mountain Wildlife Management Area is from the south because a ski area blocks access from the north. The main access point is from the signed parking lot on the north side of NJ 23 about one mile east of County 517. A woods road leaves the northeast corner of the lot. There is a much smaller parking area on the south side of NJ 23 just west (across a bridge) though a small space in the guard rail. It gives access to the Beaver Lake Rail Trail (see below). Another entrance is from the Silver Lake fishermen's parking area, which is reached by turning north from NJ 23 at the western junction with Silver Grove Road and very shortly turning left on Silver Lake Road. Follow the signs.

On the east side of the wildlife management area, there is access from the Newark Watershed Conservation and Development Corporation (NWCDC) property, which is on both sides of County 515 for 5 miles north of NJ 23. Several small pull-off parking areas are on both sides of the road. Permits are required to hike or park on NWCDC land. For more information or permits, contact NWCDC by mail at P.O. Box 319, Newfoundland, NJ 07435, or at

©1997 ERIC M. GENDELL

their office at 223 Echo Lake Road, West Milford, NJ 07480; (973) 697-2850.

On the western side of the WMA, Sand Lake Road leads east into the area from County 517 north of the town of Franklin. The wildlife management area begins where the paving ends. There is a small parking area and a woods road leading off to the left. Further up Sand Lake Road, a larger parking area is on the right just before the road is gated where it enters the land of the Morford Conservation Corporation.

The Beaver Lake Rail Trail is south (across NJ 23) of the main tract. Part of the abandoned Hanford Branch of the New York, Susquehanna and Western Railroad, it runs for three miles from Beaver Lake Road to Ogdensburg through an upland forest. To maintain the rail grade, cuts were made into the limestone hillside. Over most of its length, it parallels an active railroad line, separated by a small strip of trees. To reach the rail trail, either use the small parking area mentioned above and walk east to Beaver Lake Road (limited parking) and return to head west and south, or start by entering the woods directly across County 517 from the Ogdensburg Fire Station and proceed east and then north. At the northern end, shortly before reaching Beaver Lake Road, the trail turns right at a point where there is a wooden bridge over a stream on the left (that leads to a private house) and it crosses the active railroad line (stop, look, and listen).

Since there are no marked trails in the Hamburg Wildlife Management Area, users of the area should obtain the Franklin, Hamburg, and Wawayanda USGS topographic quadrangle maps. For more information, contact New Jersey DEP, Division of Fish, Game and Wildlife, 501 East State Street, P.O. Box 400, Trenton, NJ 08625; (609) 292-2965.

JENNY JUMP STATE FOREST

This 2,014-acre forest is like an emerald jewel rising out of the surrounding farmland. From the high areas, there are panoramic views over the valley, including one of the Delaware Water Gap. Bare rocks on the hilltops show glacial striations and are littered with large glacial erratics. Created in 1931, Jenny Jump State Forest is situated in Warren County, along Jenny Jump Mountain, between Hope and Great Meadows. Lying about 12 miles southeast of the Delaware Water Gap, it is typical of the mountain country in northern New Jersey, with elevations ranging from 399 to 1,108 feet.

According to folklore, Jenny Jump Mountain derives its name from Jenny

Lee, a young woman living with her aged father on the mountain. While in a remote area on the mountain, she was accosted by (depending on the account) either a spurned suitor or a Native American. After being chased to the edge of the cliff, she chose "death before dishonor" and jumped. In one account, however, she lived to tell the tale. The authenticity of this pre-Revolutionary story is difficult to assess.

The state forest has a picnic area with sites for family-size groups. Near the forest headquarters, eight camp shelters can be rented between April 1 and December 31. The shelters are completely enclosed buildings, each with a wood stove for heating, an outdoor fireplace for cooking, and bunk facilities for four people. Twenty-two campsites are available for tents or small camp trailers. For more information, contact Jenny Jump State Forest, P.O. Box 150, Hope, NJ 07844; (908) 459-4366.

To reach Jenny Jump State Forest, take I-80 to Exit 12 (Hope-Blairstown). Turn left on County 521 to the old Moravian village of Hope, one mile from I-80. Turn left at the blinking traffic light onto County 519 (Johnsonburg Road), and take the third right, onto Shiloh Road. In approximately two miles, turn right on State Park Road and proceed to the park entrance.

Birders will enjoy both the trails in Jenny Jump State Forest and the roads that border the park. Common birds are scarlet tanager, rose-breasted grosbeak, and a variety of warblers.

Trails in Jenny Jump State Forest

To the hiker, the main features of Jenny Jump State Forest are the views from forest roads and trails. The contrast of black soil with rows of green vegetables between the hillsides sprinkled with farms and woodlands provides striking panoramic views. The five trails, which can be combined to form loops, offer a variety of hiking experiences, from eagle-view vistas over wide expanses of countryside to quiet strolls through low-lying swampy areas.

Ghost Lake Trail   *Length: 1.3 miles Blaze: turquoise*
From the parking lot at Group Campsite B, the Ghost Lake Trail and the Summit Trail (yellow) run jointly for a short distance and then the Summit Trail turns right. The Ghost Lake Trail begins as a woods road and then becomes a narrow footpath as it traverses a ridge. On its descent, it passes glacial erratics and then ends at Ghost Lake on Shades of Death Road. Public access to the State Forest is available from this road. Cars may be parked at the boat launch area at Ghost Lake.

Orchard Trail   *Length: 0.7 mile Blaze: white*
Starting at the Orchard Park picnic area, the Orchard Trail runs along the northwest edge of the park in the woods, skirting farmland. The half of the trail near the entrance of the park is a wide woods road. At the midpoint, it turns into a narrow footpath, which terminates at East Road, 0.2 mile from the Ghost Lake/Summit trailheads. It is a quiet walk through the woods, with some clear views of the Delaware Water Gap (10 miles to the west) along the route.

Spring Trail   *Length: 0.7 mile Blaze: blue*
Beginning at the far end of the main parking area, the Spring Trail runs along the south side of the base of the ridge. It climbs steeply to the ridge, crosses the Summit Trail (yellow), and descends to end at the Swamp Trail (red). Rock outcroppings and glacial erratics appear along the route.

Summit Trail   *Length: 1.5 miles Blaze: yellow*
Beginning at the main parking area, the Summit Trail travels east along the top of
the ridge, with two vistas near the southwest end. The striations along the ridge are
evidence of glacial activity. The trail drops down off the ridge, turns northeast to
meet the Ghost Lake Trail (turquoise), and ends near Group Campsite B.

Swamp Trail   *Length: 0.3 mile Blaze: red*
Starting at the main parking area, this wide woods road runs along a swamp at
the base of the ridge, connecting the Spring Trail (blue) with the Summit Trail
(yellow). A large glacial erratic is on the left side of the trail just past Campsite 21.

KITTATINNY VALLEY STATE PARK

Within 1,618-acre Kittatinny Valley State Park, there are two lakes and extensive wetlands. The Andover-Aeroflex Airport, operated by the New Jersey Forest Service, is quite visible from the park entrance. Trails are open to hiking,
mountain biking, and horseback riding. To reach the trailheads, cross the run-
way, paying attention as a sign cautions Low Flying Aircraft - No Loitering. There
is a connection to the Sussex Branch Trail. Hunting is permitted in certain
areas of the park.

To reach the main portion of the park and the administration building,
take US 206 to Andover and turn north onto County 669. It is 1.1 miles to the
park entrance on the left. For more information, contact the Kittatinny Valley
State Park, P.O. Box 621, Andover, NJ 07821; (973) 786-6445.

Rail Trails in Kittatinny Valley State Park
Western New Jersey has a network of abandoned railroads, some of which
have been converted into rail trails. Two of them, the Paulinskill Valley Trail
and the Sussex Branch Trail, are administered as part of Kittatinny Valley State
Park. There are breaks in the routes because of missing bridges.

Paulinskill Valley Trail   *Length: 27 miles Blaze: unmarked*
The Paulinskill Valley Trail is the abandoned cinder bed of the western portion
of the New York, Susquehanna and Western Railroad. It is open to all forms of
non-motorized recreation. Acquired by the state in October 1992, the right-of-
way parallels the Paulinskill River and for most of its course borders working
farm fields and lowland forests.

The western end of the trail is at Brugler Road near NJ 94. The trail reaches Vail at 3.8 miles and Blairstown at 7.4 miles. A detour must be made around the edge of Blairstown Airport. The 11.5 miles between Blairstown and Swartswood Station traverse hilly terrain. In 1998, private property blocks a filled-in road crossing at County 610. Waterfalls and views of Paulinskill Lake lend interest as the trail approaches Swartswood Station. The trail's eastern-most section passes through the flatter and more developed portions of the Kittatinny Valley as it crosses US 206 and NJ 94. Soon it again reaches rural farm and forest landscape and crosses several streams. It crosses the Sussex Branch Trail at Warbasse Junction. As of 1998, the last two of nine bridges, on the eastern end of the trail, are not covered with planking and can be crossed only on the girders remaining from the railroad.

Parking is available at Station Road in Knowlton Township in Warren County, Footbridge Park in Blairstown, Spring Valley Road off NJ 94 in Marksboro, County 622 at Swartswood Station in Sussex County, and Warbasse Junction Road (County 663).

For more information, contact Kittatinny Valley State Park, P.O. Box 621, Andover, NJ 07821; (973) 786-6445, or the Paulinskill Valley Trail Committee, P.O. Box 7076, Hackettstown, NJ 07840. The committee leads organized hikes on the trail and has a modest membership fee.

Sussex Branch Trail   *Length: 21 miles Blaze: unmarked*
The Sussex Branch Trail follows the route of the abandoned Sussex Branch of the Erie-Lackawanna Railroad. This rail line originated as the Sussex Mine Railroad, built by Peter Cooper and Abram Hewitt to transport iron from the Andover mines to the Morris Canal beginning in 1851. By 1854, there was steam service from Newton to Waterloo. Additional extensions brought the railroad to Branchville and Franklin Furnace, and established connections with other railroads. The Delaware, Lackawanna and Western Railroad (DL&W) acquired the Sussex Mine Railroad in 1881, and it soon carried agricultural produce and passengers, as well as iron and zinc from local mines.

The DL&W merged with the Erie in 1960, but by that time both freight and passenger traffic on the Sussex Branch had greatly declined. Passenger service was discontinued in 1966, and the line was abandoned shortly thereafter. The state acquired the right-of-way between Netcong and Andover Junction in 1979 and between Andover Junction and Branchville in 1982. The rail trail traverses part of Kittatinny Valley State Park, farms, and forested lands, and passes by lakes and streams. In some sections, it is in the midst of commercial and residential development.

The trail travels due north past Cranberry Lake, then parallels US 206 to Andover Township (about 5 miles). A missing bridge necessitates a detour on the highway. After crossing US 206, the trail leaves that road, reaching County 616 and Hicks Avenue (County 663) in Newton in another 3 miles. North of Hicks Avenue, the 1.5 miles of rail bed which pass through the town of Newton are not state owned, and there is a missing bridge at a stream crossing. To avoid this section, hikers can walk north along Hicks Avenue for about a mile, then cross the guardrail to regain access to the Sussex Branch, which briefly parallels the road to the left. From here, it is 2.5 miles to the Sussex Branch Trail's intersection with the Paulinskill Valley Trail just south of NJ 94 at Warbasse Junction. In 1998, this is effectively the end of the trail, since there are six missing bridges as the railroad parallels the south side of NJ 15 and US 206, ending at Branchville. However, these bridges are scheduled to be replaced by the summer of 1999. For more information, contact Kittatinny Valley State Park, P.O. Box 621, Andover, NJ 07821; (973) 786-6445, or the Paulinskill Valley Trail Committee, P.O. Box 7076, Hackettstown, NJ 07840. The committee offers outdoor activities and has a modest membership fee.

MERRILL CREEK RESERVOIR ENVIRONMENTAL PRESERVE

Located in Warren County, Merrill Creek Reservoir Environmental Preserve offers opportunities for year-round recreational activities on over 3,000 acres of open space. The reservoir was constructed to store water for release to the Delaware River during periods of low flow. During droughts, the stored water can be released to replace river water used by seven electric utilities for their generating facilities along the Delaware. Completed in 1988, it took 6 months to fill the 650-acre reservoir with over 16 billion gallons of water. Exhibits at the Visitors Center display the wildlife found in the area and explain the operation of the reservoir and history of the area. Hunting is restricted to club members in designated areas.

To reach Merrill Creek Reservoir Environmental Preserve from the intersection of NJ 31 and NJ 57 in Washington, go west on NJ 57 for 6.5 miles and make a right turn onto Montana Road. Continue for 2 miles, bearing left at a

Y junction. At 0.3 mile, turn left onto Merrill Creek Road. The Visitors Center is at the end of the right fork. For more information, contact Merrill Creek Visitors Center, 34 Merrill Creek Road, Washington, NJ 07882; (908) 454-1213.

Trails in Merrill Creek Reservoir Environmental Preserve

The 290-acre Merrill Creek Environmental Preserve is located on an arm that juts into Merrill Creek Reservoir. Seven trails within the preserve wind their way through a wide range of habitats. The easy-to-moderate grades and ample opportunities to view wildlife make the area ideal for families. Hikers pass through mixed hardwood forests, orchards, evergreen plantations, and fields, and travel along the lake shore, wetlands, and a stream.

Creek Trail   *Length: 0.9 mile or 1.1 miles Blaze: orange*
Beginning at the intersection of the Shoreline (blue) and Timber (red) trails, the Creek Trail proceeds along spring-fed Merrill Creek. At 0.3 mile, it reaches a footbridge at the end of the Perimeter Trail (black) and follows close to Upper Merrill Creek. After intersecting with the Orchard Trail (green) at 0.4 mile, it reaches a junction at 0.7 mile. At this point the hiker can either take the right branch to head directly to Merrill Creek Road at 0.9 mile, or take the left branch to proceed through wetlands along the way before reaching the road at 1.1 miles.

Eagle Trail   *Length: 0.4 mile Blaze: unmarked*
This trail is accessible for wheelchairs. Starting at the entrance drive, it passes through farm fields and an apple orchard to end at a wildlife observation blind.

Farmstead Trail   *Length: 0.4 mile Blaze: yellow*
This old farm road connects the Shoreline Trail (blue) with the Timber (red) and Eagle (unmarked) trails. It passes through a hardwood forest between two farm sites.

Orchard Trail   *Length: 0.9 mile Blaze: green*
From the Visitors Center parking lot, the trail splits at 0.1 mile. The right fork rejoins the direct route at 0.2 mile and shortly crosses the Visitors Center Road to join the Eagle Trail (handicapped accessible). After passing the terminus of the Farmstead Trail (yellow) on the left, the two trails separate, with the Orchard Trail continuing straight ahead. The Orchard Trail passes through an abandoned

orchard and ends at 0.9 mile at the junction with the Creek Trail (orange).

Perimeter Trail   *Length: 3.8 miles Blaze: black*
Since the Perimeter Trail is a circular route, it can be started at three different points. Arbitrarily beginning at the boat trailer parking area and proceeding clockwise around the reservoir, at 0.5 mile the trail enters the woods and crosses the first of four earthen dams. After passing through fields, the trail splits at 1.3 miles, to cross over the half-mile-long main dam. The route to the left crosses Lower Merrill Creek and Reservoir Road and is a tenth of a mile longer.

After crossing the main dam, the Perimeter Trail goes through a stand of red pine trees. At 1.6 miles, the trail reaches the Overlook parking lot. An 0.2-mile side trail connects the parking lot and the observation deck. The trail reaches the third dam at 2.5 miles. After passing the Inlet/Outlet Tower at 2.6 miles, there are panoramic views of the countryside and the reservoir. The Perimeter Trail crosses the fourth dam at 3.0 miles. The remaining 0.8 mile of trail passes intermittently close to the reservoir before crossing a footbridge which leads to the hiking trails within the Environmental Preserve around the Visitors Center. The shortest path can be followed by turning left on the Creek Trail (orange) and Orchard Trail (green) for 0.1 mile, then continuing on the Orchard Trail (green) for 1.0 mile back to the boat trailer parking lot. Care should be exercised at turns.

Shoreline Trail   *Length: 1.7 miles Blaze: blue*
To reach the Shoreline Trail, take the gravel path on the side of the building that leads into the woods and bear left at a Y junction. Passing through a dense oak, tulip, and sassafras woods, the Shoreline Trail descends towards the reservoir. In 0.5 mile, it intersects an unmarked trail, then continues for another 0.2 mile, passing several ruins on the right, to the Farmstead Trail (yellow) and more ruins. At 0.8 mile, the trail reaches a connection to the Timber Trail (red), with a lime kiln visible to the left. The trail passes close to the shore of the reservoir, including an area of flooded timber, in the final half mile. It ends at an intersection with the Timber (red) and Creek (orange) trails at 1.7 miles.

Timber Trail   *Length: 0.7 mile Blaze: red*
Leaving from the Visitors Center, the Timber Trail takes an interior route through the preserve, passing though pine plantations in various stages of succession. After crossing the Farmstead Trail (yellow) at 0.3 mile, it ends at the Creek

(orange) and Shoreline (blue) trails at 0.7 mile.

PEQUEST WILDLIFE MANAGEMENT AREA

Paralleling the Pequest River east of the intersection of US 46 and NJ 31, the approximately 4,000-acre Pequest Wildlife Management Area is managed for hunting upland game and trout fishing. It has three marked hiking trails, two abandoned rail beds, and the Trout Hatchery and Natural Resource Education Center. From parking areas, farm roads and woods roads lead into the interior.

The marked trails lead from the trout hatchery. The Red Trail is an interpretive trail with numbered stops and is used to gain access to the Blue and Yellow trails. The Blue Trail begins just before the pond and goes through a glacial deposit of sand and gravel, fields, and mixed woodlands. The Yellow Trail begins at the pond, climbs through mature woods, and passes through old fields. Both the Blue and Yellow trails have views of the surrounding countryside.

Abandoned routes of the Lehigh and Hudson River Railroad (L&HR) and the Delaware, Lackawanna and Western Railroad (DL&W) which pass through the wildlife management area have not been formally converted to rail trails but are open to hikers. Constructed in 1881-82, the L&HR served the dairy industry and as an interstate connection between Pennsylvania and New England.

Within the wildlife management area, a 4.1-mile segment of the L&HR parallels US 46 and the Pequest River. In 1998, the walking surface is either ties or ballast. There are mile markers, signposts, piles of slag, remnants of an iron furnace, and a livestock underpass, which allowed livestock access to the river. The three access points to the rail trail are in Townsbury (a half-mile from the intersection of US 46 and Pequest Road), on the access road to the hatchery, and at the northeast corner of the intersection of US 46 and NJ 31. At this last access point, the L&HR passes under a concrete viaduct of the cinder-surfaced DL&W. A woods road connects the two rail beds further to the north.

To reach the Pequest Wildlife Management Area, take US 46 north from its intersection with NJ 31. The road to the fish hatchery and Natural Resource Education Center turns right at 2.6 miles. Users of the Pequest Wildlife Management Area who want to explore the area off trail should obtain the Washington USGS topographic quadrangle map. For more information, contact New Jersey DEP, Division of Fish, Game and Wildlife, 501 East State Street, P.O. Box 400, Trenton, NJ 08625-0400; (609) 292-2965, or the Pequest Trout

Hatchery and Natural Resource Education Center, 605 Pequest Road, Oxford, NJ 07863; (908) 637-4125.

SWARTSWOOD STATE PARK

The park is named for the Swartout family who were killed in a Native American raid on the family farm in 1756. Located in the Kittatinny Valley, this 1,470-acre state park offers facilities for camping, swimming, boating, and fishing. In the fall, Swartswood Lake attracts a variety of migrating ducks. Hunting is permitted in designated areas. In addition to small woodland animals, black bears live in the area. There are three marked trails totaling 5 miles, of which one is for equestrian use and cross-country skiing and another is accessible for the handicapped.

To reach Swartswood State Park, take NJ 94 or US 206 to Newton. From just north of the NJ 94/US 206 split in Newton, take County 519 0.4 mile north to County 622. Turn left on County 622 and follow it 3.6 miles to County 619. Turn left to the park entrance in 0.6 mile. Parking for the trails is on the left at Duck Pond multi-use trail area. For more information, contact Swartswood State Park, East Shore Drive, Swartswood, NJ 07875; (908) 213-1891.

WHITTINGHAM WILDLIFE MANAGEMENT AREA

The fact that there are no marked trails into the 1,514-acre Whittingham Wildlife Management Area should not deter anyone from enjoying a visit. The mowed paths along the edges and through the centers of former farm fields beckon hikers to savor a pastoral setting. Hedgerows and small stands of hardwoods separate the fields. Woods roads cutting through adjacent forests pass by limestone rocks, some looking like well-crafted stone walls.

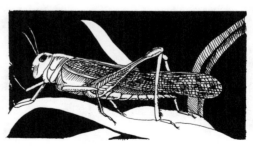

Three types of forests are dominant in the area: north Jersey mixed oak, sugar maple mixed hardwood, and hem-

Grasshopper

lock mixed hardwood. Visitors can find colorful wildflowers, abundant grasses, and humming insects in the summer. Wild turkey, pileated woodpecker, and ruffed grouse are year-round residents.

A 400-acre state-designated natural area contains a spring-fed swamp and the headwaters of the Pequest River. It can be reached via a one-mile hike along a woods road and includes access to a pond. Hunting is permitted in season, although not in the natural area. During hunting season, hikers are advised to wear blaze orange or restrict their hikes to Sundays.

To reach Whittingham Wildlife Management Area, take Exit 25 (US 206 North) from I-80 to Andover. Go 2.9 miles past the only light in Andover and turn left onto County 618 (Springdale-Fredon Road). One parking area is on the left at 1.1 miles. To reach the second parking area, drive 0.3 mile past the first area and turn left at the junction. Since there are no marked trails, users of the area should obtain the Newton West and Tranquility USGS 7.5-minute topographic quadrangle maps. For more information, contact New Jersey DEP, Division of Fish, Game and Wildlife, 501 East State Street, P.O. Box 400, Trenton, NJ 08625; (609) 292-2965.

EIGHT

THE KITTATINNIES

Paralleling the 40-mile stretch of the Delaware River from Port Jervis to the Delaware Water Gap is the long, wooded ridge of the Kittatinnies, the Native American name for "Big Mountain." The ridge continues on the Pennsylvania side of the Water Gap southwest to Wind Gap and beyond; northeast, the ridge continues into New York State as the Shawangunk Mountains. With elevations of 1,400 to 1,800 feet, the Kittatinnies offer panoramic views from High Point, Sunrise Mountain, and innumerable other overlooks. In addition, approximately 43 miles of the New Jersey section of the Appalachian Trail run along the ridge.

Geologically the Kittatinnies are the ridge of the Ridge and Valley physiographic region and are comprised of Paleozoic rocks. Most of the ridge is publicly owned and is divided into four administrative areas: High Point State Park, Stokes State Forest, the Delaware Water Gap National Recreation Area, and Worthington State Forest. The land between the ridge and the Delaware River contains three New Jersey Wildlife Management Areas.

HIGH POINT STATE PARK

The 14,193-acre High Point State Park extends south 10 miles from the New York state line. High Point has a natural landscape of unusual beauty onto

which a designed landscape was placed. Recreational facilities are centered around the Lake Marcia and High Point Monument area, located north of NJ 23. As suggested by its name, the park includes the highest point within the state—1,803 feet. In 1930, a memorial modeled after the Bunker Hill Tower was erected on the highest point in New Jersey to honor the men of New Jersey who served in the nation's wars. When open, this 220-foot-high monument offers views in all directions. The park also contains the 1,327-acre Dryden Kuser Natural Area.

Campsites and group camping are available in the park. In 1998, limited hunting was permitted. For information about hunting season, hikers should contact the New Jersey Department of Environmental Protection, Office of Fish, Game and Wildlife, P.O. Box 400, Trenton, NJ 08625; (609) 292-9410. For more information about the park, contact High Point State Park, 1480 State Route 23, Sussex, New Jersey 07461; (973) 875-4800. Hikers making overnight trips on the Appalachian Trail may use a special parking area after obtaining a permit from the park office.

History

For more than 150 years, High Point State Park has been a recreational area reflecting four phases in the region's leisure and vacation trends: summer hotels, gilded summer homes, the state park movement, and the work of the Civilian Conservation Corps (CCC). Each phase has left distinct historic and architectural imprints on the park property.

As early as 1855, the public used the Lake Marcia/High Point area for picnics and outings. By that time, the High Point area had been cleared for farming, but it was not suitable for agriculture and was poor in timber. In 1890, Charles St. John, a Port Jervis newspaper publisher, built the High Point Inn. Representative of the era of grand mountaintop hotels, it operated with great success until 1908, when a combination of hard economic times, the threat of forest fires, and St. John's health forced the inn into bankruptcy. Much of the estate was purchased in 1911 by John Fairfield Dryden, who intended to use the land as a nature preserve but did not live to do so. At the same time, the unaltered natural landscape was improved with the addition of carriage roads, paths, trails, rustic seats, and ornamental trees.

As the era of grand hotels waned, Dryden's son-in-law, Anthony Kuser— a New Jersey industrialist, philanthropist, and conservationist—converted the High Point Inn into a lavish summer residence. High Point's ultimate destiny as a state park reflects John Dryden's wish to use the property as a preserve.

In 1923, when the Kuser family donated the property to the state, High Point became a state park and so entered its third phase. Like Bear Mountain State Park and other pioneers in the state parks movement, High Point was within one to two hours of a major urban area. It provided recreational facilities that low- and middle-income residents could afford—in contrast with the national parks, which required considerable time and money to visit.

Soon after the park was created, the Olmsted brothers were hired to design both a general development plan and specific features. Their design reflected the American romantic style of landscape architecture, with an emphasis on natural scenery, use of native raw materials, a lack of formal design, and curvilinear roads. During its first two decades, under the High Point Park Commission, the park flourished. The park was provided for as long as it remained a product of people with wealth, political connections, and vision. When they vanished, the era of vast improvements vanished with them. Although not all of the improvements from that time have survived, High Point still has one of the finest assemblages of rustic park architecture in the northeast.

In 1933, High Point entered the last of its four historic eras with the establishment of a Civilian Conservation Corps camp. Men stationed at Camp Kuser worked under the direction of the National Park Service to expand and improve the park. Although the work the men did at High Point typifies CCC activities elsewhere, the plan they implemented was more ambitious than most others in New Jersey.

Several sets of master plans were drawn up between 1937 and 1941. The basic document that guided CCC efforts faithfully accepted the Olmsted brothers' plan to spread activities across the park and relieve pressure on the Lake Marcia area. Extensive recreation facilities that were planned but never constructed included ball fields, tennis courts, a museum, an eastern perimeter park drive, and more picnicking and parking areas scattered throughout the park. The rustic architectural elements that the CCC added to High Point provide far more tangible evidence of their efforts than their conservation work. Unfortunately, many of their improvements—including a beach complex at Sawmill Pond, sections of boulder guard rail and curbing, a boardwalk around Lake Marcia, and actual buildings of the camp—did not survive.

After 1945, the state's ambitious improvement plans for the park were abandoned. It was not until the late 1950s that the park received its next major slate of improvements, which involved upgrading or replacing deteriorating facilities at Lake Marcia. By the early 1960s, the state's primary concern was the acquisition and creation of new parks, and monies were no longer funneled into expanding the facilities of existing parks. By the 1990s, the intense park development planned for High Point in the 1930s had fallen into environmental, planning, and aesthetic disfavor, as it became clear that non-native species crowd out native ones and altered landscapes are expensive to maintain.

🚶

Trails in High Point State Park

High Point State Park has ten named and marked trails as well as sections of the Appalachian and Shawangunk Ridge trails. The trails range from 0.4 to 4.5 miles in length. It is possible, by using park roads in conjunction with these paths, to walk a number of circular routes and to extend shorter hikes. Except for the Appalachian, Monument, and Shawangunk Ridge trails, all trails in High Point State Park are open to mountain bikes. Trails that are blazed with two colors have half of the dot in one color and the other half in another color.

During the winter when conditions are suitable, the Ayers, Parker, Fuller, Mashipacong, and Iris trails, all south of NJ 23, are reserved for snowmobile and dogsledding use. North of NJ 23, the trails and unplowed roads are open for snowshoeing and cross-country skiing. The park started offering groomed trails and cross-country ski rentals in 1995.

Appalachian Trail   *Length: 10.1 miles Blaze: white*
This major trail traverses the park. See chapter 14, "Long Distance Trails," or the *Appalachian Trail Guide to New York-New Jersey* for a complete descrip-

tion of the 10.1 miles in High Point State Park.

Ayers Trail   *Length: 0.9 mile Blaze: black*
This east–west woods road cuts through a mixed hardwood forest and an old
farm site, built soon after the Civil War. The west end is on Ridge Road where
there is parking. Parking is available 0.3 mile north of the eastern trailhead on
Sawmill Road near the Mashipacong Trail and 0.4 mile south of the eastern
trailhead at the Sawmill Lake parking area.

Blue Dot   *Length: 0.4 mile Blaze: medium blue dot*
This short trail, one of the steepest in the park, starts in the Sawmill Camping Area
across from Campsite 15. It connects the Appalachian Trail (white) to the camping
area. Rising slowly at first through an oak and maple forest, it becomes steep
halfway to the top. Along the way are views of the pond and surrounding countryside. Parking is available at the camping area or Sawmill Lake parking area.

Fuller Trail   *Length: 0.8 mile Blaze: light blue/red dot*
Blazed in 1994 to provide yet another circular opportunity for hikers and cross-
country skiers, the Fuller Trail starts at Sawmill Road, adjacent to the
Mashipacong Trail (yellow) on the west side of the road. It runs next to a low
boggy area for about 0.5 mile before reaching the mid-point of the Life Trail
(brown). Turning right, it then runs jointly with the Life Trail for another 0.3
mile before reaching the winter-use parking area on Ridge Road.

Iris Trail   *Length: 4.2 miles Blaze: red*
The Iris and Mashipacong (yellow) trails start from a point on the Appalachian Trail (white) 0.2 mile south of the park office on NJ 23. The Iris Trail
turns left; the Mashipacong Trail (yellow) turns right. The first 1.5 miles of the
Iris Trail meander along a woods road through rolling country under a canopy
of trees until the trail reaches Lake Rutherford. Heading south, the trail crosses
a stream and, within another 0.25 mile, makes a hard right and becomes a
narrower track for the remaining 2.4 miles. En route, the trail intersects the
Appalachian Trail (white) twice, first at approximately 3 miles, and next at
4.2 miles. The trail ends at the Deckertown Turnpike, where parking is
available. The Iris Trail is frequently used with the Appalachian Trail to
make a loop hike.

LAKE... FARMS. ROAD TO OVERLOOK...WATERGAP. SOUTHWEST............ POCONO MTS......DELAWARE RIVER.

MOUNTAIN PROFILES ACCENTUATED

LAKE TEENYKILL

1801 FEET.   STATE PARK 11,000 ACRES

FROM HIGH POINT MOUNTAIN TO KITTATINNY MOUNTAINS···LAKE MARCIA AND LODGE.

Life Trail   *Length: 0.6 mile Blaze: brown*
The Life Trail is in the shape of a horseshoe beginning and ending on Ridge
Road. Its western end is just east of where Ridge Road and Steeny Kill Road
join. Its eastern end is near the group camping area, where parking is available
even in the winter. The junction with the Fuller Trail (light blue/red) is at the
midpoint. The Life Trail is adjacent to a low, boggy area, with rich soil that
supports a myriad of vegetation, including wildflowers, ferns, and fungi.

Mashipacong Trail   *Length: 2.8 miles Blaze: yellow*
The Iris and Mashipacong trails start from a point on the Appalachian Trail
(white) 0.2 mile south of the park office on NJ 23. The Iris Trail (red) turns left;
the Mashipacong turns right. After doubling back behind the ranger station,
the Mashipacong Trail turns left, crosses an old service road, and heads into
the woods. After rising slightly, the trail descends steadily for 0.6 mile. At the
intersection of Sawmill Road, Ridge Road, and an unused service road, the
Mashipacong turns left onto the service road and runs jointly with it for about
0.5 mile. It then takes a hard right into the woods and heads approximately
100 yards to a wooden post in the middle of an old farm field clearing, before
making another left into the woods. It meanders back and forth between the woods
and the field for another 0.6 mile. The Mashipacong Trail turns left at Sawmill
Road, running jointly with it for a very short distance before again turning right
onto a woods road. The trail ends 0.9 mile later at its western terminus on Ridge
Road. Following Ridge Road south to the Ayers Trail (black) provides a loop.

Monument Trail   *Length: 3.7 miles Blaze: red/green*

For most of its length, this circular footpath passes through pristine backcountry unspoiled by the sounds of road traffic. The Shawangunk Ridge Trail (turquoise) is coaligned with or crosses parts of the Monument Trail and is marked only at intersections. At the north end of the Monument parking lot, the Monument Trail goes into the woods, reaching an outcrop in a short distance, with a vista to the east. The trail continues northward along the ridge, descending, at 1.0 mile, to Cedar Swamp, where it crosses a bridge, and swings around to go south through a level wooded area. It goes through two rock outcrops with scraggly pitch pines and vistas to the west, continues south for another mile, and descends to a second wooden bridge just before the intersection with the Steeny Kill Trail (blue). For the next 0.2 mile, the Monument Trail climbs, levels, and then descends gradually. It joins the road to the High Point Nature Center (just opposite the center) and continues its descent toward Lake Marcia. After turning east along the northern shore of Lake Marcia, the Monument Trail reaches the Appalachian Trail (white) and turns left. The Shawangunk Ridge Trail (turquoise) also starts at this intersection and runs jointly with the Monument Trail. The two trails climb to the ridge, passing west of the High Point Monument and along the west side of the parking lot back to the starting point.

Old Trail   *Length: 0.5 mile Blaze: yellow/brown*

The Old Trail, a woods road, is heavily used by campers going to Lake Marcia or to the day-use area. It has a stream along one side and a striking array of geologic rock formations. In the summer, the canopy of tall, old hardwood trees lends serenity and grandeur. Parking is available at the winter-use parking area on Ridge Road. The other trailhead is at the rear of the picnic area across from the new Lake Marcia beach parking area.

Parker Trail   *Length: 3.0 miles Blaze: blue*

Three miles of the Parker Trail are in High Point, with the final 0.5 mile in Stokes State Forest. The northern trailhead is on Ridge Road, 0.1 mile west of the parking area on Ridge Road. After a 1.3-mile walk west on a narrow trail, the trail crosses Deckertown Turnpike. In wet seasons, hikers can hear the Big Flat Brook, which closely parallels this section. The 1.7-mile section between Deckertown Turnpike and Crigger Road is a woods road, with stately hardwoods providing shade in the summer. The trail continues into Stokes State

Forest (see trail description on page 133), where it ends at Grau Road.

Shawangunk Ridge Trail *Length: 3.1 miles Blaze: turquoise*
See *Guide to the Long Path* for a complete description of the 3.1-mile section
of the Shawangunk Ridge Trail in High Point State Park.

Steeny Kill Trail *Length: 0.7 mile Blaze: blue*
Although the trailhead is on NJ 23 just north of Steeny Kill Lake, the best
parking is at the Steeny Kill boat ramp just off NJ 23, south of the trailhead.
The Steeny Kill Trail goes southeast along the northern shore of Lake Steeny
Kill and ends at the Monument Trail.

STOKES STATE FOREST

Named in honor of Governor Edward Stokes, who donated the first 500 acres,
this public area is managed for recreation and for timber, wildlife, and water
conservation. Its 15,482 acres include some of the first land purchased for
public use by the State of New Jersey.

The effects of human activities are everywhere. Lenni Lenape grew crops
in the fertile areas and hunted in the forest-covered mountains. The English
and Dutch were known to farm the area in the early 1700s. During the 1800s,
the area was deforested through heavy harvesting of wood for lumber and for
domestic and industrial fuel. Even into the twentieth century, many areas had
no trees at all.

Like High Point, Stokes State Park was the site of Civilian Conservation
Corps camps. During the 1930s, the young men in the CCC constructed Sunrise Mountain Road, developed the Lake Ocquittunk, Kittle Field, and Shotwell
areas, and built the park's extensive trail system. As part of their conservation
efforts, they established evergreen plantations, which are evidence of early forest management in that area.

Camping is available at four locations and at shelters on the Appalachian
Trail. Hunting is permitted in parts of Stokes State Forest. For information about
the hunting season, hikers should contact the New Jersey Department of Environmental Protection, Office of Fish, Game and Wildlife, P.O. Box 400, Trenton, NJ
08625; (609) 292-9410. For more information about the park, contact Stokes
State Forest, 1 Coursen Road, Branchville, NJ 07826; (973) 948-3820.

Trails in Stokes State Forest

The majority of the 42 miles of marked trails in Stokes State Forest provide quiet, pleasant walks in the woods. They range in length from less than 0.5 mile to a 9.3-mile section of the Appalachian Trail. Many of the trails are short and, as in High Point, trails and park roads can be combined for interesting circular routes. Some of the roads are recommended only for four-wheel-drive vehicles. In winter, under suitable snow conditions, the Lackner, Coursen, Parker, Swenson, and Tinsley trails are snowmobile and dogsled routes. The area southwest of US 206 is set aside for snowshoeing and cross-country skiing.

Acropolis Trail   *Length: 1.0 mile Blaze: gold/brown*
The Acropolis Trail begins on US 206 at the park boundary on the northwestern shore of Culvers Lake. It climbs steeply to the top of the ridge, crossing the Appalachian Trail (white) at 0.6 mile. The trail's path is rocky, becoming grassy and open at the crest of the ridge, where there are views of Culvers Lake. Limited parking is available at a restaurant 0.1 mile south on US 206 (northbound side).

Appalachian Trail   *Length: 9.3 miles Blaze: white*
This major trail traverses the park. See chapter 14, "Long Distance Trails," in this book or the *Appalachian Trail Guide to New York-New Jersey* for a complete description of the 9.3 miles in Stokes State Forest.

Blue Mountain Trail   *Length: 1.4 miles Blaze: brown/green*
This relatively level trail begins at the Lake Ocquittunk camping area (parking available). Following a woods road which parallels the Big Flat Brook, it goes along a sandstone ridge bordered by stream-cut limestone valleys. A wide variety of wildflowers, shrubs, and trees are in evidence along the route, which ends at Kittle Road.

Cartwright Trail   *Length: 0.9 mile Blaze: brown/red*
The Cartwright Trail descends somewhat steeply west from Sunrise Mountain Road near its northern end. The trail ends at the Swenson Trail (red). Forest succession can be observed at a 1900s former farm site along the route. As the Cartwright Trail approaches the Swenson Trail, it resembles a streambed. Parking is available at the trailhead for the Howell Trail, less than 0.5 mile farther

north on Sunrise Mountain Road.

Coursen Trail *Length: 1.3 miles Blaze: blue*
From Stony Lake, the Coursen Trail runs south, initially sharing its route with the Swenson (red), Station (light green), and Stony Brook (brown) trails, and ending at Sunrise Mountain Road. The Station Trail intersects with the Coursen Trail twice. During June and July, mountain laurel and rhododendron bloom along the gently sloping route. Wetlands and portions of Stony Brook are encountered along the way. Parking is available at Stony Lake.

Criss Trail *Length: 2.0 miles Blaze: green/gray*
This moderately sloped trail follows an old woods road along a boulder-strewn hillside. Stone striations are further evidence of glacial action in the area. Wildflowers are common. The trail loops from Grau Road near Cabin 15 to Grau Road near Forked Brook, on the way crossing DeGroat Road (passable for four-wheel-drive vehicles), where parking is available.

Deep Root Trail *Length: 1.0 mile Blaze: red/yellow*
This trail is for hikers looking for a more isolated experience. Beginning on DeGroat Road (passable for four-wheel-drive vehicles), it is mostly a wide open grassy trail that ends on a small hilltop. Return is via the same route. Parking is available on DeGroat Road.

Howell Trail
Length: 1.6 miles Blaze: gray
Beginning at the Parker Trail (green) and heading east, the rock-strewn route of the Howell Trail winds over small, gently sloping hills to end at Crigger Road. An unmarked trail connects it to the Appalachian Trail. Parking is available at Steam Mill camping area and at the trailhead on Crigger Road.

Mountain laurel

Jacob's Ladder Trail   *Length: 0.4 mile Blaze: blue/gray*
Aptly named, this trail provides hikers with a steep climb from the junction of
Woods Road and Coss Road to the Appalachian Trail (white) on the top of the
ridge, where there is a view to the east of several lakes. Mountain laurel and
blueberries bloom along the route. The closest parking is at the junction of
Woods Road and Brink Road, over a mile away.

Lackner Trail   *Length: 2.0 miles Blaze: black*
The Lackner Trail follows the slope of a low ridge, with blueberries and mountain laurel along the route. It begins north of Stony Lake, goes south, passes
the Lead Mine Trail (blue/gray), and continues west to end at the Stokes State
Forest Office. Retreating glaciers exposed red sandstone beds, which can be
seen along the way. Parking is available at the Stokes State Forest Office and
Stony Lake.

Lead Mine Trail   *Length: 1.0 mile Blaze: blue/gray*
This connector trail provides an alternate route from Coursen Road to the
middle of the Lackner Trail (black). The terrain is generally level and passes
through an area that was clear-cut in the mid-1980s. Parking is available at the
Stokes State Forest Office and Stony Lake.

Parker Trail   *Length: 0.5 mile Blaze: blue*
From Grau Road, about 0.5 mile south of Crigger Road, the Parker Trail passes
through new growth and reaches the confluence of Parker Brook and Big Flat
Brook, where the sounds of water rushing down a rocky stream predominate as
the trail follows the brook. The trail turns left on Crigger Road after 0.4 mile,
proceeds for 0.1 mile, and then turns right into the woods, continuing into High
Point State Park for another 3 miles (see trail description above) to Ridge Road.
Parking is available at the Steam Mill camping area on Crigger Road.

Rock Oak Trail   *Length: 1.5 miles Blaze: blue/yellow*
As the Rock Oak Trail traverses a small ridge from Deckertown Turnpike southwest to DeGroat Road, it passes through forests in various stages of succession. Along the lower portions of the trail there are boulder fields and glacial
till. Limited parking is available on Deckertown Turnpike.

Silver Mine Trail   *Length: 1.0 mile Blaze: orange*
From the parking area at Kittle Field to a waterfall, this trail is accessible to the handicapped. Past the waterfall the treadway is rocky and uneven as it ascends a gently sloping hill. After 0.5 mile, the trail descends and reaches a fork. The Silver Mine Trail takes the left fork, while a shorter trail heads right to an old silver mine that was active in the 1870s. An unmarked trail between the two forks leads to ruins.

Spring Cabin Trail   *Length: 0.4 mile Blaze: blue*
This short trail connects the Tinsley (yellow) and Swenson (red) trails, passing a Department of Environmental Protection cabin on the Swenson Trail.

Station Trail   *Length: 0.9 mile Blaze: light green*
Beginning at the Stony Lake parking area, this trail goes northeast and provides access to the Coursen (blue), Stony Brook (brown), Swenson (red), and Tower (dark green) trails. It ends at the Stony Brook Trail.

Steam Mill Trail   *Length: 0.8 mile Blaze: blue*
Starting near the Steam Mill camping area, the trail goes west up a low ridge with no steep climbs. Along the route, the vegetation changes from a hemlock forest near Big Flat Brook to pitch pines and laurel on the dry rocky ridgetop. It ends at Skellinger Road.

Steffen Trail   *Length: 1.8 miles Blaze: black/gray*
This moderately-sloped trail runs southwest along a low ridge from Struble Road to Coss Road. Moss, fern, and lichen-covered rocks demonstrate the early stages of how rocks are broken down into soil. It provides access to the Jacob's Ladder Trail at the Coss Road end.

Stoll Trail   *Length: 0.7 mile Blaze: light blue/gray*
This relatively level trail passes through a forest with large beech, hemlock, white pine, and oak trees. The rhododendron thickets bloom in mid-June. The trail runs east from Dimon Road to Coss Road (near the Struble Road intersection). Limited parking is available at both ends.

Stony Brook Trail   *Length: 0.7 mile Blaze: brown*
Starting from the Stony Lake parking area, this trail runs jointly with the Coursen

(blue) and Tower (dark green) trails. After passing through an old farming area, the Stony Brook and Tower trails turn left together. When the Tower Trail turns right, the Stony Brook Trail continues straight and goes uphill, passing a small waterfall. It reaches the Appalachian Trail (white) near the Gren Anderson Shelter, where it ends.

Swenson Trail *Length: 3.8 miles Blaze: red*
Named for a local subsistence farmer, the Swenson Trail begins at Stony Lake and meanders northeast up a low ridge. About halfway, the Tinsley Trail (yellow) comes in steeply from the right, briefly runs jointly with the Swenson Trail, and then leaves to the left. The Swenson Trail continues downhill and then up a small rise, passing the Spring Brook Cabin. It passes through a clearcut area, which is part of the forest management program. After going through a wide wet area, the Swenson Trail reaches the terminus of the Cartwright Trail (brown/red) at 3.0 miles before descending for 0.8 mile to Crigger Road. Parking is available at both ends of the trail.

Tibbs Trail *Length: 0.5 mile Blaze: blue/green*
Starting from the Shotwell camping area (no parking), the Tibbs Trail crosses a brook on stone footings. The trail then widens, and a swamp with abandoned beaver lodges is visible to the left. It ends at Coursen Road, where there is parking.

Tillman Ravine Trail *Length: 1.0 mile Blaze: unmarked*
The Tillman Ravine became part of the Natural Areas System in 1978 because of its geological features and forests of hemlock, mixed hardwoods, and mixed oaks. The steep banks of the ravine are covered with rhododendron and hemlock. In high-water season, there are cascades near its upper end. The trail begins at the Walpack Cemetery and parallels a section of Brinks Road (closed January 1 through March 30) before ending on Brinks Road near Dimon Road (parking available). The well-used path follows Tillman Brook.

Tinsley Trail *Length: 2.8 miles Blaze: yellow*
Starting on Skellinger Road south of Lake Ocquittunk, the Tinsley Trail runs southeast, climbing until it ends at the Appalachian Trail (white). En route it passes through oak, maple, hickory, and birch forests, and stands of mountain laurel. At 1.4 miles it joins the Swenson Trail (red) for 0.1 mile and then turns left, away from it. Glacial features include *kettle holes* (depressions left when large blocks of ice

trapped in sand, gravel, and rock melted) and *moraines* (piles of earth and rocky debris). Limited parking is available at Skellinger Road and Sunrise Mountain Road, which is crossed just before reaching the Appalachian Trail (white).

Tower Trail   *Length: 1.0 mile Blaze: dark green*
Starting with the Coursen (blue) and Stony Brook (brown) trails at the Stony Lake parking area, the Tower Trail first turns left off the Coursen Trail and then right off the Stony Brook Trail. On its steep ascent to the Appalachian Trail (white), the Tower Trail passes through a small marsh, mixed hardwood forests, and a scrub oak forest. The trail ends at the Normanock (Culver) Lookout Tower on the Appalachian Trail (white). Limited parking is available where the trail crosses Sunrise Mountain Road.

DELAWARE WATER GAP
NATIONAL RECREATION AREA

Archeological evidence indicates that Native Americans came to the Delaware River Valley almost ten thousand years ago. Descendants of these early settlers participated in the Indian Wars of the eighteenth century. During the American Revolution, the valley was a vital communication link between New York and Philadelphia.

The first tourists came to the Gap around 1830 to marvel at its rocky crags, forested slopes, and winding river. When the railroad penetrated the Gap in 1855, the floodgates of tourism opened. The area soon acquired a body of legends and romance, as well as hotels and saloons. All kinds of natural features were given names—not a creek, crag, or vista escaped.

The idea of damming the Delaware River has danced in the heads of schemers for almost as long as industry has existed along the river. In 1868, powerful Trenton manufacturing interests defeated such a bill, but local supporters correctly predicted that someday a dam near the Water Gap would be proposed again. A devastating flood in 1955 convinced federal officials that the river should be dammed. Six major dams were proposed, but only one developed beyond paper. Beginning in 1956, plans were under way to construct a huge dam on Tocks Island that would span the valley, impounding a 28-mile-long lake for the purposes of flood control, electric generation, water supply, and, as an added benefit, recreation. In 1962, Congress authorized the construction

DELAWARE WATERGAP

of the Tocks Island Dam. In a frenzied attempt to prepare for the building of the reservoir, the Army Corps of Engineers condemned properties, evicted families, and razed thousands of homes and many historic structures. Eventually, the government purchased 55,161 acres from the Water Gap north almost to Port Jervis. The public attacked the project and its projected environmental consequences.

On September 1, 1965, President Lyndon B. Johnson signed into law the act authorizing establishment of the Delaware Water Gap National Recreation Area, with the dam and its man-made lake envisioned as its centerpiece. But opposition to the dam remained steadfast. Finally, after years of acrimonious debate, the Tocks Island project was shelved by the Delaware River Basin Commission in 1975. It was not until 1992, however, that the proposed dam was officially de-authorized. Since water is an ever-important commodity and powerful lobbies exist that would like to be a part of a multi-billion-dollar construction project, it is conceivable that the project could be revived.

Parcels of private land are scattered throughout the recreation area. Please respect the rights of these landowners and do not trespass.

NEW JERSEY WALK BOOK

For more information, visit the Kittatinny Point Visitor Center just off I-80 in New Jersey or contact the Delaware Water Gap National Recreation Area, Bushkill, PA 18324; (717) 588-2451.

Trails in the Delaware Water Gap National Recreation Area

The trails on the New Jersey side of the Delaware Water Gap vary in length, many being unmarked woods roads. The roads around Blue Mountain Lakes are open to mountain bikes. They reportedly offer the best cross-country skiing in the state, given enough snow cover. The trails on both sides of the Water Gap are described in detail in the New York-New Jersey Trail Conference's *Delaware Water Gap National Recreation Area Hiking Guide*. Only a brief description of several trails is provided below.

Appalachian Trail   *Length: 11.7 miles Blaze: white*
This major trail traverses the park. See chapter 14, "Long Distance Trails," or the *Appalachian Trail Guide to New York-New Jersey* for a complete description of the 11.7 miles in the Delaware Water Gap National Recreation Area.

Coppermines Trail   *Length: 2.1 miles Blaze: red*
The trail begins on the east side of the Old Mine Road, across from the Coppermines parking area, 7.8 miles north of Kittatinny Point Visitor Center. This grassy woods road is joint with a branch of the Kaiser Road Trail (blue) for the first 0.2 mile. The woods road passes the foundation of an old wayside hotel on the left and then turns left and proceeds uphill. The Kaiser Road Trail turns right at a sign, while the Coppermines Trail continues straight ahead to the upper mines. At 0.3 mile, the Coppermines Trail passes a mine on the left, approximately 50 feet off the trail. The trail crosses a stream on a wooden bridge and then passes through a rhododendron grove. It leaves the grove at 0.6 mile and continues to ascend moderately, paralleling a stream and passing through a hemlock glen for the next 0.2 mile. At 0.9 mile, a blue-blazed trail leaves on the right and leads to the Kaiser Road Trail in 0.2 mile. After crossing a seasonal brook, the Coppermines Trail steadily ascends the ridge, leveling out at 1.1 miles and passing rock ledges to the right and a boggy area at 1.3 miles. It then turns right and continues to ascend, reaching a height of land

atop a knoll at 1.9 miles. After descending gradually, the Coppermines Trail reaches the Appalachian Trail (white) and ends at 2.1 miles.

Kaiser Road Trail   *Length: 3.5 miles Blaze: blue*
The Kaiser Road Trail (also known as the Kaiser Trail) is a former jeep road that climbs over the Kittatinny Ridge. The western trailhead is on Old Mine Road, 7.6 miles north of I-80, with an alternative trail leaving Old Mine Road 0.2 mile farther north. To reach the eastern trailhead from I-80, take Exit 4 (NJ 94) to Hainesburg and turn left onto Walnut Valley Road. Follow the road to its end at the Lower Yards Creek Reservoir. Parking is available at both ends.

From the western end, the Kaiser Road Trail turns right at the Kaiser Trail sign and begins to ascend steeply. The Coppermines Trail (red) continues straight ahead to the upper mine. At 0.5 mile, a blue-blazed spur joins the Kaiser Road Trail at the Coppermines Trail sign and both turn left, beginning a steady climb to the top of the ridge. At 0.9 mile, the trail enters a rhododendron grove, and at 1.2 miles, it passes an old foundation on the left. Another blue-blazed trail to the left leads 0.2 mile to the Coppermines Trail. The Kaiser Road Trail swings right and passes a large talus field on the left. From there, it continues its gradual ascent of the ridge toward Mt. Mohican, also known as Raccoon Ridge. At 2.2 miles, it turns right to join the Appalachian Trail (white), which it follows for the next 0.2 mile. It leaves to the left, going down the ridge. At 2.8 miles, the Kaiser Road Trail passes a woods road to the right, and then, at 2.9 miles, a spring and a springhouse. At 3.3 miles, the Kaiser Road Trail passes a brook on the right. In another 200 feet, it turns left onto a road, then turns right onto a dirt road, and ends at the parking area near the Boy Scout camp in the Yards Creek Lower Reservoir area.

WORTHINGTON STATE FOREST

Located within the boundaries of the Delaware Water Gap National Recreation Area, but administered separately by the State of New Jersey, Worthington State Forest contains some of the most rugged terrain in the state. Comprising the bottom part of the Kittatinny Ridge, the state forest extends approximately seven miles along the ridge and includes 5,878 acres.

Worthington was once called Buckwood Park, a private deer preserve of engineer Charles Campbell Worthington. His retirement home, Shawnee-on-Delaware, was later developed as a resort. Buckwood Park was first leased to the state as a game preserve in 1916, and was purchased from the Worthington estate in 1954. Among the forest's features is a glacial lake, Sunfish Pond, which was restored to the state after a long fight by conservationists defeated a planned pumped-storage utility project there.

At the southern end of the forest is the Dunnfield Creek Natural Area. The creek tumbles over a waterfall on its way from Mount Tammany to the Delaware River, and it is one of the few in the state to support native brook trout. Overlooking this rocky stream are stands of hemlock, maple, and birch. Mountain laurel adds color to the area when in bloom.

For more information, contact Worthington State Forest, HC62, Box 2, Columbia, NJ 07832; (908) 841-9575.

Trails in Worthington State Forest

Since Worthington State Forest is within the Delaware Water Gap National Recreation Area, its trails and woods roads are also included in the New York-New Jersey Trail Conference's *Delaware Water Gap National Recreation Area Hiking Guide*. A sampling of what the area offers is given here.

Appalachian Trail   *Length: 7.8 miles Blaze: white*

This major trail traverses the park. See chapter 14, "Long Distance Trails," in this book or the *Appalachian Trail Guide to New York-New Jersey* for a complete description of the 7.8 miles in Worthington State Forest.

Beulahland Trail   *Length: 1.3 miles Blaze: yellow*

The Beulahland Trail begins as a woods road on the east side of the Old Mine Road, adjacent to the Farview parking area. The area is 1.7 miles north of the Kittatinny Point Visitor Center on the Old Mine Road. Overnight parking is not permitted.

After passing through the parking area on a well-worn foot path, the Beulahland Trail ascends the ridge, turns right onto a woods road, and continues to ascend steadily through a mature hardwood forest. At 1.3 miles, the trail ends at the Appalachian Trail (white). The Holly Springs Trail (red) begins directly ahead and descends the other side of the ridge.

Blue Dot Trail   *Length: 1.8 miles Blaze: blue*

The Blue Dot Trail starts with the Dunnfield Creek Trail (green), turning right from the Appalachian Trail (white) 0.4 mile from the Dunnfield Creek parking area off I-80. Both trails cross the creek, and in 100 yards the Blue Dot Trail splits off to the right to begin the ascent of Mount Tammany. At 1.5 miles, it reaches the ridge at an intersection with the Mount Tammany Fire Road. The Blue Dot Trail turns sharply right along the ridge to meet the Red Dot Trail (red). A view is to the right of the summit. The Red Dot Trail may be used to return to the parking area.

Douglas Trail   *Length: 2.5 miles Blaze: blue*
The Douglas Trail—named for the late U.S. Supreme Court Justice William O. Douglas, in recognition of his conservation efforts—begins on the east side of Old Mine Road. Parking is on the opposite side of the road, at the Douglas parking area, 3.9 miles north of I-80.

The trail turns right onto a woods road and begins a moderate ascent through a mature maple forest. Narrowing down to a wide trail, it continues to climb along several switchbacks, passing a backpacker camping site at 1.7 miles. Overnight usage is restricted to Appalachian Trail thru-hikers. There is no water, and ground fires are not permitted. The trail terminates 250 feet later at the Appalachian Trail (white).

Garvey Springs Trail   *Length: 1.2 miles Blaze: yellow/orange*
The Garvey Springs Trail goes from the Douglas parking area to the Appalachian Trail, following a woods road for most of its length. Ascending moderately, the trail turns left and joins the Rockcores Trail (unmarked) at 0.5 mile, with which it runs jointly for approximately 0.1 mile before turning right and beginning a steep and rocky ascent. At 1.1 miles, the trail passes Garvey Springs. After a gradual ascent, the trail descends slightly to its junction with the Appalachian Trail (white) at 1.2 miles, where it terminates.

Red Dot Trail   *Length: 1.3 miles Blaze: red dot on white*
The Red Dot Trail starts from the rest area off of I-80 and climbs relentlessly. There is a view at 0.4 mile into the Water Gap and across the river to Mount Minsi. At the top of Mount Tammany, a rocky viewpoint is to the right. The Water Gap was not, as many people guess, formed by the river cutting its way through the mountains; rather, it evolved as the mountain slowly rose up around the already-existing river. At the top, the trail meets one end of the Blue Dot Trail, which may be used to return to the parking area.

WILDLIFE MANAGEMENT AREAS

Flat Brook and its tributaries flow between the Kittatinny Ridge and the Delaware River. Along its banks are three wildlife management areas. Although primarily managed for wildlife, there are many acres to explore during non-hunting seasons. All three areas are covered on the NY-NJ Trail Conference Kittatinny Map set, or see the appropriate USGS topographic quadrangle maps mentioned below.

Hainesville Wildlife Management Area

The eastern edge of the Hainesville Wildlife Management Area narrowly touches High Point State Park. It is one of the smaller, older WMAs and is managed for upland game hunting, with planted fields, hedgerows and a pond which is fast becoming a swamp. Wild turkeys, deer, grouse, black ducks, mallards, and wood ducks are some of the species found within the area.

To reach the Hainesville WMA from Hainesville on US 206, proceed north for about 0.5 mile to Shaytown Road, continue east for about 0.5 mile, then go north on Cemetery Road 0.5 mile to parking at the entrance to the wildlife management area.

Since there are no marked trails, users of the area should obtain the Milford USGS topographic quadrangle map. For more information, contact New Jersey DEP, Division of Fish, Game and Wildlife, 501 East State Street, P.O. Box 400, Trenton, NJ 08625; (609) 292-2965.

Flatbrook-Roy Wildlife Management Area

Noted for its trout streams, the Flatbrook-Roy Wildlife Management Area contains 2,334 acres adjoining Stokes State Forest to its west. Birdwatching and winter cross-country skiing opportunities are also found here.

Parking is available on a road leading east from County 615 (Kuhn Road) just north of Peters Valley Craft Center on County 615 about 0.25 mile east of the intersection with County 640, and at the intersection of Flat Brook Road and the road leading south from Peters Valley Craft Center (continuing straight when County 615 takes a right turn).

Since there are no marked trails, users of the area should obtain the Culvers Gap USGS topographic quadrangle map. For more information, contact New Jersey DEP, Division of Fish, Game and Wildlife, 501 East State Street, P.O. Box 400, Trenton, NJ 08625; (609) 292-2965.

Walpack Wildlife Management Area

The Walpack Wildlife Management area (387 acres) is a narrow strip extending for about two miles along County 615 north of Flatbrookville and is entirely contained within the Delaware Water Gap National Recreation Area. It offers fishing on Flat Brook and also has high ground along Pompey Ridge which overlooks the Delaware River. Parking is available.

Since there are no marked trails, users of the area should obtain the Flatbrookville and Lake Maskenozha USGS topographic quadrangle maps. For more information, contact New Jersey DEP, Division of Fish, Game and Wildlife, 501 East State Street, P.O. Box 400, Trenton, NJ 08625; (609) 292-2965.

NINE

THE WATCHUNGS

uring the late Triassic Epoch, separate lava outflows onto the Newark Basin formed two 50-mile-long ridges now known as the Watchungs. Stretching from Paterson toward Bridgewater, the two ridges follow roughly parallel courses while keeping a distance of one or two miles between one another. Consisting primarily of basalt (traprock), they show cross-faulting at Paterson, Great Notch, Summit, Plainfield, and Bound Brook. The views from the First Watchung are their chief attraction.

Because of their height, the Watchungs played an important part in the American Revolution. Their walls form natural ramparts that could have been designed by a military engineer for General Washington's needs. The fronts of the ridges were steep and easy to protect and afforded many places for American scouts to watch the movements of the British Redcoats across the New Jersey flatlands to the east. The double line of the Watchungs was further engineered by nature, with curving flanks from Bound Brook back to Bernardsville on the south and from Paterson around to Oakland on the north, right up to the older, solid mass of the Precambrian granites of the Ramapos.

At the northern end of the First Watchung, Garrett Mountain overlooks the city of Paterson. From here, the ridge runs southwest to Eagle Rock Reservation and on to South Mountain Reservation in Essex County. The First Watchung then continues southwest into Union County, where the Watchung Reservation runs between Summit and Scotch Plains. At Bound Brook, the ridge swings northwest, its tip having an elevation of 589 feet. Two peaks, High Mountain and Beech Mountain, mark the northern end of the Preakness Hills. Southwest along the Second Watchung, the only public areas are in the South Mountain and Watchung reservations, both of which straddle the two ridges.

Over two centuries after the American Revolution, these hills, which rise as high as 900 feet, still provide views of the plains below. High above the city settlements and wildlife preserves, hikers can see how the state has fared since the War for Independence. In 1998, the surrounding area is extensively urbanized. Areas for hiking and respite are concentrated around the various county parks and reservations. Suburban developments have covered all but isolated sections.

History

Because of their height, the Watchungs played an important part in the American Revolution. After Washington captured the Hessian garrison at Trenton and fought the British at Princeton, he eluded the superior forces that gathered and escaped via the northern branch of the Raritan River into the hill fortress around Morristown where the enemy was afraid to pursue him. The only occasion when the British penetrated the Watchung barrier was in December 1776, when a small cavalry patrol surprised General Charles Lee and his aides in a tavern at Basking Ridge. After that, no British or Hessian soldier ever passed these ridges. Every month, Washington strengthened his main camp at Morristown and its outposts, which served as a rallying place and source of supplies for the rest of the war.

After the American Revolution, the series of events taking place within the Watchungs had far-reaching effects on the United States. In 1791, the federal government gave Alexander Hamilton the authority to create the Society for Useful Manufactures (S.U.M.). The society was to promote the formation of American industries and to establish a planned industrial city to be named Paterson. After considering other sites, a location on the Passaic River was chosen because of the power from a large waterfall and the close proximity to natural resources.

As the Industrial Revolution developed and a variety of industries emerged, Paterson's population soared, and it became a major industrial city. The first

cotton mill opened in 1794 and the first silk mill in 1839. After 1837, Paterson became noted for its steam locomotives, producing nearly half of America's locomotives. In 1858, Dundee Manufacturing Company built a 450-foot dam across the Passaic River to produce power and by 1873, 15 mills were located along the Dundee water power canal. Paterson's reputation as a silk manufacturer was established, such that by the late 1880s, it was known as the Silk City. The first Colt revolver was made in Paterson, as well as the first submarine, and the engine in Charles Lindbergh's plane, *The Spirit of St. Louis*.

With such a concentration of industry, it is not surprising that Paterson gave rise to a strong and effective reform movement in the early 1900s. A series of welfare acts providing workmen's compensation and protection for laborers were among the social reforms associated with Woodrow Wilson, the governor of New Jersey. His efforts with the progressive movements brought him to national attention, and eventually to the presidency of the United States.

HACKENSACK MEADOWLANDS

In 1969, the State of New Jersey enacted legislation to preserve, enhance, and develop the 32 square miles now known as the Meadowlands. The wetlands and tidal marshes of the Hackensack River and the adjacent area had been threatened with haphazard zoning, unregulated waste disposal, and lack of planning. Since its inception, the Hackensack Meadowlands Development Commission has worked to protect the environment and, at the same time, create jobs and office space. The part of the project of interest to walkers and birders is the creation of wildlife management areas and parks.

Although the area is often thought of as landfill, a visit to the Meadowlands is definitely not a trip to the dump. The capped landfill is landscaped, water levels in pools are regulated, and trails take visitors out into observation areas and bird blinds. Over 250 species of birds have been sighted here, but birds are not the only reason to visit. The Environmental Center Trash Museum is the country's first museum devoted to trash. Its purpose is to increase public awareness of the garbage disposal problem and its impact on the environment.

DeKorte State Park

Named for a state senator, Richard DeKorte, this 2,000-acre state park is reclaimed landfill and revitalized wetlands. Behind the parking lot is the Field-to-Forest Trail which, in a small area, shows plant succession. Two trails lead out

to the brackish wetlands. The Marsh Discovery Trail is on a recycled plastic boardwalk for its entire length and meets the gravel-based Transco Trail to make a loop.

To visit DeKorte State Park, take the New Jersey Turnpike to Exit 16W. Follow NJ 3 west to the exit for NJ 17 south. Follow the ramp to Polito Avenue and turn left. At the end of Polito Avenue, turn left on Valley Brook Avenue and go to the end, where there is parking. Signs along the route direct you to the park. During the week, public transportation to the office buildings on Valley Brook Avenue is available via NJ Transit Buses 76L and 76T. A walking lane on Valley Brook Avenue is called the Meadows Path and leads to the marsh. For more information, contact De Korte State Park, 2 DeKorte Park Plaza, Lyndhurst, NJ 07071; (201) 406-8300.

Lyndhurst Nature Reserve

Adjacent to De Korte State Park, this 3.5-acre garbage island is an environmental study park, with two management zones. In one zone, there will be unlimited access for education and recreation. The other zone is seasonally restricted to make sure that sensitive wildlife areas remain undisturbed during critical times. To reach Lyndhurst Nature Reserve, follow the directions to DeKorte State Park.

Saw Mill Creek Wildlife Management Area

Known for its birding opportunities rather than for hiking, the Saw Mill Creek Wildlife Management Area is comprised of tidal flats and landfill on both sides of the New Jersey Turnpike. The expanse of open wetlands is visible to anyone traveling south on the New Jersey Turnpike and looking west just past Exit 16W. Railroads, old roads, and a gas line cross the area.

To reach the wildlife management area from the New Jersey Turnpike, take Exit 15W (I-280, Newark, The Oranges). After the toll booths, stay right, follow the signs to Harrison Avenue, and go west 0.7 mile to Schuyler Avenue. Turn right and proceed north to Belleville Pike. Turn right, and go 1.4 miles to the power substation on the right, just before reaching the New Jersey Turnpike. Walk north along the gas line.

Since there are no marked trails in the Saw Mill Creek Management Area, users of the area should obtain the Weehawken USGS topographic quadrangle map. For more information, contact New Jersey DEP, Division of Fish, Game and Wildlife, 501 East State Street, P.O. Box 400, Trenton, NJ 08625; (609) 292-2965.

GARRETT MOUNTAIN RESERVATION

Garrett Mountain Reservation, located in Paterson and West Paterson, consists of 550 acres in two parts—Garrett Mountain and Rifle Camp Park. They are part of the Passaic County park system.

The Garrett Mountain section includes Lambert Castle, built in 1891 by Catholina Lambert, a wealthy silk manufacturer. It houses a combined museum and library, the Passaic County Historical Society, and the Passaic County Parks Department. Entrance to the Garrett Mountain section is from Mountain Park Road, which leads uphill from the intersection of Valley Road and Fenner

Avenue in Paterson. For more information, contact the Passaic County Parks Department at (973) 881-4832.

Rifle Camp Park consists of 225 acres and features an amphitheater, toboggan run, nature trail, and astronomical observatory. The John Crowley Nature Center sponsors songbird and hawk watches during migration and houses the observatory's seismograph. Entry is on the east side of Rifle Camp Road, 1.4 miles north of US 46 in West Paterson. For more information, contact Rifle Camp Park, Rifle Camp Road, West Paterson, NJ 07424; (973) 523-0024.

Trails in Garrett Mountain Reservation

Both Garrett Mountain and Rifle Camp Park have trails that circle the park, thus providing opportunities for a short hike or a longer circuit one. The parks are connected by the Rifle Camp Connector Trail, a marked route along Weasel Drift Road.

Garrett Mountain Trail *Length: 3.8 miles Blaze: yellow*

From the entrance, proceed 0.6 mile straight ahead to the observation tower parking lot and take the trail in a northerly (counterclockwise) direction. Soon there is a side trail to the edge of the ridge, offering a wide view of most of

chimney rock Bound Brook

northern New Jersey, with Manhattan on the distant horizon. The trail comes out into a small parking lot, crosses into an open field, and bears right along the tree line. It enters woods in a short distance and, at 0.6 mile, emerges at the Paterson Overlook and the north end of the White Trail. The Garrett Mountain Trail crosses the road and passes the Benson Memorial, commemorating an early Parks Commissioner, on the right, then follows the road uphill to Veterans Memorial Point, with views to the north and northeast. On a clear day, and with the help of binoculars, Schunemunk Mountain can be picked out to the northwest, along with High Mountain in Wayne and Turkey Mountain in Montville. Turning left (southwest) along the ridge and crossing the White Trail at 1.0 mile, the Garrett Mountain Trail makes a sharp left, then a right, and descends along a switchback.

At the bottom of the switchback, the trail makes a sharp right turn and, at 1.3 miles, crosses a paved road leading to other parking lots on the western side of the park and the Mountain Avenue exit. After crossing a small bridge, it comes to Barbour's Pond and, continuing along its western shore, crosses several side trails. At the fork it bears left downhill and passes a seasonal boat rental on the left. After crossing a brook, the trail turns right and follows the brook to a small culvert. It bears uphill, with an old quarry on the right. At 2.1 miles, the Garrett Mountain Trail reaches the Weasel Drift picnic area. The trail to the right is the Rifle Camp Connector Trail (yellow), which follows Weasel Drift Road. Keeping to the left, after a few ups and downs, the Garrett Mountain Trail crosses the paved circular drive around the reservation. In 300 feet, it meets the south end of the White Trail and turns right. The Garrett Mountain Trail crosses the circular road again at a stable entrance, then turns right along it after some turns. It soon turns right and goes between concrete tank supports. The trail follows the ridge east of the stables and, with further turns and passing several side trails, it reaches views to the east and returns to the parking lot, completing its 3.8-mile loop.

Rifle Camp Park Trail   *Length: 2.0 miles Blaze: yellow*

Rifle Camp Park Trail is a circular trail which is accessible from several points in the park. From the first parking lot on the right from the park entrance at the handicapped picnic area, the trail turns left and goes downhill on a paved path, which continues right onto a gravel trail. The trail turns left to cross a brook and then turns right at an intersection. After a few turns, it comes to a fitness station and soon bears right from the drive. In a short distance, an unblazed trail comes in from the left. The trail turns left at a T junction at 0.5 mile, and, after another left turn, reaches a pond on the left. The unblazed trail on the right loops out to a view overlooking a quarry and returns to the Rifle Camp Park Trail 100 feet farther along. After continuing around the pond, the Rifle Camp Park Trail goes uphill into a rock cut, then jogs left and right to come out into a parking circle. Across the circle, a paved path goes to the nature center at 1.0 mile. Heading east, the trail comes to a panoramic view east to south.

The trail soon comes to another fitness station, crosses a dry brook bed, and passes a large house with a red roof, behind a fence. Turning left from the fence, it winds down to a small brook, then reaches a gravel path with a concrete pad on the right. In 500 feet, a path comes in from the left, and the Carney Bragg Memorial Picnic Area

can be seen ahead. After turning right (north), the trail crosses several culverts and, at 1.6 miles, meets a foot-path coming in from the left and swings right, parallel to the office fence. The trail winds through woods and heads southwest to the entrance drive. The Rifle Camp Park Connector Trail (yellow) can be reached with a right turn. The Rifle Camp Park Trail crosses the road and makes a left at an exercise station. After more turns, the amphitheater comes into view on the left. The long concrete trough at the right is the tobog-gan slide. The return route to the starting point is at the top of the hill.

Rifle Camp Connector Trail   *Length: 0.7 mile Blaze: yellow*
This road walk begins 200 feet from the Weasel Drift Picnic Area, where park-ing is available. It follows Weasel Drift and Rifle Camp roads past a firehouse and an entrance to a bank office building on the left before reaching Rifle Camp Park and the Rifle Camp Park Trail (yellow).

White Trail   *Length: 1.5 miles Blaze: white*
The White Trail starts at Benson Drive and the Garrett Mountain Trail (yel-low), at the north end of the Garrett Mountain North Viewpoint parking lot. It heads north down a set of stairs and follows a stone wall. At the end of the wall, it enters the woods, goes over logs crossing a ditch, and enters an open area with a radio tower on the left. The trail heads west downhill into a ravine and a dry brook bed, turns left uphill to a large rock, then turns left again, and crosses the Garrett Mountain Trail (yellow). The White Trail reaches the paved circular road at 0.6 mile, crosses it, and heads southeast up a gravel road, bearing left on a bridle path at the fork. In another 400 feet, the trail turns right down a slope and right over a brook. It follows the base of a cliff and makes a left on a bridle path, which it follows for 0.3 mile. After turning down-

hill, it crosses a brook and comes out on another bridle path by a large cedar tree. After a right turn, the White Trail ends at the Garrett Mountain Trail (yellow).

PREAKNESS RANGE AND HIGH MOUNTAIN

Although much of the Preakness Range is occupied by William Paterson State University, a golf course, and private homes, its northern end contains some 1,700 acres of wild wooded country, including an unobstructed view in all directions from High Mountain. Set north of Paterson, it is a continuation of the Second Watchung. Thanks to unremitting efforts by conservationists, Wayne Township, The Nature Conservancy, and the State of New Jersey became the owners of 1,057 acres on High Mountain in August 1993.

Geologically similar to the Palisades to the east and Packanack Mountain to the west, the Preakness Range is the middle of a three-layer basalt series lying roughly parallel to one another. A gap lets the Passaic River flow between the Watchung and Preakness ranges. During a glacial retreat, a great stream of ice flowed through Franklin Clove, creating a deep shady pass. It has counterparts in Long Clove and Short Clove below Haverstraw in New York. Franklin Lake is the largest of a series of ponds occupying depressions along the irregular knolls left by the glacial ice as it retreated. Stratified sand and gravel deposited along the ice front are typical of this area. The shallow soil has given rise to stunted vegetation, allowing an unobstructed, 360-degree view at the summit of High Mountain.

Cars may be parked at William Paterson University parking lot #6. College Road, leading to parking lot #6, turns off Hamburg Turnpike just east of Duncan Lane. NJ Transit Bus 197 travels along Hamburg Turnpike, and buses 703 and 744 from Passaic provide access to the eastern portion of the area from Belmont and High Mountain avenues in North Haledon.

Trails in High Mountain Park Preserve

In 1998, the trail system is undergoing major renovations. The combination of the need to protect habitat and withdrawal of permission of private landowners has resulted in hiking trails being rerouted and segments closed. Before hiking in the area, check with Wayne Township, Department of Parks and Recreation, 475 Valley Road, Wayne, NJ 07479; (973) 694-1800. Groups of 10 or more need to obtain a permit from the Parks and Recreation Department.

Pancake Hollow Trail   *Length: 2.8 miles Blaze: blue*
From Hamburg Turnpike (County 504), proceed north 1.3 miles on Valley Road to Point View Parkway. Turn right, then immediately right again onto Chicopee Drive, where parking is available. The trailhead is on the right near a large rock, 0.3 mile from Point View Parkway.

Shaped like a lollipop, the Pancake Hollow Trail traverses the northwestern portion of the Preakness Range. The trail reaches a rocky ridge at 0.6 mile. Beech Mountain is to the east, Franklin Lake to the northeast, and Franklin Clove directly below. Passing a housing development, the trail heads uphill. At 0.9 mile, the Point View Reservoir comes into view. At 1.3 miles, the trail turns left, with a woods road coming in on the right. In 100 feet, the trail reaches a Y junction. The trail loops back to this point and may be walked in either direction. If one chooses to take the left fork, the trail descends, crosses two brooks, and passes a large glacial erratic on the left at 1.9 miles. Reaching Berdan Avenue at 2.4 miles, the Pancake Hollow Trail turns to go through a stand of red cedar. It skirts a wet area and closes the loop at 2.8 miles. Hikers need to retrace their steps back to the trailhead, having hiked 4.1 miles.

Red Trail   *Length: 2.1 miles Blaze: red*
The Red Trail is accessible west of William Paterson University parking lot #6, starting at the upper west corner of the parking lot opposite the entrance driveway. From there, it climbs and passes the southern end of the Yellow Trail on the right at 0.5 mile and the White Trail on the left a short distance beyond. Continuing north, the trail works its way uphill, passing over the shoulder, and descends. The Yellow Trail crosses at 1.6 miles from the start. Skirting the side of the hill, the Red Trail continues north to end at 2.1 miles on Reservoir Road, where there is curbside parking. This northern trailhead is 0.4 mile west of High Mountain Road (between Navaho Trail and Pawnee Lane).

Waterfall Trail   *Length: 0.3 mile Blaze: orange*
Accessible from the northern end of the Yellow Trail, the Waterfall Trail is a short loop that leads hikers to the seasonal waterfall of Buttermilk Falls, which consists of fractured basalt rock.

White Trail   *Length: 1.3 miles Blaze: white*
The White Trail starts from the Red Trail 0.6 mile from its southern trailhead. It passes two large glacial erratics and a red cedar grove before turning right at

0.5 mile. It goes by the reservoir and fairways of the North Jersey Country Club and gently climbs to end at the Yellow Trail at 1.3 miles.

Yellow Trail
Length: 4.5 miles Blaze: yellow

Featuring both views from High Mountain and interesting geological formations, this trail is the longest one in the Preakness area. Parking is at William Paterson University parking lot #6.

The Yellow Trail starts from the Red Trail, 0.5 mile north of its trailhead. It climbs a small rise and then heads downhill to cross a stream. It begins a gradual ascent, turns, and reaches the ridge at 0.3 mile. The Yellow Trail turns left, proceeds north along the shoulder of Mount Cecchino, and then climbs High Mountain, reaching the first summit at 1.0 mile. The barren summit rewards the hiker with a 360-degree view. Northwest and north lie the Ramapos, with Suffern and the gap of the Ramapo River slightly east of north. To the east, the horizon is bounded by the Palisades, with Hook Mountain at the northeast. Southeast, the skyscrapers of Manhattan are visible, with the towers of the George Washington Bridge north of them. Nearer are the towns of Wyckoff and Ridgewood (northeast), and Fair Lawn (east), with Paterson lying in the bowl of the valley. Directly opposite is the long slope of the *goffle*, or ridge, of the First Watchung. The eastern cliff is almost vertical, as is the eastern side of the Second Watchung, of which High Mountain is the highest summit at 885 feet. To the near south is Veterans Memorial Point, above the abrupt drop of Garrett Mountain.

After following the ridge to the north and then steeply descending the shoulder of High Mountain, the Yellow Trail contours along the western side to cross the Red Trail at 1.7 miles. The Yellow Trail heads west briefly before turning north to make a U turn at 2.2 miles, where an unmarked side trail leads out to the circle on Reservoir Road. The Yellow Trail gradually ascends and meets the northern end of the White Trail on the flank of Beech Mountain. The Yellow Trail wanders along the ridge to two sweeping views of Point View Reservoir, Wayne, and the Pompton Hills.

From the second view at 3.0 miles, the trail again heads north and then descends, sometimes steeply, with long switchbacks. At the bottom of the descent, at 3.7 miles, it enters the south end of Franklin Clove, where slant rock formations are on the left and talus is to the right. At the north end of the clove, at 4.2 miles, the Waterfall Trail (orange) is at the Y junction to the right. The Yellow Trail goes to the left and ends at the edge of the preserve at Indian

Trail Drive at 4.5 miles, where there is parking.

SOUTH MOUNTAIN RESERVATION

Wooded hiking trails, picnic areas, and views are the main reasons for South Mountain Reservation's popularity. The park's 2,047 acres provide 19 miles of hiking trails, including the Lenape Trail (which begins here), and views of falls, millponds, and—off in the distance—Manhattan. Two year-round skating rinks, Turtle Back Zoo, and horseback riding also draw people to the reservation. In the northeastern section, Turtle Back Rock is an interesting formation, and the Turtle Back Zoo is the home of animals from many parts of the world. Numerous picnic areas, with views, can be found along Crest Drive. By park regulation, bikes are not permitted.

Essex County was one of the first in the nation to establish a network of open-space parks. Efforts here set the standard for county and state parks elsewhere. The South Mountain area had been environmentally damaged since the 1750s, when lumber crews chopped its hemlock groves to provide timber for New York City and Philadelphia. Lumberjacks were later replaced by foulsmelling paper mills. Then, in the 1890s, Essex County cried "Enough!" and began a program of buying and restoring land. A century later, the benefits of that decision are still there for people to enjoy. The Friends of South Mountain Reservation, Inc., NJ Transit, and the Essex County Department of Parks, Recreation, and Cultural Affairs strive to preserve and restore the reservation's beauty.

The reservation can be reached by NJ Transit train to Millburn, or by car via I-280 to Exit 7 and then south on Pleasant Valley Way into the park. Picnicking permits are required for groups of more than twenty people. For information on the park, or to obtain permits, contact Essex County Department of Parks, Recreation, and Cultural Affairs, 115 Clifton Avenue, Newark, NJ 07104; (973) 268-3500.

Lenape Trail   *Length: 30 miles (partially complete) Blaze: yellow*
A joint undertaking of the Sierra Club and the Essex County Department of Parks, Recreation, and Cultural Affairs, the Lenape Trail will, when complete, link a dozen county and municipal parks, the Patriots' Path, historic areas, and other landmarks along a 30-mile route. The entire path is only open to foot

WASHINGTON ROCK.

POND & SOUTH MOUNTAIN
RESERVATION NEAR MILBURN

traffic and cross-country skiing (when conditions are suitable). A 6-mile sec-tion in South Mountain Reservation, another 6-mile section from West Orange to West Caldwell, and a 12-mile section from Cedar Grove to Newark are complete as of 1998. Two significant gaps in West Orange and North Caldwell remain to be filled in.

The first section of the Lenape Trail starts in the Locust Grove picnic area, just north of the Millburn train station, and goes 6.1 miles north to Mayapple Hill. From the picnic area, the trail follows a long path to the top of the First Watchung, where, at 0.8 mile, it turns back to Washington Rock, from which George Washington surveyed the countryside during the American Revolution.

Continuing west, then north, the Lenape Trail passes an old quarry, Maple Falls, and Beech Brook Cascades, reaching Lilliput Knob at 2.0 miles. It comes to Mines Point (a circa-1800 copper excavation site) at 2.4 miles and Balls Bluff at 2.8 miles, with a shelter built in 1908. The trail crosses South Orange Avenue on a footbridge at 3.4 miles, and turns left through a pine grove, reach-ing Tulip Spring at 3.6 miles, where parking is available. After crossing the West Branch of the Rahway River, the trail goes uphill to cross Cherry Lane at South Orange Avenue at 4.0 miles. It continues further up to the western ridge on the Second Watchung. Continuing northward, it passes views of the Orange Reservoir and the ice skating arena. After crossing Northfield Avenue on a foot bridge at 5.6 miles, the Lenape Trail ends at the Mayapple Hill parking area at 6.1 miles. A variety of return routes to Locust Grove can be taken from many points along the trail by way of various footpaths and bridle paths. Maps are available at the park office.

In 1998, a gap of two miles exists between Mayapple Hill and the next section of the Lenape Trail which starts at the north end of Ellison Avenue in West Orange. It is off Mt. Pleasant Avenue, at the top of the Second Watchung, and is accessible via NJ Transit bus 71 from Newark.

After passing through O'Conner Park, the Lenape Trail reaches the Public Service Electric & Gas Company power line, and goes west under the wires. After crossing and following several streets, it goes through the undeveloped Becker Tract, formerly the Henry Becker Dairy Farm. The Lenape Trail then enters undeveloped West Essex Park, a largely wooded wetland along the Passaic River.

At the northwest corner of Eisenhower Parkway and Eagle Rock Avenue, yellow blazes with a green dot mark a link to Morris County's Patriots' Path. This link goes westward along Eagle Rock Avenue several hundred feet, along the power lines to Foulerton's Brook, and then west to Charm Acres. It crosses Eagle Rock Avenue again to the Center for Environmental Studies and connects with the Patriot's Path (white), which leads across the Passaic River one mile through swampy Lurker Park to a temporary end at Ridgedale Avenue in East Hanover.

From the Eisenhower Parkway-Eagle Rock Avenue intersection, the main Lenape Trail (yellow) continues north along the west side of Eisenhower Parkway to cross Foulerton's Brook. It winds its way westerly and goes under I-280 near the Passaic River. At times of high water in the Passaic River, the area in the vicinity of Foulerton's Brook and I-280 may be impassable. North of the underpass, the trail parallels I-280 to the power line, and then goes north for 2.0 miles under the wires, ending at Bloomfield Avenue. NJ Transit bus 71 from West Orange and bus 29 from Montclair and Newark provide access.

A 4-mile gap in the trail exists between Bloomfield Avenue and the beginning of the next section at the Morgan Farm on NJ 23 in Cedar Grove, near its intersection with Fairview Avenue. NJ Transit buses 11 from Newark and Montclair and 195 from New York serve NJ 23. The trail passes through the Morgan Farm to reach Community Park, crosses the West Essex Trail, and then goes through the woods to cross Ridge Road. It passes around the north

Summit — *Hospital* — *Hook Mountain in distance*

Summit

The Watchung ranges from Summit Observatory tow[er]

end of the Cedar Grove Reservoir to enter the 157-acre Mills Reservation.

After a short, steep descent into Mountainside Park, a site of iris gardens, the Lenape Trail follows Montclair streets 0.8 mile to Yanticaw Brook Park, and then continues to Brookdale Park in Bloomfield. Going through town streets and past a schoolyard, the trail crosses the Garden State Parkway on a footbridge. Passing along streets in Nutley, the Lenape Trail enters Yanticaw Park and turns south. Running along 1.5 miles of quiet streets, the trail enters Belleville Park. Across Mill Street is the north end of Branch Brook Park, a turn-of-the-century John Charles Olmstead design. A festival every April at the Japanese cherry blossom area celebrates the flowering of hundreds of trees and draws thousands of visitors.

Wending its way south for three miles, the trail passes Sacred Heart Cathedral, leaves the park, and crosses Clifton Avenue to follow Nesbit and James streets. In this historic area, nineteenth-century brownstones struggle against urban blight on the west and downtown commercial activity on the east. Passing the restored Ballantine House and Newark Museum, both of which are open to the public, the Lenape Trail crosses Washington Park before reaching Trinity Episcopal Cathedral, which served as a hospital during the Revolution. The trail terminates at the south end of Military Park near the Wars of America Monument by Gutzon Borglum.

For more information on the Lenape Trail, contact the Essex County Department of Parks, Recreation, and Cultural Affairs at (973) 268-3500.

Second Mountain   First Mountain with Quarry and Washington Rock   The Oranges Baltusrol

the oranges

links

Looking North to First & Second Mountain & the Oranges

WATCHUNG RESERVATION

Watchung Reservation, managed by the Union County Division of Parks and Recreation, is a 2,000-acre wooded tract where animal and plant life are protected. Highlights of the park include Surprise Lake, Seeley's Pond, the Deserted Village of Feltville/Glenside Park, the Trailside Nature and Science Center, the county nursery, and the Watchung Stables. In May and early June, the dogwood and rhododendron near Surprise Lake are outstanding. Although I-78 traverses its northwestern flank, most of the reservation remains in a natural, wild state, and sound barriers muffle the road noise.

A map showing the reservation's hiking trails is available at the Trailside Nature and Science Center. The Visitor Center has live reptiles and an auditorium, with talks scheduled most weekends. Opened in 1941, the Trailside Museum was New Jersey's first nature museum. It has a large collection of birds' eggs, as well as many native animals and birds. Nearby is a small planetarium. The Visitor Center and museum are open daily (except holidays) from the end of March to Thanksgiving. There are four short nature trails: green (0.2 mile), orange (0.5 mile), blue (0.9 mile), and red (0.5 mile.) Some of the reservation trails are used by horses. Hikers may notice some wet areas and erosion due to this traffic.

To reach Watchung Reservation by car, take Exit 44 from I-78 east, and turn left at the traffic light onto Glenside Drive. Turn right, at 1.2 miles, onto County 645. At the traffic circle, turn right at Summit Road and then right again at New Providence Road. The Trailside Museum and parking are directly ahead. From Port Authority Bus Terminal in Manhattan, take NJ Transit bus 114 and walk for 1.5 miles up New Providence Road and W. R. Tracy Drive to a traffic circle, where there are signs to the Visitor Center and parking. For more information, contact the Watchung Reservation, 452 New Providence Road, Mountainside, NJ 07092; (908) 789-3670.

Sierra Trail　　*Length: 10.8 miles*
　　　　　　　　Blaze: white squares
The circular Sierra Trail roughly follows the perimeter of the reservation. It starts on the Red Trail near the entrance to the Visitor Center. After crossing Tracy Drive at 0.7 mile, it follows the ridge of the First Watchung, reaching a water tower at 1.1 miles and then heading back southeast. It crosses Summit Lane near a traffic circle at 1.6 miles, then heads down into the valley separating the two Watchung ridges. At 2.2 miles, the trail passes near Union County Watchung Stables. After reaching its northernmost point at 2.8 miles, it turns south. It crosses a bridge on Tracy Drive at Surprise Lake at 3.4 miles.

The trail follows dirt roads southwest, passing near Surprise Lake Dam at 4.2 miles before plunging back into the woods. It continues along the hillside through woods, passing an old graveyard at 4.8 miles, then moves onto a blacktop road through a deserted village. The village, known as Feltville, thrived from 1845 to 1860 with a paper mill built by David Felt. Between 1882 and 1916, it was revived as a Victorian retreat known as Feltville. Several of the houses have been refurbished and, although the village is deserted, some of the houses are inhabited by park employees.

At 6.2 miles, the trail crosses Skytop Drive near Seeley's Pond and heads uphill, with a paper mill ruin at 6.8 miles. After running along Green Brook and an escarpment, it reaches the southwest corner of the park at 7.3 miles. A second crossing of Skytop Drive is reached at 8.4 miles, where there is parking. It crosses a stream near Blue Bridge at 10.0 miles. The Sierra Trail briefly follows the blue nature trail, then leaves it to the right. It joins the orange nature trail, which soon ends on the green nature trail, which bears to the right and returns to the Visitor Center parking lot at 10.8 miles.

TEN

MORRIS COUNTY

ntil the 1730s when surveyors found iron in the hills, few people settled in the Jersey Highlands because it offered poorer farming than land to the south. The iron-rich hills, more than any other factor, shaped the development of the area and gave birth to an industry that forged a nation. With mines supplying the iron used for weaponry, New Jersey played an important role in the fight for independence. Establishment of routes through the Ramapo Mountains allowed munitions and supplies to reach the fighting forces in the Hudson Valley. As the iron industry developed, an effective means of transportation was needed to bring coal from Pennsylvania and take iron out of the area. Thus, in the early nineteenth century, the iron industry and the Morris Canal were woven together. But canals cannot operate in the winter, and the arrival of railroads in the 1850s sounded the canal's death knell.

The decline of the Morris Canal did not harm the area. Boatmen and canal workers found other employment. Small villages had already become towns. Farming and mining continued. By the time railroads crisscrossed the county, Morris County had become an industrial and agricultural area. But when higher-grade iron ore was discovered in the Mesabi Range of Minnesota in the 1890s, the New Jersey iron industry quickly faded away. The railroads continued to bring coal to metropolitan New York for heating and industry until just after World War II.

In the 1990s, with three major interstate highways crossing the area, open space in Morris County competes for existence with development and suburban sprawl. However, wooded areas and farmlands have not given way entirely to development. Although much of the area has been taken up by single-family housing, Morris County has wildlife management areas, watershed property, and parks. These open spaces enhance the quality of life by preserving wildlife habitat, protecting aquifers and watersheds, and offering people places to hike, bird, hunt, and fish.

As of 1998, two trails are being developed across Morris County—the Highlands Trail (teal diamond) and the Patriots' Path (white). Some forty miles are in use in 1998. Linking parks with small trail systems, they create opportunities for longer hikes. When trails cross private lands, hikers should stay on the trails to respect the privacy of the landowners and to help ensure the existence of these trails in the future. In 1998, the Morris County Park System is reviewing its system of trail usage and blazing. They wish to alert hikers, bicyclists, equestrians, and other trail users that significant changes may be made.

Geology

Most of Morris County is part of the Reading Prong of the Jersey Highlands, which goes from Wawayanda State Park in the north through the Pequannock Watershed to Phillipsburg on the Delaware River. The steep ridges have rounded to flat tops with frequent rock outcroppings. Underlying rocks on the ridges are predominately Precambian, the oldest in New Jersey, while the valleys are composed of Paleozoic sandstone, limestone, or shale.

There is evidence of glaciation throughout the Highlands. As the Wisconsin glacier moved across the region, it cut scratches in bedrock, smoothed out rock formations, and left erratics perched on ridges. Its terminal moraine, almost one mile wide and 25 to 100 feet high, is a heterogeneous mixture of rocks and gravel. It stretches between Hackettstown and Morristown and then turns southeast, terminating in what is now Perth Amboy. Sand and gravel left as glacial lake or outwash deposits are sometimes as thick as 250 feet. In the past they have been mined, and are likely to be mined in the future.

Picatinny Arsenal

The 6,500-acre Picatinny Arsenal has long figured in the history of the region. In 1749, at the base of Picatinny Peak, an iron forge was constructed on a site that had water from a brook and iron from nearby mines. Known as the Middle Forge, it produced bar iron, cannon shot, shovels, and axes. Later, a powder mill was established, and both sites were productive during the War of 1812 and the Civil War. In 1880, an arsenal was built on the site. Named for the Picatinny Brook (Picatinny means "water by the hill" in the language of the Lenape), the site was chosen because water was readily available, the steep sides of the 10-mile-long valley could protect the surrounding area from the site's hazardous activities, and it was close to local commerce. First used as a site for high explosives, Picatinny Arsenal has played a major role in arms manufacture and technology. During World War II, the arsenal manufactured vital armaments, large arms, and large quantities of munitions. It continued developing and manufacturing arms during the Korean and Vietnam wars. In the 1990s, the arsenal not only contributes to military research, but also has undeveloped land which, although not open to the public, serves as a wildlife habitat.

BAMBOO BROOK OUTDOOR EDUCATION CENTER

Known originally as Merchiston Farm, Bamboo Brook Outdoor Education Center was the home of William and Martha Brookes Hutcheson from 1911 to 1959. The Center's 100 acres include fields, forest, and a formal garden designed by Mrs. Hutcheson, one of the first women trained as a landscape architect in the United States. Trails wind through fields and along the brook. A variety of birds, butterflies, and other animal life are found at the Center. A section of the Patriots' Path crosses the property.

To reach the outdoor education center, take Exit 18 from I-287, go north on US 206 for 4 miles, and turn left onto Pottersville Road (County 512). In 0.5 mile, turn right onto Lisk Hill Road and then at the T junction turn right. At the Y junction, turn left onto Longview Road. The entrance to Bamboo Brook Outdoor Education Center is on the left, one mile from the Y junction. For more information, contact the Morris County Park Commission, P.O. Box 1295, Morristown, NJ 07962-1295; (973) 326-7600.

BERKSHIRE VALLEY
WILDLIFE MANAGEMENT AREA

Located north of I-80 and west of NJ 15, the Berkshire Valley Wildlife Management Area encompasses approximately 1,800 acres of wetlands and upland mixed hardwood forest. Wild turkeys, deer, grouse, rabbits, black ducks, mallards, and wood ducks are the wildlife in the area.

There are three access points to Berkshire Valley WMA. To reach the first access point, take Exit 34 (NJ 15) from I-80. Turn right at the jug handle for Berkshire Valley Road and proceed west. The parking area is on the left, opposite Minisink Road. A woods road leads south from the parking area to an old gravel pit. This piece is cut off from the main portion of the management area by the river and an adjacent housing development. It is a good birding spot for warblers.

To reach the second access point, follow the directions above, but from the jug handle, make a U turn and go south on NJ 15. Just after a "Right Lane Ends" sign, turn onto a dirt road which leads into a former gravel pit, with wetlands extending along the Rockaway River. Hikers heading away from the river go uphill into upland mixed hardwood forest. Caution should be exercised, as an active railroad line passes through the area.

The third access point is reached by taking Exit 30 of I-80 and heading north on Howard Boulevard. The parking area is on the right as the road climbs uphill. There are no obvious trails out of the parking area. However, after scrambling up the side of the parking area opposite the entrance, hikers cross a berm leading to a woods road which goes into the interior of the wildlife management area.

Users of the Berkshire Valley Wildlife Management Area should obtain the Stanhope and Dover USGS topographic quadrangle maps. For more information, contact New Jersey DEP, Division of Fish, Game and Wildlife, 501 East State Street, P.O. Box 400, Trenton, NJ 08625; (609) 292-2965.

BLACK RIVER

Known in some areas as the Lamington River, the Black River flows into the Raritan River near Burnt Mills in Somerset County. Its route is protected in the area near Chester. Along its course, the Black River sustains a freshwater marsh and passes through the Black River Wildlife Management Area and the Black River Natural Area. A short distance away, it powers a grist mill at Cooper Mill Park. In both Black River Park and Hacklebarney State Park, the river tumbles over rocks as it passes through a gorge. The Black River Natural Area encompasses 1,820 acres of emergent marsh, swamp hardwood forest, and mixed hardwood forest.

Black River Park

Black River Park, part of the Morris County Park System, consists of 510 acres located west of US 206 near Chester. The property was formerly the summer home of the Kay family. Elizabeth Donnell Kay was the driving force behind the Great Swamp Outdoor Educational Center in Chatham. The former Kay house is now the Kay Center for Environmental Studies and the New Jersey Field Office of The Nature Conservancy, which helps provide public programming for the park.

The Black River, which traverses the property, can be viewed from many vantage points along its wandering path. Within the confines of the park, there are many miles of unpaved roads and unmarked trails, with elevation changes of about 200 feet. Some stands of conifers within the park are over fifty feet tall. A portion of the park is the Black River Natural Area, which may be accessed by permit only; for permission, call the Morris County Park Police at (973) 326-7632.

Black River Park may be reached by driving south on US 206 for 1.5 miles, from the intersection of US 206 and NJ 24, to Pottersville Road. Turn right on Pottersville Road and go 0.9 mile to the park entrance. Or, from the south, follow I-287 to Exit 18B and take US 206 north. Travel 5 miles to Pottersville Road (County 512), where there is a traffic light. Continue through the intersection on US 206 and proceed for another 3.4 miles to the second Pottersville Road on the left. Turn left here and travel 0.9 mile to the park entrance.

Black River Wildlife Management Area

Located along the Black River, this 3,000-acre Black River Wildlife Management Area encompasses river bottom, swampy woodland, freshwater marsh, fields, and upland deciduous woods. Woods roads cross the mixed hardwood forest, with a heavy understory and an occasional pine plantation. Some of the fields are filled with wildflowers and grasses, while others are still cultivated.

They provide habitat for grasslands species. The wildlife management area is well known for good birding, as more than 200 species have been found here, with about 100 nesting species. During spring migration, the area attracts a wide variety of waterfowl.

A four-mile section of the abandoned Chester Branch of the Delaware, Lackawanna and Western Railroad basically parallels the Black River within the wildlife management area. Built in 1868 to serve the needs of the local iron industry, it carried iron ore from area mines and ingots from the Chester Furnace to Wharton and Dover, but was no longer needed for this purpose when the iron boom in the area ended in 1892. In early 1933, passenger service ended, and the tracks were removed later in the year. The railbed with its gentle grade offers hikers easy walking and views of the freshwater marsh. Horses require an annual permit. A section of Patriots' Path (white) goes on part of the railbed between Pleasant Hill Road outside of Chester and Hugg Road in Ironia. It connects with the unmarked woods roads to create interesting loops.

The Black River Wildlife Management Area is located outside of Chester, which is at the intersection of US 206 and NJ 24/County 513. There are five access points. To reach the two parking areas on Pleasant Hill Road, follow NJ 24/County 513 to Hillside Road and turn left. At the Y junction, bear right onto Pleasant Hill Road. The first parking area is just after crossing the Black

Bobolink

River. The Patriots' Path (white) crosses the road on the southern bank. To reach the second parking area, continue on Pleasant Hill Road 1.7 miles past the parking area by the Black River. At a dirt road marked with a sign, turn right and follow the road to a large parking area. To reach the third area, continue on Pleasant Hill Road, turning right at 1.8 miles, at the Y junction with Ironia Road. The parking area is 1.3 miles from the junction. The other two areas are off County 513, 1.7 and 2.6 miles from the NJ 24/ County 513 split. The headquarters for the wildlife management area is located at the first of the two parking areas off of County 513.

Since there are few trails in Black River WMA, users of the area should obtain the Chester USGS topographic quadrangle map. For more information, contact New Jersey DEP, Division of Fish, Game and Wildlife, 501 East State Street, P.O. Box 400, Trenton, NJ 08625; (609) 292-2965.

Cooper Mill Park

Cooper Mill is a restored mill that was originally built in 1826 by Nathan Cooper with then state-of-the-art technology. Purchased by the Morris County Park Commission in 1963, the mill was opened to the public in 1978. Visitors may observe the stone grinding of whole wheat flour and corn meal. To reach this park, travel one mile west on NJ 24 from its intersection with US 206. The Cooper Mill Park entrance is on the left. Access to Black River Park is possible from Cooper Mill Park. For more information, contact the Morris County Park Commission, 53 East Hanover Avenue, P.O. Box 1295, Morristown, NJ 07962-1295; (973) 326-7600.

Hacklebarney State Park

Lying about three miles southwest of Chester, Hacklebarney State Park is situated along the deep hemlock and boulder lined glacial gorge of the Black River. The park is traversed by a six-mile trail system of winding footpaths. Its topography, with its ridges of gneiss, is rugged. The highest elevation on the west side of the Black River is 804 feet. Wildlife in the park includes bear, bobcat, deer, and coyote. This 893-acre park has 273 acres designated for hiking with the remainder for hunting. The Lamington Natural Area portion of the park protects the gorge and endangered plant species. A section of the Patriots' Path (white) through the park is proposed.

One story about the origin of the park's name states that a quick-tempered iron ore foreman in the vicinity was persistently heckled, and soon *Heckle Barney*, as he was called, became Hacklebarney. Another theory is that the name is of Lenni Lenape derivation, meaning "to put wood on a fire on the ground," that is, a bonfire.

To reach Hacklebarney State Park, take NJ 24 west from Chester for 1.2 miles, then turn left at the bridge after Cooper Mill onto Hacklebarney State Park Road. Continue for another 3 miles; the park entrance is on the left. For more information, contact Hacklebarney State Park, RD 2, Long Valley, NJ 07853; (908) 879-5677.

FARNY HIGHLANDS

Nestled between I-80 and NJ 23 in north central New Jersey lie 35,000 acres of rugged land known as the Farny Highlands. Headwater streams flow though the area to reach, ultimately, the Passaic, Delaware, and Hudson river basins. In the process, they not only supply clean drinking water to one-third of New Jersey's residents, but also make the region a waterscape and a forested, mountainous landscape. About two-thirds of the area is open space—Farny State Park, Mahlon Dickerson Reservation, Rockaway River, Wildcat Ridge and Weldon wildlife management areas, Pyramid Mountain Natural Historical Area, watershed lands, and reservoirs.

This area supports a vast array of wildlife: bobcat, black bear, mink, otter, porcupine, native brook trout, timber rattlesnake, coyote, wood turtle, and wood rat. Birders can find 21 varieties of warblers, along with vireos, eight flycatchers, and six owls. Seven species of hawks breed in the area. In the spring and summer, whip-poor-wills can be heard calling from the tops of the wooded ridges.

Bedrock in the region dates back to Precambian times. Massive glacial erratics and extensive boulder fields are common. They are a result of the Wisconsin glaciation which receded from this area 10,000-15,000 years ago. The glaciers also spread puddingstone—a conglomerate containing white quartzite pebbles in a purple matrix. With magnetic iron ore in the geological matrix of region, anyone using a compass should question its accuracy.

Relics of the iron mining and smelting industry—mine shafts, charcoal pits, forges, tailing piles, and machinery—dot the area. Forges and cast-off machinery can still be found near old stone walls and cellar holes in the region. Extensive acreage was

clear-cut to provide wood for the production of charcoal used to fuel the iron forges. It difficult to imagine that the iron industry in the middle of the nineteenth century cut down virtually all the trees.

Trails in the Farny Highlands

In 1995, the Morris Parks and Land Conservancy conceived the idea of a hiking trail to link these open spaces and asked the New York-New Jersey Trail Conference for assistance. With the additional support from both the public and private sectors, the Farny Highlands Trail System was underway. The Trail Conference began securing public access to private lands, and its volunteers, by 1998, had constructed three trails totaling 32.6 miles. Another thirty miles are planned. For more information, contact the Trail Conference at (212) 685-9699.

Beaver Brook Trail   *Length: 4.9 miles Blaze: white*
Completed in 1997, the Beaver Brook Trail crosses the 2,700-acre Rockaway River Wildlife Management Area. It is easiest hiked from north to south. To reach either end of the trail, take I-80 to Exit 34B (NJ 15 North, Jefferson, Sparta). For the southern trailhead, follow NJ 15 north for 2.0 miles, then turn right onto Berkshire Valley Road. At 2.0 miles, pass a bridge and Taylor Road, with parking in a clearing on the left. Access to the northern end is via the Highlands Trail (teal diamond) in Mahlon Dickerson Reservation. Follow NJ 15 north for 5.0 miles, and exit right at Weldon Road/Milton Oak Ridge turnoff. Follow Weldon Road north for 4.4 miles and turn left into the picnic parking area. Hikers should follow the Highlands Trail (teal diamond) south past the interpretive sign board on the east side of the parking area. The junction with the Beaver Brook Trail is on the left, 1.6 miles from the parking area.

From the northern end, the Beaver Brook Trail gently climbs through a mixed-hardwood forest and enters a young hardwood pole stand. This area had commercial grade iron ore close to the surface, so prospectors removed the overburden, leaving behind the pits and piles. The presence of the pits suggests that the area was stripped of trees used to manufacture charcoal for the iron ore smelting furnaces. The trail switchbacks down to a boulder-strewn draw at 1.1 miles, only to climb back out of it into a dense laurel thicket. There has been extensive black bear activity in this area. The Beaver Brook Trail turns south, following a ridge along the western side of Lost Lake, an expansive beaver meadow. The trail passes through "Split Rock" and crosses a rocky glen. The trail parallels Beaver Brook, and passes numerous iron ore test pits. At 2.0 miles, the trail goes under power lines and crosses Beaver Brook.

After crossing a woods road, the trail, at 2.2 miles, briefly follows a mining road. The extensive road network and overburden excavated in this area facilitated the removal of iron ore. After meandering its way through outcrops, the trail, at 2.7 miles, traverses the lip of a 50-foot escarpment and enters a forest dominated by expansive oaks. At 3.3 miles, the trail reaches an overlook, with views south down the Berkshire Valley. From this point, the trail becomes far more rugged. Hikers should take care as the trail follows or crosses woods roads and crosses intermittent streams along a rocky route. After a steep descent, the trail turns right onto a woods road.

At 3.8 miles, the trail turns and follows a demarcation between two distinct forests. To the east, along the steepest parts of the valley, are hemlocks; to the west is a mixed hardwood forest. The trail begins a steep climb to reach the highest point along the eastern slopes of Mase Mountain. At 4.4 miles, there is view across the valley towards Green Pond Mountain and the roof of a guard tower at Picatinny Arsenal. The trail descends over several exposed ledges with views to the east, and gradually levels off as it enters a field adjacent to the trailhead parking at 4.9 miles.

Four Birds Trail   *Length: 19.4 miles Blaze: white*

Trails of this length are rare in New Jersey. Completed in 1996, the Four Birds Trail crosses only one paved roadway throughout its course. Views are abundant along the trail year round; however, those hiking during the leaf-off seasons will have views along over half of the trail. Although elevation gains and losses are a maximum of 400 feet, hikers will have plenty of exercise, as the trail ascends and descends numerous times along its undulating route.

The trail traverses four principal biomes—old-growth mixed deciduous forests, lake shore, wetlands, and cliff/rock outcrops. The Four Birds Trail is so named to symbolize the biological diversity. Wild turkeys, ospreys, great blue heron, and red-tailed hawks are regularly spotted in these four biomes, respectively. Black bear, river otter, white-tailed deer, beaver, and raccoon were also spotted during trail construction. Timber rattlesnakes are also known to exist in the area, so caution should be exercised when hiking through the rockier regions of this trail.

The Newark Watershed Conservation and Development Corporation

(NWCDC) regulates the use of the northern half of this trail (from Riley's Rise to NJ 23). Hiking and parking permits must be obtained before utilizing this stretch of trail. For permits or more information, contact NWCDC by mail at P.O. Box 319, Newfoundland, NJ 07435, or in person at their office at 223 Echo Lake Road, West Milford, NJ 07480; (973) 697-2850.

There are three access points. To reach the southern trailhead, take Exit 37 (Hibernia/Rockaway) from I-80 west. Turn left onto County 513 (Green Pond Road), continue north for 2.7 miles, and turn right onto Sunnyside Road. The trailhead is on the left 300 feet from the intersection, at the beginning of a gated woods road. A second access point is located 7.4 miles north of Sunnyside Road on County 513. The gravel turnout is on the left, 100 feet north of the trail intersection. (A parking permit is required from NWCDC.) The northern trailhead is located 11.5 miles north from I-80 on County 513. Just before crossing the railroad tracks, turn left onto Bigelow Road. Park in the ballfield parking lot on the left and walk 0.2 mile to the road's end. The trail begins about 100 feet up the dirt road extension on your left. (A parking permit is required from NWCDC.)

From the southern trailhead, the Four Birds Trail immediately enters a clearing once used to facilitate the removal and processing of high-grade iron ore from the area. The trail passes an abandoned, barricaded mine shaft. Extending 2,500 feet into the earth, it is home to an estimated 26,000 little brown bats. At 0.4 mile, the trail straddles a mining berm, merges with a woods road, and bears left. The ditch alongside the berm once contained the water pipes to Marcella Mine, used to operate the steam-powered machinery. The abandoned Hibernia Cemetery is 360 feet to the right down the woods road. Many of the plots belong to immigrant workers in the mines; the headstones date back to the mid-nineteenth century.

At 1.1 miles, the trail crosses a mine road and begins a moderate descent to an intermittent stream crossing. After excessive rainfall, a cascade develops just to the right of the stream crossing. Dreamer's Rock is at 1.5 miles, where the trail begins its ascent to the ridge. At 1.8 miles, a yellow-blazed spur trail leads 0.5 mile to Graffiti Cliffs, with views to the west of the Hibernia valley. The main trail climbs to the ridge, where it crosses a heavily-used woods road. Hikers need to stay alert in this area as extensive, illegal use by dirt bikes and ATVs has obscured parts of the trailway. The Four Birds Trail crosses the road and, at 2.6 miles, crosses a gravel road, which leads north 0.2 mile to a cable television tower with a panoramic view of Rockaway Valley.

The Four Birds Trail begins a moderate descent and then climbs steeply to reach, at 3.7 miles, an exposed outcrop with a view to the east. At 4.0 miles, it passes the southern terminus of the Split Rock Loop Trail (blue) on the right, goes by a huge glacial erratic, and reaches Split Rock Road at 4.6 miles. After crossing the road, the trail makes a short, steep climb up a rock outcrop. It crosses a stream at 5.0 miles to enter a region locally known as the Bumps. The highest point in the Bumps is at 6.1 miles. In this area, trees have grown to an impressive size, including Sentinel Oak, a majestic red oak nearly 4 feet in diameter.

After passing a small marble corner post, the trail descends to Split Rock Reservoir and follows the shore for nearly 1.5 miles. At 9.6 miles, the trail crosses a boulder-strewn glade where, during spring thaw and times of excessive rainfall, water can be heard flowing beneath the stones. The trail steeply climbs Riley's Rise to reach Tom-Tom Lookout at 9.8 miles. The view to the east across the valley is of Indian Cliffs over which the Split Rock Loop Trail traverses. The trail gradually descends and crosses, at 9.9 miles, a red-blazed woods road. At 10.0 miles, the Split Rock Loop Trail (blue) leaves to the right. The Four Birds Trail, at 10.6 miles, begins a gradual climb up Big Bear Peak, then descends and passes through several stone walls. At 11.2 miles, the trail begins a circuitous route up and down exposed bedrock. It crosses Timberbrook Road at 11.6 miles. (A left turn on Timberbrook Road leads, in 0.8 mile, to the main entrance of the Winnebago Boy Scout Reservation.)

The Four Birds Trail reaches, at 12.0 miles, a lake or a beaver meadow, depending upon current beaver activity. At 12.7 miles, after crossing an old railroad grade and woods road, the trail bears left to ascend Copperas Mountain. Reaching the crest at 13.8 miles, the trail turns right onto a woods road, bears right at the fork, and follows the road for 0.6 mile. There are views to the east towards Charlottesburg Reservoir. The trail turns sharply to the left, passes through a laurel grove, and enters open deciduous forest at 14.5 miles. It gradually descends to emerge, at 15.6 miles, on County 513 (Green Pond Road), where parking is available.

After crossing Green Pond Road, the Four Birds Trail enters a small tamarack/spruce plantation and follows a berm. The trail makes several creek crossings as it winds its way to the foot of Green Pond Mountain at 16.2 miles. After climbing, the trail reaches Notch Road at 16.6 miles and turns right. It follows this road for 900 feet and then turns right onto a lesser woods road. At 17.2 miles, the trail makes a sharp left off the road, re-entering the forest. The trail descends and, at 17.5 miles, crosses an- other woods road. After crossing a small stream, the trail reaches the base of cliffs at 17.7 miles. The trail bears right and begins a moder- ate-to-steep ascent, reaching the ridge at 18.1 miles, with views from White Pine

Osprey

Bluff. The trail follows the ledges and turns away from the edge of the escarp- ment to weave its way through an old upland pasture delineated by a series of stone walls. At 19.4 miles, the Four Birds Trail descends to its northern termi- nus near NJ 23 in Newfoundland, where there is parking.

Split Rock Loop Trail · *Length: 7.8 miles Blaze: blue*
Passing through the high country to the south and east of Split Rock Reservoir, the Split Rock Loop Trail completes a loop with the Four Birds Trail. The geomorphic features found along this route are rockier and more abrupt than those on the western side of the reservoir, and hiking grades tend to be steeper. The views af- forded the hiker on this trail far surpass those from the western shore.

Trailside parking for the Split Rock Loop Trail is not available. The Jersey City Water Commission does not want vehicles parked close to the reservoir on their lands (the restrictions are for the reservoir side of Split Rock Road and the entire length of Charlottesburg Road). Vehicles parked in these areas are subject to towing and ticketing. Parking is available on Split Rock Road at two pullouts, with space for three to four cars at each one. The first pullout is 0.4 mile east of the trailhead on the south side of the road, almost under the power lines. The second site is located 1.1 miles west of the trailhead on the west side of the road. Though farther from the trail than the first site, the second site is only 0.3 mile north of the Four Birds Trail. When parking along Split Rock Road, vehicles need to be pulled far enough off the road so as not to obstruct traffic flow.

To reach the trail crossings on Split Rock Road, take Exit 37 (Hibernia/ Rockaway) from I-80 west. Turn left onto County 513 (Green Pond Road), continue north for 1.7 miles, and turn right onto Meriden Road. Follow Meriden Road for 2.1 miles, then turn left onto Lyonsville Road. Go 0.3 mile, bear left, and proceed 1.0 mile to a stop sign. Turn left onto Split Rock Road, continue 0.3 mile to the next intersection and bear left, staying on Split Rock Road. The trail crossing is 0.6 mile ahead on the right.

The southern trailhead of the Split Rock Loop Trail is on the Four Birds Trail (white), 0.6 mile from Split Rock Road. From that trail junction, the Split Rock Loop Trail winds its way through a scrub oak and hickory forest to reach, at 0.2 mile, a seasonal viewpoint. The trail descends through a more mature forest along an outcrop to a boulder-strewn glen at 0.5 mile. Entering the Maze at 0.7 mile, the trail snakes its way through large glacially deposited boulders, some of which are only a couple of feet apart. After crossing an abandoned mine road, the trail passes over a massive finger of mine tailings and enters a mixed hardwood forest. The trail descends to Split Rock River at 1.0 mile. Care should be taken in crossing the river, particularly during periods of high water. It is best negotiated by following the marked route, stepping from boulder to boulder.

The Split Rock Loop Trail, at 1.2 miles, passes Cedar Point, with unob-structed views down the river valley, and crosses a rocky slope where, at the height of land, there are abundant views to the south. After the next high point at 2.1 miles, the trail gently descends through a young-growth forest before going under power lines. From Split Rock Road at 2.3 miles, the Split Rock Loop Trail heads north, staying within sight of the reservoir. The trail gently meanders through a hardwood forest. After reaching a shoreline vista over the reservoir, the trail goes uphill. At 3.3 miles, it crosses Charlottesburg Road, climbs a hill, and turns sharply left. The stone walls, cedars, and trees with broad full crowns suggest that this area was once open pasture.

At 3.8 miles, the trail reaches a glacially balanced boulder and passes an excavation pit with scattered tailings. Continuing along the ridge, the trail passes two 0.1-mile-long side trails to the right. The first one leads to a rock outcrop with a limited view of Buck Mountain, and the second one climbs steeply to the open crest of Double D Peak with 360-degree views. Shortly after the junction with the second side trail, the Split Rock Loop Trail turns left and descends through a mixed hardwood forest. At 4.9 miles, the trail crosses a broad creek on stepping stones, and over the course of 0.9 mile, passes over three ridges with views. The trail crosses Charlottesburg Road at 6.4 miles and closely par-allels the shoreline, with views of the small wooded islands in the reservoir. It crosses Charlottesburg Road again and ascends Indian Cliffs. The trail briefly merges with a woods road at 6.8 miles and climbs along the ledges to reach the pinnacle of Indian Cliffs, with the best views of the reservoir.

After descending steeply at 7.3 miles, the Split Rock Trail follows the base of the cliffs past several huge boulders before turning right. It crosses Charlottesburg Road for the last time and enters a small tamarack (larch) forest. Commonly referred to as a deciduous evergreen, the larch loses its needles in the fall after turning a beautiful shade of yellow. The trail reaches Misty Pond, formed and maintained by beavers. Care should be taken in this area, as occasionally beaver stop gnawing through a tree, leaving it precariously balanced on a thin spindle of wood. The trail leaves Misty Pond and begins a moderate climb, ending at the Four Birds Trail at 7.8 miles.

FRELINGHUYSEN ARBORETUM

In the late nineteenth century, Morristown was a fashionable summer address for prominent families. In 1891, George and Sarah Frelinghuysen built a Colonial Revival-style summer home and carriage house, naming it Whippany Farm. Their daughter, Mathilda, inherited the property, turned it into a public arboretum and, in 1969, donated the estate to Morris County. The 127-acre tract is well known for its rose garden and other floral displays. The Frelinghuysen Mansion, an official historic site, houses the administrative headquarters of the Morris County Park Commission. A section of the Patriots' Path (white) is on the property.

To reach the Arboretum from I-287 north, take Exit 36A. Proceed east in the center lane of Morris Avenue to turn left on Whippany Road. Continue to the second light and make a left turn onto East Hanover Avenue. The entrance to the arboretum is on the left, opposite the Morris County Library. From I-287 south, take Exit 36 and follow signs for Ridgedale Avenue. Bear right on the exit ramp and turn right at the traffic light onto Ridgedale Avenue. At the first traffic light, make a right turn onto East Hanover Avenue. The entrance to the Arboretum is on the right, opposite the Morris Country Library. For more information, contact the Morris County Park Commission, P.O. Box 1295, Morristown, NJ 07962-1295; (973) 326-7600.

THE GREAT SWAMP

In 1708, members of the Delaware Nation exchanged a 30,000-acre tract which included what is now the Great Swamp for a barrel of rum, 15 kettles, 4 pistols, 4 cutlasses, plus other goods, and 30 pounds cash. Settlements began to dot the area and, by 1844, farms appeared on the cleared uplands. As small farming operations became uneconomical, they disappeared. Gradually, much of the cleared uplands reverted to woodlands, and the lower flat areas again became wet.

In 1959, the Great Swamp was proposed as the site for a new metropolitan-area airport. An alliance of concerned citizens waged an extended battle and halted the construction. Their efforts raised more than a million dollars to purchase 3,000 acres which were donated to the U.S. Department of the Interior to establish the Great Swamp National Wildlife Refuge. Subsequently, more acreage has been added to the original tract. In 1968, under the Wilderness Act of 1964, Congress designated the eastern portion as a wilderness area. Today, the Great Swamp is also protected by two county park systems, which operate outdoor education centers.

Swamp woodland, hardwood ridges, grasslands, cattail marshes, ponds, and meandering streams characterize the area. Trails bring the hiker into contact with an unusual variety of plant life, produced by the area's converging climatic zones. Plants varying in size from tiny duckweed to the towering red oak are visible from the trails and boardwalks. Here one will find some three hundred species of birds, mammals, reptiles, am-

Jack in the Pulpit

phibians, and fish. There are approximately 600 species of plants, including 215 species of wildflowers. The yellow marsh marigold in early April, the blue iris in May, and the pink-and-white mountain laurel in June are great attractions. The twenty-six threatened or endangered species include the bog turtle, wood turtle, and blue-spotted salamander. Of the more than 200 species of birds that are found in the Great Swamp, over 90 nest there.

Great Swamp National Wildlife Refuge

Almost nine miles of trails meander through the federally administered 7,400-acre portion of the Great Swamp. The refuge's mission is to provide migrating, nesting, and feeding habitat for migrating birds. It also provides environmental education and compatible recreation opportunities. The Wildlife Observation Center provides wetland vistas and offers opportunities for wildlife observation and photography. There are interpretive displays, an information kiosk, and two boardwalks into the Great Swamp.

To reach the National Wildlife Refuge, take I-287 to Exit 30A. From the exit, take North Maple Avenue to the traffic light at Madisonville Road, turn left, and follow the signs. Maps are available at the refuge headquarters. For more information, contact the refuge at 152 Pleasant Plains Road, Basking Ridge, NJ 07920; (973) 425-1222.

Great Swamp Outdoor Education Center

Dedicated in 1963, the Great Swamp Outdoor Education Center is administered by the Morris County Park Commission. The 40-acre park is on the eastern edge of the Great Swamp, off Southern Boulevard in Chatham Township. A boardwalk and series of paths enter the swamp at this point and penetrate into it for a short distance. There is a boardwalk and wildlife observation blind accessible to the handicapped.

To reach this area from the center of Chatham on NJ 124, turn onto Fairmount Avenue. Turn right on Southern Boulevard and drive about one mile to the sign that marks the dirt road leading to the Outdoor Education Center. For more information, including a map, contact the Morris County Park Commission, 53 East Hanover Avenue, P.O. Box 1295, Morristown, NJ 07962-1295; (973) 326-7600.

Lord Stirling Park

The Somerset County Park Commission administers 900 acres on the western border of the Great Swamp National Wildlife Refuge. It was originally the estate of William Alexander, the so-called Lord Stirling (whose title was legitimate but was never recognized by Parliament). Alexander served with distinction as an officer in the Revolutionary War. His estate was one of the grandest in the middle colonies. Alexander also owned vast tracts of mountain land, including one on the New York-New Jersey border, which still bears his name: Sterling Forest.

In addition to an environmental education center, over eight miles of hiking trails loop their way around and through 430 acres, providing visitors with opportunities to visit a variety of habitats. A short boardwalk trail is handicapped accessible. The remaining acres are for equestrian use on 10 miles of trails. For more information, contact the park commission at 190 Lord Stirling

Road, Basking Ridge, NJ 07920; (908) 766-2489.

HEDDEN PARK

The original 40 acres of Hedden Park were donated by the Hedden family of Dover in 1963, and in the ensuing years its size has been increased to 285 acres. In 1997, the park was the site of Morris County's most accessible beaver colony. The lodge of mud and sticks is clearly visible right behind the boat house.

The park contains four blazed footpaths. To reach the Ford Street entrance, take US 46 west in Dover. After the hospital, make a left onto Hurd Street. Turn left on Oak Street, and continue a short distance to Ford Street and the entrance. For more information, contact the Morris County Park Commission, P.O. Box 1295, Morristown, NJ 07962-1295; (973) 326-7600.

JOCKEY HOLLOW

It was to Jockey Hollow in January 1777 that George Washington brought his troops after their successful campaign against the Hessians at Trenton and the British at Princeton. The natural fortifications of the hills and ready source of supplies gave the army a chance to rest and regroup before the summer's campaign. The troops returned to Jockey Hollow during the winter of 1779-80, during which time twenty-eight storms blasted the area, keeping critical supply routes closed. The bitter cold weather added more hardships to a commander already plagued with the inability to pay for supplies. In May 1780, the Marquis de Lafayette arrived with the news that 6,000 French troops were en route to Rhode Island. Washington began to rebuild his starved and threadbare army.

Connected by the hiking trail branch of the Patriots' Path, each of the three adjacent parks offers something different. Sitting on the southern edge of a terminal moraine, the trail system in the Jockey Hollow portion of Morristown National Historical Park wanders through giant trees and past reconstructed encampments. Lewis Morris Park has recreational facilities and trails for mountain bikers and horses. Birders will find a haven at the Scherman-Hoffman Sanctuaries.

Lewis Morris County Park

This 1,154-acre park, whose southern border is contiguous with the Jockey Hollow Encampment Area of Morristown National Historical Park, was named for New Jersey's first governor. It offers camping, picnic sites, lake swimming, softball fields, sledding, and ski touring. The Sunrise Lake area is the center of water recreation.

Within the park, there are over 11 miles of trails, including one for horses and another for mountain bikes. Four marked hiking trails form loops. The 2.4-mile red-blazed trail goes through Group Camping Areas A and B in the southwest part of the park, just northeast of Ledell's Pond. It can also be reached via short connecting trails from the Grand Loop that traverses the outer perimeter of adjacent Morristown National Historical Park. The red trail joins the 1.6-mile green-blazed trail. The bike trail (yellow) is 5.4 miles long and extends throughout the park. With the trail system linked via the Patriots' Path (white) and several short unmarked spurs to Jockey Hollow, visitors can enjoy much longer hikes.

To reach Lewis Morris County Park, take Exit 36 (Morristown) of I-287 to NJ 24 west. The park entrance is 3.0 miles from the center of Morristown on the left side of NJ 24. NJ Transit trains from Hoboken and from Penn Station in New York City run to Morristown, from which a taxi can be taken to the park. The group campsite can be reached from Tempe Wick Road. For more information, including a map, contact the Morris County Park Commission, 53 East Hanover Avenue, P.O. Box 1295, Morristown, NJ 07962-1295; (973) 326-7600. Groups of 25 or more and all groups arriving by bus must make advance reservations with the Morris County Park Police, by calling them at (973) 326-7631.

Morristown National Historical Park

Jockey Hollow, Fort Nonsense, and the Jacob Ford Mansion were of importance during the American Revolution. Today, they are part of the Morristown National Historical Park. The Jockey Hollow Encampment Area housed 10,000 soldiers of the Continental Army during the winters of 1777 and 1779–80. This area of about a thousand acres includes all but three units of the campsite of the Revolutionary Army. Log huts, typical of hundreds once used as quarters for officers and men, have been reconstructed. The Wick House, built about 1750, has been restored and furnished. It served as military quarters for Major General Arthur St. Clair during the encampment of 1779–80.

A 1937 reconstruction of Fort Nonsense is located north of the encampment area. Just why the place is called Fort Nonsense has been forgotten. One story says that the soldiers building it felt the project was merely labor meant to keep them busy, and as such was "Nonsense." The third site is the Jacob Ford Mansion, which served as Washington's headquarters during the 1779– 80 encampment. An historical museum is located at the same site, just off I-287 in Morristown.

The Cross Estate Gardens, located at the New Jersey Brigade Encampment Area on Old Jockey Hollow Road, has parking for larger groups. The house, built in 1905, is not open to the public. The estate included a carriage house, a five-story water tower, and a gate house. In 1929, Julia Cross made extensive improvements to the gardens, which included a formal walled garden and a native plant area. Volunteers of the New Jersey Historical Garden Federation maintain the gardens, which are open daily. The Gardens are also an access point for the Patriots' Path (hiking trail) and are either a destination or a side trip (0.2 mile each way).

There are 27 miles of trails (including fire trails and footpaths) in the national historical park. Maps of the park are displayed at trail intersections. Each map has an arrow indicating the hiker's current location. All of the parking areas provide access to the trails.

A branch of Primrose Brook runs past the central parking area and is followed by trails on both sides, one being the Wildflower Trail. The Patriots' Path, marked with metal discs, brown on a white background—depicting a tree along a winding path—also passes through the central parking area.

Morristown National Historical Park can be reached by car from US 202 or I-287 (Exit 30). NJ Transit trains from Hoboken and from Penn Station in New York City also run to Morristown, from which a taxi can be taken three miles to Jockey Hollow. Maps and brochures are available at the Visitor Center. For more information, contact the park headquarters at (973) 539-2085 or the Jockey Hollow Visitor Center, (973) 543-4030.

Scherman-Hoffman Sanctuaries

Owned by the New Jersey Audubon Society, this 260-acre site is made up of two adjacent parcels, donated by Mr. and Mrs. Harry Scherman and Frederick Hoffman. The property encompasses 600-foot-high ridges, fields, streams, deciduous woodland, and flood plain. Over 60 breeding birds and 20 mammals are found on the property.

Although there are only 3.2 miles of trails, the Patriots' Path (white) links them to the Cross Estate and Jockey Hollow sections of the Morristown National Historic Park and ultimately to Lewis Morris County Park. Thus, hikers can enjoy a full day's excursion. The main route is the 2.5-mile Dogwood Trail (red). The cutouts leading to the river invite hikers to pause for awhile.

Birds are the primary focus of the sanctuaries, particularly evident when visiting the book/gift shop. The extensive array of books on bird identification and birding sites could easily persuade one to begin a new hobby.

To reach the Scherman-Hoffman Sanctuaries, take Exit 30B from I-287 and go across US 202 to Childs Road. Turn right on Hardscrabble Road, following signs that say "NJ Audubon." Go uphill to the center or continue to the parking area on the right for the trails. For more information, contact the New Jersey Audubon Society, Scherman-Hoffman Sanctuaries, 11 Hardscrabble Road, P.O. Box 693, Bernardsville, NJ 07924; (908) 766-5787.

LOANTAKA BROOK RESERVATION

Tucked almost next to I-287, Loantaka Brook Reservation stretches along the Loantaka Brook. Loantaka is a combination of two Native American words which mean "the place of cold water," and refers to the Loantaka Brook, which flows into the Great Swamp and the surrounding area. The park contains nearly five miles of marked trails for biking, jogging, hiking, horseback riding, and cross-country skiing. The recreation area includes stables, a riding ring, ball fields, and a picnic area. Also located on the property is the Helen Hartley Jenkins Wood, with a rich variety of wildflowers and bird life.

To reach Loantaka Brook Reservation, take Exit 35 from I-287 and turn east onto NJ 124. At the traffic light at South Street, turn left, and proceed 0.5 mile. The park is on the left. For more information, including a map, contact the Morris County Park Commission, 53 East Hanover Avenue, P.O. Box 1295, Morristown, NJ 07962-1295; (973) 326-7600.

MAHLON DICKERSON RESERVATION

Mahlon Dickerson Reservation, named after the former governor and United States senator active during the early nineteenth century, is the largest of the Morris County Park Commission's holdings (3,042 acres). The reservation, which also offers year-round trailer, tent, and lean-to camping, is located on Weldon Road in Jefferson Township, east of NJ 15 near Lake Hopatcong.

Trails in the reservation follow old logging roads and, as such, are especially well-suited for cross-country skiing, when conditions are favorable. The Pine Swamp Trail (white) is a 3.5-mile loop trail that goes to the edge of the Great Pine Swamp, a wet area densely covered with spruce, rhododendron, and native azalea. The trail climbs to the highest point in Morris County (1,388 feet), although it has no views. The three other marked trails in the Pine Swamp Trail loop are the 0.5-mile Boulder Trail (green) and two unnamed trails that are 0.4 mile (blue) and 0.3 mile (yellow) in length. The Pine Swamp area is very remote—a plane that crashed here in May 1974 was not found until December of that year.

Additional trails in the reservation include the Highlands Trail (teal diamond), a portion of the Beaver Brook Trail (white), and 2.5 miles of an abandoned rail line. The railbed was originally built in 1864 as the Ogden Mine Railroad and served the iron mines in the area. At the time of its abandonment, it was part of the Edison Branch of the Central Railroad of New Jersey. The only available parking for direct access to the rail trail is at Saffin Pond, on Weldon Road, 3 miles north of NJ 15.

To reach the reservation, take I-80 to Exit 34B (NJ 15 North, Jefferson, Sparta) and go north for 5.0 miles. Turn right at the Weldon Road (Milton/Oak Ridge) turnoff and follow Weldon Road north. Park at Saffin Pond, the picnic parking area, or the third reservation entrance (second on left) for access to the trails. The Highlands Trail (teal diamond) is accessible from all three entrances. For more information, including a map, contact the Morris County Park Commission, 53 East Hanover Avenue, P.O. Box 1295, Morristown, NJ 07962-1295; (973) 326-7600.

MORRIS CANAL

Completed in 1831, the Morris Canal was built to transport coal from Pennsylvania and, hopefully, revitalize the New Jersey iron industry. Its main line stretched 102 miles from Phillipsburg on the Delaware River to Jersey City. After 1870, the canal ceased being profitable, but continued to operate. It was not until 1918 that legal issues concerning water rights to the major bodies of water in northern New Jersey were finally settled, and the canal ceased operations in 1924.

Morris Canal boats were towed by a team of two mules connected to the boat by a 100-foot-long rope. The boat crew included at least a driver, walking

along the towpath to lead the mules, and a captain steering the boat constantly to prevent it from being pulled into the towpath embankment. To bypass rapids, locks and inclined planes were constructed to raise or lower canal boats, sometimes with 70-ton loads of cargo. Reminders of the canal can be seen at Hopatcong State Park and at Saxton Falls, one mile north of Stephens State Park. The remains of one of the twenty-eight locks of the canal are at the falls, while a section of the canal filled with water still exists in Hugh Force Park.

In 1998, much of the Morris Canal is gone, and the people who are looking for long stretches of canal filled with water and a towpath alongside for walking will be disappointed. Modern development has obliterated portions, and private property owners have restricted access. The county has placed markers at sites where the canal crossed what is now a major road. For those who accept the challenge of discovering where the canal was, the rewards are there— finding one's way, learning local history, and investigating the environment.

Joseph J. Macasek's book *Guide to the Morris Canal in Morris County* is a walking guide to the remains of the canal. Published by the Morris County Heritage Commission, it is available from him at 19 Budd Street, Morristown,

NJ 07960. The Canal Society of New Jersey has an exhibit at Waterloo Village. For more information, contact the Canal Society of New Jersey, P.O. Box 737, Morristown, NJ 07963.

Hugh Force Park   *Length: 0.5 mile Blaze: unblazed*

Within Hugh Force Park is one of the best preserved sections of the canal, which appears much as it would have during its period of operation. The half-mile round trip is suitable for families with young children as it is along the level towpath and provides an ideal opportunity for experiencing the historic canal.

To reach this section from US 46, turn onto South Main Street in Wharton. Proceed one mile and turn left onto Pine Street. Continue for 0.9 mile and turn left onto West Central Avenue. In 0.1 mile, turn right into a dirt-and-gravel parking area. The hike begins at the end of the parking area farthest from West Central Avenue and continues westward along the towpath beside the watered stretch of the Morris Canal.

When the canal was constructed in this location, its channel was excavated by hand into the toe of the adjacent steep hillside. Supporting the canal and its towpath, a 10- to 12-foot-high man-made embankment separates the waterway from adjacent Stephens Brook and the Rockaway River. The High Bridge Branch of the Central Railroad was constructed along the hillside next to the canal in 1881. It is easy to imagine a mule team walking along the towpath in this well-preserved section of canal.

At approximately 0.25 mile, the water-filled section ends at the site of Lock 2 East. A flat grassy area at the end of the watered section marks the location of the former lock. Careful inspection in the grass reveals several large, flat stones which may be traces of the lock's buried walls.

Lock 2 East allowed the canal boats to overcome an 8-foot elevation change. This 90-foot-long by 11-foot-wide chamber had timber doors or gates at each end. By opening and closing the lock gates and operating small valves in the bottom of these gates, the water level and hence a boat in the lock could be raised or lowered. This process enabled boats to change elevation and continue on their journey. After the canal was closed in 1924 and dismantled, the drained locks were filled in with earth to prevent the public from falling into the deep lock chamber.

Stone ruins of the lock tender's house are south of the filled-in Lock 2 East. Lock tenders had to reside next to their locks so they would be readily available to service passing boats. Note the apple trees in the backyard of the house site. Oftentimes the lock tender's family would supplement their income by selling pies and bread to passing boatmen. Hikers should turn around at this point, as private property is beyond the locks.

MOUNT HOPE HISTORICAL PARK

Known locally as Richard Mine, Mount Hope Historical Park was once an active industrial site where fortunes were made and lost and where iron was king. Opened in 1997, the park was part of the original Mount Hope Tract, first developed by John Jacob Faesch in 1772. Over the course of the years, three separate veins of ore—Brennan, Mount Pleasant, and Richard—were mined on the property. Over time, each mine was owned by one or more mining companies. The operations consolidated, with mining finally ceasing in 1978. Within the site are remains from nearly every major period in American history.

Four trails lead hikers through the former mining operations. The Allen and Teabo operations are visible from the Red Trail (1.5 miles) which begins at the parking area. Accessible from the far end of the Red Trail, the Orange Trail adds 1.2 miles to the hike and leads to the Richard and Allen mines. The shorter Blue and White trails lead hikers to the Old Teabo and Brennan mines, respectively. For personal safety, hikers are requested to stay on the marked trails.

To reach the park from I-80, take Exit 35 or 35B and turn left onto Mt. Hope Avenue. At 0.5 mile, turn left onto Richard Mine Road and then proceed 0.7 mile and make a right onto Coburn Road. The park entrance is 0.7 mile ahead on the left. For more information, contact the Morris County Park Commission, P.O. Box 1295, Morristown, NJ 07962-1295; (973) 326-7600.

PATRIOTS' PATH

The Patriots' Path is a trail and greenway system in southern Morris County linking federal, state, county, and municipal parks, watershed lands, historic sites, and other points of interest. It was created as a joint effort of several groups, including the Morris County Park Commission and the New Jersey Conservation Foundation (which initiated the project). The system aims to protect and maintain the environment and aesthetics of stream valleys and uplands while providing a network of hiking, biking, and horseback riding trails, most of which lie along the along the corridors of Whippany, Black, and both branches of the Raritan rivers. In 1980, a completed portion of the path was designated as a National Recreation Trail.

For driving directions to the individual segments within a park, see the description of that park. For more information about the Patriots' Path, contact the Morris County Park Commission, P.O. Box 1295, 53 East Hanover Avenue, Morristown, NJ 07962-1295; (973) 326-7600.

Trails in the Patriots' Path System

In 1998, over 20 miles of the Patriots' Path had been established, with some 50 additional miles of trail projected for future development, when permission from landowners has been obtained. Parts of the main route have been paved for bicycles, other sections have been cleared for walking, and certain sections are open to mountain biking. Use restrictions in various sections are posted.

Bamboo Brook to US 206 at Daly Road   *Length: 1.5 miles Blaze: white*
This short section of the Patriots' Path connects Bamboo Brook Outdoor Education Center, the Willowwood Arboretum, and US 206. In the county parks, the trail is through open meadows. As it leaves approaches Daly Road, it follows an old railroad grade though the woods. In 1998, this section does not connect to other sections.

Cooper Mill to Kay Environmental Center   *Length: 1.5 miles Blaze: orange*
This side trail in the Patriots' Path system starts at Cooper Mill and contours along the wooded banks and slopes of the Black River. At 1.0 mile, it leaves the river and heads uphill to end at the Kay Environmental Center. The entrance to the Center is on Pottersville Road, where an 0.4-mile driveway leads to the headquarters. Parking is available at the Kay Center and at Cooper Mill. In 1998, this section does not connect to other sections.

Frelinghuysen Arboretum   *Length: 1.0 mile Blaze: white*
Starting in Frelinghuysen Arboretum, this short spur of the Patriots' Path leads to Acorn Hill through woods and meadows in an urban setting. Parking is available at the arboretum. In 1998, this section does not connect to other sections.

Ironia to Black River   *Length: 4.0 miles Blaze: white*
One end of this section is on Hugg Road, a side street off Dover-Chester Road,

(County 513), next to a luncheonette, 1.8 miles south of Calais Road. The Patriots' Path enters the Black River Wildlife Management Area and goes into the woods. Turning onto a woods road, the trail heads downhill through a northern upland forest with heavy understory. At 0.5 mile, the Patriots' Path reaches a railbed and turns left. The path continues along a gentle grade as it parallels the Black River to reach Pleasant Hill Road, where there is parking 0.2 mile to the west. In 1998, this section does not connect to other sections.

Lewis Morris Park to Jockey Hollow   *Length: 5.5 miles Blaze: white*
Not to be confused with the multi-use trail, the hiking trail branch of the Patriots' Path follows a varied route through rolling, wooded hills in Morristown National Historical Park and Lewis Morris Park. Over its course, the trail uses six other trails, so it is important to keep track of blazes at intersections. With seven places where parking is available, hikers have many access points. Parking is available on Hardscrabble Road, at the Trail Center, on Cemetery Road, at Sunrise Lake in Lewis Morris Park, and at the northern terminus along the north side of NJ 24. Hikers using the parking areas on Old Jockey Hollow Road at the Public Gardens or Scherman-Hoffman Sanctuary reach the Patriots' Path via side trails.

From the parking area on Hardscrabble Road, the Patriots' Path goes uphill and bears left at a Y junction (the right fork leads to the Brigade Huts and loops back to rejoin the trail). The Patriots' Path climbs steeply and reaches the trail to Cross Estate Gardens at 0.4 mile and the path to the Cross Estate parking lot at 0.8 mile. Descending through the woods, the trail, at 1.2 miles, crosses the Passaic River, which at this point is a rocky brook. After climbing the hill, the Patriots' Path joins the Grand Loop Trail (white) at 1.8 miles. Together the two trails cross Tempe Wick Road at 1.9 miles and the Mendham Road Trail (unmarked) at 2.2 miles. The Mendham Road Trail leads to the Visitor Center, Wick Farm and Farm House, and parking, an 0.4-mile side trip.

Reaching the Old Camp Road Trail (blue), the Patriots' Path turns left and then goes straight when the Grand Loop Trail (white) turns right at 3.5 miles. The Patriots' Path reaches the Trail Center parking lot on Jockey Hollow Road at 3.7 miles and joins the Soldiers Hut Trail (unmarked). At 4.1 miles, reconstructed soldier huts field are visible a short distance above the clearing. Continuing past the parking lot at the intersection of Grand Parade, Cemetery and Sugarloaf roads, the trail turns right and joins the Grand Loop Trail (white) for the second time. At 4.4 miles, it turns and enters Lewis Morris Park.

Going downhill, the Patriots' Path joins the Green Trail and turns right. At 4.6 miles, it reaches a Y junction and goes right onto the Blue Trail. Both trails rejoin the Green Trail briefly. The trails separate, with the Patriots' Path and the Blue Trail crossing a stream and heading downhill. Reaching the recreation area, the trails pass Sunrise Lake. At the junction with the Yellow Trail at 5.3 miles, the Blue Trail ends and the Patriots' Path turns right. It reaches a gate at NJ 24, crosses the road and joins the main part of the Patriots' Path, along the Whippany River, at 5.5 miles from Hardscrabble Road. At this junction, it is 4.7 miles eastward to Speedwell Avenue and 5.5 miles westward to Ralston Corners.

Schooley's Mountain
Length: 2.3 miles Blaze: white

From NJ 24 just west of Bartley Road, the Patriots' Path crosses farm fields and reaches, at 0.8 mile, the abandoned railbed of the High Bridge Branch of the Central Railroad of New Jersey. After crossing the railbed and turning right, the trail continues through the woods to cross Fairview Avenue at 1.0 mile. Almost immediately it begins its ascent of Schooley's Mountain through wooded slopes and reaches a lookout on the left at 1.5 miles. The trail emerges from the woods, at 2.0 miles, into a developed area with picnic tables and athletic fields. Parking is available at the boat house and ballfield parking lots. In 1998, this section does not connect to other sections.

Speedwell Lake to Woodland Avenue
Length: 6.9 miles Blaze: white

Over most of its length, this section of the Patriots' Path roughly parallels NJ 24 as it follows the banks of the Whippany and North Branch of the Raritan rivers. There are numerous access points, most of which have parking. To reach the eastern end, take NJ 24 to the Green in Morristown and continue on Speedwell Avenue north to Speedwell Lake. The western end is near Clyde Potts Reservoir. Only 1.8 miles are paved, with the remainder either gravel or soil. Mountain bikes are permitted on the portion between Speedwell Avenue and East Main Street.

Beginning at the parking lot at Speedwell Lake, the Patriots' Path parallels the lake and crosses Lake Road. After crossing Watnong Brook, it makes a left turn onto pavement and then a right to cross Lake Valley Road, where there is parking for several cars. Heading upstream along the banks of the Whippany River, the Patriots' Path crosses Sussex Avenue at 1.8 miles. To the left, across the Whippany River and then right, a paved portion continues 0.8 mile to Washington Valley Road, where it ends. There is parking for 4 cars and an unpaved 0.5-mile connection to the main portion of the Patriots' Path.

Directly across Sussex Avenue, opposite the paved path from Speedwell Lake, the main route follows the railbed of the former Rockaway Valley Railroad through wooded wetlands. Dubbed the "Rock-a-Bye Baby" because of its rough bed, the railroad was abandoned in 1913. The Patriots' Path crosses Washington Valley Road at 2.6 miles. To the left there is a connecting link to the paved spur mentioned above.

After crossing Whitehead Road, where there is a small parking area, the Patriots' Path continues through drier terrain away from the abandoned rail bed. It turns southwest to cross the Whippany River at 4.7 miles. At this point, the 5.5-mile Patriots' Path (hiking trail) leads straight ahead into Lewis Morris Park and Morristown National Historical Park.

The main trail turns right and crosses Tingley Road. At 5.4 miles, the trail turns right, crosses a footbridge, and turns right on East Main Street. In 200 feet it turns left to enter the Dismal-Harmony Natural Area. The trail follows Dismal Brook upstream through a hilly forested area and then turns left up a steep sidehill. Its temporary end in 1998 is at Woodland Avenue near Clyde Potts Reservoir, but there is no parking.

Sunrise Lake to Ralston Corners   *Length: 5.0 miles Blaze: white*
Beginning at Dismal Brook Junction, this branch of the Patriots' Path continues westerly through the village of Brookside, crossing Cherry Lane at 0.5 mile and Cold Hill Road at 1.5 miles. Skirting a development, the trail enters the watershed of the North Branch of the Raritan River. Descending through suburban woods, it reaches Mountain Avenue, where there is parking for a dozen cars. The trail crosses the river to the north bank and reaches a short paved section just before crossing Ironia Road at 4.0 miles. The section between Ironia Road and Ralston Corners is restricted to foot traffic only. At 4.6 miles, the trail reaches NJ 24, where there is parking at the old firehouse. In 1998, the Patriots' Path ends at the edge of private property, 5.0 miles from the Dismal Brook Junction.

PEQUANNOCK WATERSHED

Adjoining the southern boundary of Wawayanda State Park, the City of Newark's Pequannock Watershed property contains clear lakes, streams, ponds, mountains, dramatic rock outcroppings, forests, and varied vegetation. Encompassing portions of Morris, Passaic, and Sussex counties, the Pequannock

Watershed is traversed east to west by NJ 23. The watershed contains five major reservoirs, totaling almost 2,000 acres, which provide a substantial portion of the water supply for the City of Newark. The Pequannock water system also serves portions of Pequannock, Wayne, Belleville, and Bloomfield townships.

The area of the Pequannock Watershed was of economic importance during the height of the iron industry in the eighteenth and nineteenth centuries. Its forests supplied wood for charcoal used at furnaces and ironworks located along the rivers. The area also produced iron ore, and several shafts and surface sites are still in existence. Later, the affluent built summer homes. In April 1900, the City of Newark acquired the property.

In 1974, the Newark Watershed Conservation and Development Corporation (NWCDC), a nonprofit corporation, was assigned responsibility for managing the property on behalf of the City of Newark. As part of a major policy shift in land use, the NWCDC subscribed to the multiple-use concept and opened the property for recreational use by the general public through a controlled access-by-permit program. At the same time, the NWCDC invited an all-volunteer trails development group to create and maintain a hiking trail system for the Clinton, Buckabear, Bearfort, Hanks Pond, and Echo Lake sections. This trails group has completed, measured, and mapped the hiking trails in these areas. The NWCDC subsequently entered into a Memorandum of Understanding with the New York-New Jersey Trail Conference to have their volunteer maintainers assist with the remarking and maintenance of the watershed trail system.

🚶

Trails in the Pequannock Watershed

Because there are many short connecting trails, a variety of hikes are possible on the 29 miles of major blazed trails. Although not described below, these blue-blazed connecting trails are noted in the appropriate places in the trail descriptions. For more information and hiking permits, contact NWCDC, by mail at P.O. Box 319, Newfoundland, NJ 07435, or in person at their office at 223 Echo Lake Road, West Milford, NJ 07480; (973) 697-2850.

To reach the Pequannock Watershed, take Exit 53 west (NJ 23) from I-287. Trail access from Echo Lake Road is 7.6 miles from the interstate interchange or 1.5 miles south of Newfoundland. Clinton Road is 0.7 mile north of Newfoundland and 9.8 miles west of I-287. Parking areas P1 to P5 and P7 are located along the road at 1.7, 2.9, 3.9, 4.8, 6.1, and 7.8 miles respectively. To reach the four trailheads on Stephens Road, take Union Valley Road (County 513), which is 9.1 miles west of I-287, and go 5 miles north. Stephens Road is unpaved beyond 0.2 mile. Parking area P9 is just after the pavement ends on Paradise Road, an exit on NJ 23 (10.4 miles west of I-287). Public transportation is available via NJ Transit buses 194/195, serving Newfoundland.

Bearfort Waters/Clinton Trail *Length: 8.5 miles Blaze: yellow*
A major north–south trail, the Bearfort Waters/Clinton Trail connects Wawayanda State Park with the Pequannock Watershed. It starts on the Old Coal Trail (red) (see Chapter 6, "Greenwood Lake Area") which is 0.4 mile from parking area P7 on Clinton Road. Crossing Mossman's Brook two times, it passes through laurel patches and over grassy slopes. At 1.7 miles, just before the second brook crossing, a woods road on the left leads, in 0.1 mile, to parking area P5 on Clinton Road.

The trail reaches an old pipeline at 2.7 miles and leaves it at 2.9 miles. Here an 0.2-mile blue trail connects to the Clinton West Trail (white), which may be followed 0.3 mile to parking lot P4 on Clinton Road. The Bearfort Waters/Clinton Trail turns southwest, reaching Buckabear Pond, where it follows the west bank to its end at the Clinton West Trail (white).

Buckabear Pond Trail *Length: 0.8 mile Blaze: red triangle on white*
This trail leaves from parking lot P3 on Clinton Road and follows an old woods

road south along the west side of Clinton Reservoir. It then goes steeply up the ridge to meet the Clinton West Trail (white) at 0.2 mile. Shortly after this crossing, the Buckabear Pond Trail turns left off the woods road and heads downslope to Buckabear Pond and the Clinton West (white) and Bearfort Waters/Clinton (yellow) trails.

Clinton West Trail   *Length: 4.1 miles Blaze: white*

At the P4 parking area on Clinton Road, the Clinton West Trail ascends the ridge through an open hardwood forest littered with rocks. It passes, at 0.3 mile, a blue-blazed trail which connects with the Clinton/Bearfort Waters Trail (yellow). At 0.8 mile, the trail begins a gradual descent, and then goes along the ridge to reach a view of the Clinton Reservoir at 1.3 miles. The trail crosses the Buckabear Pond Trail (red triangle on white) at 1.5 miles, continues down the ridge and, at 1.8 miles, passes a large boulder on the right. At 2.0 miles, it passes another view of the reservoir accessible via a herd path.

Gradually descending the ridge, the Clinton West Trail turns and becomes a woods road at 2.3 miles. It contours its way down to reach the reservoir at 2.7 miles and then continues along the shore. The trail meets the west end of the Buckabear Pond Trail (red triangle on white) and turns left to cross a dam between Clinton Reservoir and Buckabear Pond. In 1998, beaver activity determined the water level in the pond. At 2.9 miles, on the far side of the dam, the trail turns left. To the right is the southern end of the Clinton/Bearfort Waters Trail (yellow).

The Clinton West Trail parallels the west shore of the Clinton Reservoir and, at 3.1 miles, passes bronze plaques commemorating three individuals who laid out the original watershed trail system. Two of the plaques are in the woods behind the one that is along the trail. The trail joins a horse trail built by the Civilian Conservation Corps in the 1930s as it continues along the lake shore. At 3.7 miles, the Clinton West Trail goes straight ahead as the Highlands Trail turns off to the right. The trail ends at parking area P9 at 4.4 miles. All but the southern 0.7 mile of the trail is co-aligned with the Highlands Trail (teal diamond).

Echo Lake East Trail   *Length: 1.8 miles Blaze: white*

Beginning near the boat launch just north of the NWCDC office, the Echo Lake East Trail passes the sluice at the dam and a large cliff on the right. It is mostly level as it hugs the east shore of Echo Lake. Boating and fishing are by permit only. Parking is available at the NWCDC office off Echo Lake Road, 1.0 mile northeast of NJ 23. A 1.1-mile section of the trail is co-aligned with the Highlands Trail (teal diamond).

Echo Lake West Trail　　　　　　　　*Length: 1.7 miles Blaze: white*
The trailhead is reached by following the service road from the NWCDC parking area off Echo Lake Road, 1.0 mile northeast of NJ 23. A mostly level shoreline trail, the Echo Lake West Trail leads to rock formations at the north end of the lake that once provided shelter for the Native Americans living. The entire length of the trail is co-aligned with the Highlands Trail (teal diamond).

Fire Tower Ridge Trail　　　　　　*Length: 2.0 miles Blaze: red/white*
From its trailhead 0.4 mile north of parking lot P1, which is at the intersection of Clinton and Van Orden roads, the Fire Tower Ridge Trail climbs gently along a woods road leading to the site of Cross Castle. Only ruins and an old foundation of this former mansion remain. A connector trail (blue) leads in 0.4 mile to the Fire Tower West Trail and parking lot P2. The trail follows the ridge of Bearfort Mountain, continuing on the woods road and passing an old stone water tank on the left that once served the Cross Castle complex. Approximately one mile from Clinton Road, the woods road ends. The trail follows a rocky ridge with open views and then continues along vernal bogs. There is another blue-blazed connector trail at 1.2 miles, providing shortcuts on the left to Fire Tower West and on the right to Hanks West and Hanks East trails. The Fire Tower Ridge Trail ends at the Bearfort Fire Tower and the Fire Tower West Trail.

Fire Tower West Trail　　　　　　*Length: 1.9 miles Blaze: yellow*
From parking lot P2, the Fire Tower West Trail rises gently in a northeasterly direction with a rock ridge on the right, reaching the Twin Brooks Trail (white) in 0.9 mile. Another 0.2 mile farther on, a blue-blazed connector trail provides access to three parallel trails (Fire Tower Ridge, Hanks West, and Hanks East). The Fire Tower West Trail climbs the ridge, gaining views of Cedar Pond and the valley below. At 1.5 miles, it passes the Bearfort Fire Tower (staffed during high fire-danger periods only), with two picnic tables and the end of the Fire Tower Ridge Trail (red). Here, the Fire Tower West Trail descends to Stephens Road with a gate and a small parking area. The Highlands Trail (teal diamond) is co-aligned with a portion of the trail.

Hanks East Trail   *Length: 3.2 miles Blaze: white*
This trail leaves from parking lot P1 at the intersection of Clinton and Van Orden roads. Heading in a northeasterly direction, it follows a woods road, passing Hanks Pond on the left. The trail follows the ridge which provides views of Union Valley and Kanouse Mountain. At about the midpoint, a blue-blazed connector trail leads to the Hanks West and Fire Tower Ridge trails. The Hanks East Trail ends at Stephens Road.

Hanks West Trail   *Length: 2.6 miles Blaze: blue/white*
The Hanks West Trail splits left off the Hanks East Trail 0.2 mile from parking lot P1 at the intersection of Clinton and Van Orden roads. It passes Hanks Pond on the right. Remaining mostly level for the first mile, it follows a woods road past the pond and the remains of a boathouse. At 1.7 miles, the Hanks West Trail crosses a connecting trail (blue) leading left to the Fire Tower Ridge Trail and right to the Hanks East Trail. The Hanks West Trail continues through hardwood forest before ending at unpaved Stephens Road.

Highlands Trail   *Length: 8.6 miles Blaze: teal diamond*
The Highlands Trail is co-aligned on portions of the Echo Lake East Trail, Echo Lake West, Fire Tower Ridge, Fire Tower West, Twin Brooks, and Clinton West trails. See chapter 14, "Long Distance Trails," for a full description of the exact route.

Twin Brooks Trail   *Length: 0.8 mile Blaze: white*
From parking lot P4 on Clinton Road, the Twin Brooks Trail provides access to the midpoint of the Fire Tower West Trail (yellow). The trail follows a brook south through hemlocks. It crosses two low ridges and then Cedar and Clinton brooks on log bridges. The trail ends at the Fire Tower West Trail (yellow). The entire trail is co-aligned with the Highlands Trail (teal diamond).

PYRAMID MOUNTAIN
NATURAL HISTORICAL AREA

Thanks to a remarkable coalition of citizens' groups, conservation organizations, corporations, and government agencies, more than 1,400 acres of wilderness land are now in public ownership on Pyramid and Turkey mountains. The Pyramid

Mountain Natural Historical Area features include the headwaters of Stony Brook (a tributary of the Rockaway River), extensive wetlands, and waterfalls.

Made up of Precambrian gneiss and schist, Pyramid Mountain straddles the Ramapo Fault which runs along the western edge of the Newark Basin. One of the largest and most active faults in the region, the Ramapo Fault is the boundary between the Precambrian and Paleozoic rocks of the Highlands Region and the Mesozoic rocks of the Newark Basin. Glacial erratics, including several truck- to house-sized boulders, are along its ridge. Bear Rock is the one of the largest glacial erratics in the state, and Tripod Rock sits on top of three smaller boulders.

Chestnut oaks are plentiful in the high ridges. Witch hazel, maple leaf viburnum, and winterberry lend seasonal color to the hard-

Cardinal flower

wood understory. The area provides habitat for over 100 species of birds, 30 species of mammals, and over 400 species of plants. Seasonal birds include scarlet tanagers, yellow warblers, and indigo buntings. Black-capped chickadees and red-bellied and pileated woodpeckers are year-round residents. In season, fringed and bottled gentians, cardinal flowers, and wood lilies can be seen.

The area is administered by the Morris County Park Commission, which maintains a visitors center on Boonton Avenue opposite Mars Court in Montville. It sponsors various programs and guided walks. To reach Pyramid Mountain Natural Historical Area, take Exit 44 from I-287 north and proceed along Main Street to Boonton Avenue (County 511). Turn right and go 3.3 miles to the Visitors Center on the left. For more information, contact the Visitors Center at (973) 334-3130 or the Morris County Park Commission, P.O. Box 1295, Morristown, NJ 07962-1295; (973) 326-7600.

Trails in the Pyramid Mountain Natural Historical Area
Pyramid Mountain Natural Historical Area is popular place for families to hike.

The over 20 miles of marked trails provide opportunities to visit glacial erratics, enjoy expansive views, see waterfalls, and observe wetlands. The Visitors Center on Boonton Avenue in Montville is a starting point for loop hikes over either Pyramid or Turkey mountains. Access to the trails on Pyramid Mountain and the Butler-Montville Trail (blue) is via an unmarked trail from the Visitors Center. The Yellow Trail on Turkey Mountain is across Boonton Avenue.

Butler-Montville Trail   *Length: 7.1 miles Blaze: blue*

The Butler-Montville Trail is the connecting route between Turkey and Pyramid mountains. Its features include a walk along the reservoir and Bear Rock, one of the largest glacial erratics in New Jersey. The periodic intersections with blacktop roads and other trails permit the hiker to complete shorter portions. Parking is available at Kiel Avenue in Butler and at the Visitors Center on Boonton Avenue. Public transportation is via NJ Transit bus 194 to Meadtown Shopping Center in Butler.

The Butler-Montville Trail begins at the gate on Bubbling Brook Road. At 0.1 mile, it reaches a fisherman's parking lot. The pavement ends at 0.4 mile, where the Butler Connecting Trail goes off to the left across the dam. Becoming a narrow trail, the Butler-Montville Trail continues close to the shore of Butler Reservoir, which is dotted with white pines. It crosses the footbridge over Stonehouse Brook at 1.5 miles and reaches Fayson Lakes Road at 1.8 miles. Passing through a former meadow at 2.4 miles, the trail crosses another stream and turns southeast, with a gentle climb to Miller Road at 3.0 miles. After crossing the road, the trail meanders southeast along the valley floor and reaches the terminus of the Red Trail on the left at 3.7 miles.

Continuing, the Butler-Montville Trail joins, at 4.1 miles, the Kinnelon-Boonton Trail (white) at Bear Rock, a glacial erratic with an uncanny resemblance to a giant bear. In quick succession, the two trails turn left, cross a brook, and pass the terminus of the Yellow Trail on the right. The Kinnelon-Boonton and Butler-Montville trails make a steep ascent through a stand of laurel. Reaching a T junction at 4.5 miles, the Butler-Montville Trail turns right. A side trip of 400 feet to the left, along the Kinnelon-Boonton Trail (white), leads to Tripod Rock.

At 4.6 miles, the Butler-Montville Trail passes a side trail (blue-with-white bars) that leads, in 100 yards, to Lucy's Overlook. Soon, the Butler-Montville Trail joins the Yellow Trail, which comes in from the right. At 4.7 miles, the two trails split, with the Yellow Trail going left. After a gradual ascent, the

Butler-Montville Trail reaches the summit of Pyramid Mountain, which features views east toward Manhattan and points south. Descending steeply, the Butler-Montville Trail turns left under the power line at 5.3 miles. The end of the Kinnelon-Boonton Trail (white) is on the right. Following the power line, the Butler-Montville Trail passes the end of the Yellow Trail on the left at 5.4 miles and reaches the junction with the trail to the Visitors Center at 5.5 miles.

After crossing Boonton Avenue (County 511) at 5.6 miles and still following the power line, the Butler-Montville Trail passes through a meadow. At 5.8 miles, the trail begins to climb, going up what is known locally as the "100 Steps." At the top of the climb, there is a view to the west. At 6.1 miles, there is a post marking a right turn, with another post marking the end of the Turkey Mountain Trail (red) visible 50 feet straight ahead. At 6.2 miles, the trail reaches a T junction with a woods road, with the end of the Waterfall Trail (green) to the left, and then, at 6.5 miles, it crosses the Yellow Trail. The Visitors Center and Boonton Avenue are 0.5 mile to the right via the Yellow Trail. As the Butler-Montville Trail continues south, it passes one end of the Red Dot Trail (red) at 6.7 miles. After going through laurel, it ends at a viewpoint overlooking a quarry at 7.1 miles.

Butler Connecting Trail   *Length: 0.3 mile: Blaze: blue on white*
This trail skirts the north end of the Butler Reservoir, connecting the trails on the reservoir's east and west sides. Its terminus at the Butler-Montville Trail (blue) is at the point where the paved reservoir road turns east to cross the dam/causeway. Hikers should be careful not to confuse the paved and lighted dam/causeway with a narrow, crumbling, concrete reservoir spillway 0.2 mile downstream, which should not be crossed under any circumstances. After crossing the dam, the trail leads up to the turnaround at the end of paved Seabert Lane, which it follows to Birch Road. It turns right on Birch Road and in 0.3 mile reaches the trailhead of the Kinnelon-Boonton Trail (white).

Green Trail (Pyramid Mountain)   *Length: 0.7 mile Blaze: green*
The Green Trail provides easy access to the ridge overlooking the Taylortown Reservoir. Parking is available at the athletic field on Fayson Lakes Road just north of its junction with Boonton Avenue. The trail begins at the northwest corner of the tennis courts. After climbing the ridge, the Green Trail ends at the Kinnelon-Boonton Trail (white), where Tripod Rock is 0.7 mile to the left.

Kinnelon-Boonton Trail   *Length: 4.3 miles Blaze: white*

Located along the east side of Butler Reservoir, the Kinnelon-Boonton Trail affords more level walking than the Butler-Montville Trail (blue) does. Parking is available at the Visitors Center on Boonton Avenue or at the end of Birch Road, a mile south of the intersection of NJ 23 and Kiel Avenue, reached via Kakeout Road. If parking at the end of Birch Road, hikers should park off the road and leave a note on the dashboard indicating that they are using the trail. Public transportation is via NJ Transit bus 194 to Meadtown Shopping Center in Butler.

To reach the Kinnelon-Boonton Trail, take the trail from the parking lot at the Visitors Center to the Butler-Montville Trail (blue), turn left, and continue for 0.4 mile. The Kinnelon-Boonton Trail continues ahead, following the power line, when the Butler-Montville trail turns right. At 0.4 mile from its start, the Kinnelon-Boonton Trail crosses Bearhouse Brook on a bridge. After turning right and leaving the power line at 0.5 mile, the trail reaches Bear Rock at 0.8 mile. Here, it turns right to rejoin the Butler-Montville Trail (blue). In 100 yards, the two trails pass the end of the Yellow Trail and ascend steeply through a stand of laurel. At a T junction at 1.1 miles, the Kinnelon-Boonton Trail goes left and reaches Tripod Rock at 1.2 miles. After passing a small pond on the left at 1.3 miles, the trail reaches the end of the Red Trail at 1.6 miles.

Continuing along the ridge, the Kinnelon-Boonton Trail passes a side trail to a view to the east at 1.7 miles and the end of the Green Trail at 1.9 miles. The path rises and falls through fairly rugged terrain, with the rocks on the left concealing most of the houses on Reality Drive below. At 2.4 miles, the trail crosses Reality Drive and immediately turns left onto Glen Rock Drive. Following Glen Rock Drive, the trail passes Lynnbrook Road on the left and then, at 2.6 miles, turns right onto Brentwood Drive. It turns right onto Lakeview Drive and turns left and re-enters the woods at 2.7 miles. Crossing Fayson Lakes Road at 3.0 miles, the trail first follows Toboggan Trail (a paved road, not a trail) and then turns left and leaves the road at 3.2 miles. After reaching the crest of a hill at 3.7 miles, the Kinnelon-Boonton Trail turns left off an ATV track at 4.0 miles. The trail ends at Birch Road at 4.3 miles, where there is parking.

Red Dot Trail (Turkey Mountain)   *Length: 0.7 mile Blaze: red* dot

Accessible from the Yellow Trail (Turkey Mountain), the Red Dot Trail meanders along a woods road and, at 0.1 mile crosses a stream. At 0.3 mile, it turns left and leaves the woods road. It gently climbs to its terminus at the Butler-Montville Trail (blue).

Red Trail (Pyramid Mountain)   *Length: 0.8 mile Blaze: red*
The beginning of the Red Trail on Pyramid Mountain is on the Kinnelon-Boonton Trail (white), 0.3 mile south of the junction of the Kinnelon-Boonton (white) and Green trails. Wiggling along with small ups and downs, the Red Trail reaches the foot of Eagle Cliff and turns right at 0.3 mile. A glacial erratic is on the left, and in another 100 feet, the trail turns left and ascends the ridge. At the top of the cliff, the trail continues to meander and reaches on the left, at 0.5 mile, Whale Head Rock, which looks like a whale's head coming up out of the water. The trail turns right over a rocky area, and goes down to a westerly overlook. Turning left at 0.6 mile, it starts a steep descent through laurel and rocks. After two stream crossings, it reaches the Butler-Montville Trail (blue), where it ends.

Red Trail (Turkey Mountain)   *Length: 0.9 mile Blaze: red*
The Red Trail is accessible from Boonton Avenue (County 511) via the Butler-Montville Trail (blue). The Red Trail starts under the power line, 0.5 mile east of Boonton Avenue and 50 feet east of a right turn in the Butler-Montville Trail (blue). The Red Trail heads uphill and, at 0.5 mile, reaches the top of Turkey Mountain where, in the middle of a red cedar grove, there are seasonal views. The Yellow Trail begins here. Descending steeply, with better views, the Red Trail reaches a junction with the Waterfall Trail (green) at 0.7 mile. The trails join for 0.1 mile and then split, with the Red Trail continuing straight ahead. At 0.9 mile, the Red Trail ends at the Yellow Trail.

Waterfall Trail (Turkey Mountain)   *Length: 1.5 miles Blaze: green*
The Waterfall Trail starts on the Butler-Montville Trail (blue) 0.6 mile east of Boonton Avenue and 0.1 mile south of the junction with the power line. At 0.1 mile, the Waterfall Trail reaches the Lake Valhalla Overlook, from which the Manhattan skyline is visible on a clear day. The trail turns sharply left and reaches a stone ruin. Descending, the Waterfall Trail turns left to join the Red Trail. At 0.5 mile, the two trails pass under a power line and split, with the Waterfall Trail turning right. The trail reaches the waterfall at 0.9 mile, where there is a level resting area. The Waterfall Trail turns away from the stream, gradually climbs the side of Turkey Mountain, and ends at the Yellow Trail at 1.5 miles.

Yellow Trail (Pyramid Mountain)   *Length: 1.0 mile Blaze: yellow*
The Yellow Trail provides an easier alternate route to Pyramid Mountain. To reach

the Yellow Trail, take the trail from the parking area at the Visitors Center to the Butler-Montville (blue), turn left, and cross the stream. The Yellow Trail begins to the right in another 0.1 mile. Ascending first gently, and then steeply, the trail reaches the Butler-Montville Trail (blue) at 0.7 mile and briefly joins it. At the split, the Yellow Trail goes left while the Butler-Montville goes straight ahead. The Yellow Trail descends to end a short distance from Bear Rock.

Yellow Trail (Turkey Mountain)   *Length: 3.7 miles Blaze: yellow*
Starting from the east side of Boonton Avenue directly opposite the Visitors Center, the Yellow Trail is a level, gravel-surfaced path that provides access to the Butler-Montville Trail (blue). It reaches the start of the Red Dot Trail at 0.2 mile and crosses the Butler-Montville Trail at 0.5 mile. After a gentle descent, the Yellow Trail turns left at a T junction and begins a gradual ascent. It passes a limestone quarry on the right and then the Red Trail on the left at 1.2 miles. After a short descent, the Yellow Trail makes a sharp left turn and ascends. Seasonally, Botts Pond may be visible about 100 yards off to the right. Reaching a power line at 1.6 miles, the trail turns right and then left. After crossing a bridge over North Valhalla Brook at 1.8 miles, the trail continues and makes a left turn just before Stony Brook Road. Paralleling the road, the Yellow Trail crosses Valhalla Brook on a road bridge and turns left into the woods at 2.8 miles. Continuing through a wet area, the trail crosses a small stream. At 3.3 miles, it passes the northern terminus of the Waterfall Trail and begins a gradual ascent of Turkey Mountain. The Yellow Trail ends at a T junction with the Red Trail at 3.7 miles, with the top of the mountain 100 feet to the left.

SCHOOLEY'S MOUNTAIN PARK

Schooley's Mountain Park is the former site of Camp Washington, a YMCA camp from the 1920s to the 1950s. This 782-acre park is named after the Schooley family, who were landowners in the area in the late 1700s. Opened in 1974, the park offers hiking, picnicking, boating, swimming, fishing, and winter activities. A two-mile section of the Patriots' Path (white) has been established through the park from East Mill Road (NJ 24), west of Bartley Road, to Springtown Road. No bicycles are permitted on the section between Fairview Avenue and Springtown Road. The Highlands Trail (teal diamond) will also be part of the trail system.

To reach Schooley's Mountain Park from Chester on US 206, take NJ 24 west 5.1 miles through Long Valley to Camp Washington Road on the right. The information center is about 0.5 mile from the turn. To reach the recreation facilities, continue to Springtown Road and turn right. The park entrance is on the right. For more information, contact Morris County Park Commission, P.O. Box 1295, Morristown, NJ 07962-1295; (973) 326-7600.

WILLOWWOOD ARBORETUM

Willowwood Arboretum comprises 130 acres of rolling farmland and a shallow valley with 3,500 varieties of plants. Henry and Robert Tubbs bought the property in 1908 and developed the garden for half a century, many of the specimens dating from their initial plantings. The Willowwood Farm became a private arboretum in 1950 and part of the Morris County Park System in 1980. Lilacs, magnolias, hollies, lady-slippers, and ferns decorate the area. Paths wind through open areas and woodland. A route through the formal gardens and woodland paths is described in a trail guide. A section of the Patriots' Path (white) traverses the property.

To reach the arboretum, take Exit 22B from I-287 north, go north on US 206 for 4 miles, and turn left onto Pottersville Road (County 512). In 0.5 mile, turn right onto Lisk Hill Road and then, at the T junction, turn right. At the Y junction, bear left onto Longview Road. The entrance to Willowwood Arboretum is on the left, 0.5 mile from the intersection. For more information, contact the Morris County Park Commission, P.O. Box 1295, Morristown, NJ 07962-1295; (973) 326-7600.

ELEVEN

THE JERSEY SHORE

ummertime at the Jersey Shore evokes images of Atlantic City, hordes of summer sunbathers, and traffic crawling on the Garden State Parkway. When those crowds diminish, however, walkers have a chance to enjoy brisk autumn, winter, and spring treks along miles of empty beaches. Geologically, the Jersey Shore is part of the outer Coastal Plain, a physiographic region that forms 45.2% of the land mass of the state. But behind these sandy shores, teeming marshes and patches of forest offer other delightful strolls over rolling hills, past wildflowers, and through bird-filled meadows. The county and state parks offer glimpses into the past—the American Revolution, early industry, or a businessman's country estate. Since New Jersey is on the flyway for both spring and fall bird migrations, there are many places to witness these annual events.

The Jersey Shore is not just resorts thriving on sandy beaches. It is also lighthouses, villages, cranberry bogs, and migrations. It is because of New Jersey's long association with the sea that, in 1988, Congress authorized the New Jersey Coastal Heritage Trail. The National Park Service, the State of New Jersey, and many organizations are working together to provide for public appreciation, education, understanding, and enjoyment of natural and cultural sites along the coast. Each of the five regions focuses on a different aspect of the shore—maritime history, coastal communities, wildlife habitats, resorts, and coastal habitats. Although the New Jersey Coastal Heritage Trail is designed for vehicular touring, it connects areas of interest to hikers. The trail is identified by the New Jersey Coastal Heritage Trail logo. As of 1998, the trail is not complete. For more information, contact New Jersey Coastal Heritage Trail, National Park Service, P.O. Box 118, Mauricetown, NJ 08329.

ALLAIRE STATE PARK

The 3,063-acre Allaire State Park is located on the New Jersey coastal plain. Its well-drained sandy soil is useless for agriculture. One-third of the park lies south of the Manasquan River and is on the northern fringe of the Pine Barrens, thus supporting a pine forest community. Birders will find spring migrating warblers and other songbirds as well as a variety of breeding birds such as owls, warblers, vireos, and indigo buntings.

Best known for its historic village, it provides a variety of year-round recreational activities. The park is named for James P. Allaire who, in 1822, purchased an iron furnace that dated from the 1790s. The furnace produced castings and pig iron for his foundry in New York and pots for the retail market. Under Allaire's guidance, the site became a self-contained community. As many as 500 people lived there during the years that the village prospered. With the discovery of high grades of iron ore in Pennsylvania, the village declined as an industrial community, and the furnaces were extinguished in 1848. Arthur Brisbane, a Hearst newspaperman, purchased the property in 1907. In 1941, his estate deeded 800 acres, including the village, to the State of New Jersey. Since that time, Allaire has more than tripled in size with acquisitions of land under the Green Acres program.

Through the combined efforts of the State of New Jersey and Allaire Village, Inc., most of the original working buildings from the historic village have been restored. Allaire Village, Inc., a not-for-profit organization, assists the state in preserving, maintaining, and operating the village. Open to the public from May to October on weekends only, this living museum has costumed interpreters who demonstrate crafts and recount history. Admission to the village is free. For more information about the historic village, contact Allaire Village, Inc. at (732) 938-2253.

The park also offers 23 miles of marked trails. The green, red, and yellow trails are for hiking only; the orange trail is for multi-use, with cross-country skiing allowed. Other park uses include canoeing and fishing along the

Manasquan River, tent camping, deer hunting in season, and a narrow-gauge steam train. The park is open year-round, with a parking fee in season.

To reach Allaire State Park, take Exit 98 of the Garden State Parkway, turn west onto County 524, and follow the signs two miles to the park. Or, from Freehold, go south on US 9 and turn right on County 524, which goes through the park. For more information, contact Allaire State Park, P.O. Box 220, Farmingdale, NJ 07727; (732) 938-2371.

CATTUS ISLAND PARK

This over-500-acre preserve north of Toms River, funded in part by New Jersey's Green Acres program, is 70 percent salt marshes, with some lowland and upland forests and a stand of the once-common Atlantic white cedar. John Cattus, a New York importer in 1895, purchased the land for weekend vacations. Central to the park is the Cooper Environmental Center, where visitors may see natural science exhibits and live animals, register for a variety of nature programs, or obtain a trail map and wander on their own.

Six miles of marked trails and four miles of dirt fire roads wander through the wetland and wooded areas. The marked trails are for hiking only. One mile of the trails is accessible to the handicapped. Several sections of boardwalk thread through the marshes, allowing walkers a close look at the complex life in the otherwise inaccessible wetland habitat. Trees to look for are maple, gum, magnolia, holly, and white cedar. The trailhead for the white trail, known as the Causeway, is at the park entrance, and leads out to Page's Point. An observation deck offers a view of the osprey platforms as well as shorebirds and Atlantic flyway migratory birds. The preserve is referred to as an "island" because the area is surrounded by salt marshes. As a result, there are mainland and island trails, duly identified on the map/brochures.

Cattus Island Park is open daily, dawn to dusk, but the Environmental Center has more limited hours. A ramp makes the center and its wildlife view deck accessible to the handicapped. There is no parking fee.

Lady's Slipper

Cattus Island is reached by taking the Garden State Parkway to Exit 82 (Route 37, Seaside) and traveling east on NJ 37 for 6 miles. Use the jug handle to turn north onto Fisher Boulevard. Cattus Island Boulevard, and the entrance to the park, is reached in 2 miles. For more information, contact Cattus Island Park, 1170 Cattus Island Boulevard, Toms River, NJ 08753; (732) 270-6960.

CHEESEQUAKE STATE PARK

Located in Middlesex County in a developed region on the western end of Raritan Bay, 1,284-acre Cheesequake State Park is a botanical preserve comprised mostly of salt marsh, pine barrens, and mixed oak forest. The park's three marked loop trails start at a trailhead at the Nature Center parking area, a short distance from the park's entrance and office. The Nature Center is open all year.

A green trail, 3.5 miles long, leads through pine barrens, mixed oak forest, freshwater marsh, and white cedar swamp. Scattered spoil banks remind the visitor that the area was once mined for clay, used for a thriving pottery industry in New Jersey. An 0.5-mile spur off the green trail leads to the remains of an old steamboat landing on Cheesequake Creek. Unused since the 1920s, it was here that local farmers brought their produce for shipment to market.

The 2-mile red trail leads through pine barrens and mixed oak woods, with numerous small streams. The yellow trail, one mile long, leads to Hooks Creek Lake, where swimming is allowed in summer. In May, this area abounds with pink lady's slippers, wild azalea, swamp azalea, mountain laurel, and trailing arbutus. Boardwalks cross the wet sections. A multi-use trail, 2.7 miles long, is available to mountain bikers and cross-country skiers.

A beach area with parking is one mile from the park entrance. It is open from Memorial Day to Labor Day. Brochures with maps of the park are available at the park office located at the entrance to the park.

Cheesequake Park is accessible from either the Garden State Parkway or NJ 34. From the Garden State Parkway, take Exit 120, turn right, and follow the signs a short distance to the park. From NJ 34, turn east onto Morristown Road, travel one mile before turning onto Gordon Road, and follow signs 0.5 mile to the park entrance. There is a parking fee from Memorial Day to Labor Day. For more information, contact Cheesequake State Park, Gordon Road, Matawan, NJ 07747; (732) 566-2161.

EDWIN B. FORSYTHE NATIONAL WILDLIFE REFUGE

Forsythe National Wildlife Refuge, comprising 40,000 acres of tidal wetlands and shallow bay habitat, is protected and managed for migratory birds. The Brigantine and Barnegat divisions were originally two distinct refuges established in 1939 and 1967, respectively. In 1984 they were combined and renamed to honor the late conservationist congressman from New Jersey.

The refuge's location on one of the Atlantic flyway's most active paths makes it an important link in the network of national wildlife refuges. Ninety percent of Forsythe Refuge is tidal salt meadow and marsh, interspersed with shallow coves and bays.

More than 6,000 acres are designated wilderness areas, including Holgate and Little Beach, two of the few remaining undeveloped barrier beaches in New Jersey. They protect nesting and feeding habitat for the endangered piping plover, black skimmer, and least tern. To minimize disturbance to these birds and their habitat, public access is limited. Holgate is closed to public use during nesting season, April 1 until September 1. During all other times, the beachfront is open, although the dunes are always off limits. Little Beach is closed all year except by special-use permit for research or education.

More than 3,000 acres are woodlands dominated by pitch pine, white oak, and white cedar. Fields amidst the woods provide habitat diversity. A wide variety of upland wildlife species frequent these areas.

The Brigantine Division consists of an 8-mile self-guiding Wildlife Drive, two short foot trails (0.2 and 0.5 mile), observation towers, and the refuge headquarters. Migratory birds and other wildlife may be photographed and observed from the Wildlife Drive, a one-way loop road on dikes constructed over bay water. The best wildlife viewing is in the spring and fall. The Barnegat Division is all salt marsh. Seasonal waterfowl and deer hunting, fishing, and crabbing are permitted in designated areas of both divisions.

The refuge is open year-round during daylight hours. Wildlife Drive brochures, maps, guides, and bird lists are available at headquarters. An entrance fee is charged year-round.

To reach the Brigantine Division, take the Garden State Parkway to Exit 48, then go south 6 miles on US 9 to Oceanville. At the traffic light, a sign indicates the refuge entrance to the left. Turn left and follow Great Creek Road one mile to the refuge entrance, headquarters, and parking. For the Holgate

Atlantic Highlands

Division, take NJ 72 east to the town of Ship Bottom on Long Beach Island, turn right, and drive 8 miles south to the dead end. Here, there is parking and access to the beach edge (open only from September 1 until April 1). There are no public facilities at the Barnegat Division.

For more information, contact the Edwin B. Forsythe National Wildlife Refuge, Great Creek Road, P.O. Box 72, Oceanville, NJ 08231; (609) 652-1665.

HARTSHORNE WOODS PARK

The 736-acre park is named for Richard Hartshorne, who sailed into the area in 1670, falling under its spell. He went to considerable trouble to clear his title to the lands and settled directly with the Lenape, who felt that they had not been justly paid for the land.

The trail system, open to all user groups, wanders on sandy soil through forested hillsides with large deciduous trees and seasonal wildflowers. The five marked trails range from 0.7 mile to 6.0 miles and offer varying degrees of difficulty. The mountain laurel in bloom delights visitors in late May, while summer visitors can enjoy a cool morning hike.

To reach Hartshorne Woods Park, take Exit 117 on the Garden State Parkway, and then NJ 36 east to Navesink Avenue; turn right on Navesink Avenue and go to the park entrance on the left. For more information, contact Monmouth County Park System, 805 Newman Springs Road, Lincroft, NJ 07738-1695; (732) 842-4000.

HOLMDEL PARK

In 1962, the Monmouth County park system acquired this 342-acre facility which includes a living history farm and an arboretum. Eight miles of foot trails wend their way through beech, hickory, tulip, spruce, and pine trees. When there is sufficient snow cover, the rolling terrain is suitable for cross-country skiing.

To reach the park from the Garden State Parkway, take Exit 114 (Red Hill Road) west to Crawfords Corner Road, then turn right and follow signs to Holmdel Park on Longstreet Road. For more information, contact the Monmouth County Park System, 805 Newman Springs Road, Lincroft, NJ 07738-1695; (732) 842-4000.

HUBER WOODS PARK

In 1974, the children of Hans and Catherine Huber, a manufacturer of pigments used in dry inks, donated 118 acres of woodlands to the Monmouth County Park System. Huber was enlarged with subsequent donations, including the winter residence and barns. The house was built in 1926, and in 1992 became the environmental center, dedicated to nature interpretation, programs, and classes.

The 6.5 miles of multi-use trails are open to hikers, bikers, equestrians, and cross-country skiers in season. They lead through stands of tulip trees, oak-hickory forest, and meadows. The trails provide both long and short loop hikes along several clearly marked intersecting routes. Trail maps are available at the trailhead across the grass field north of the parking lot. Trails are open dawn to dusk year-round. The park also offers an equestrian program which includes people with physical and mental disabilities.

Huber Woods Park is reached from NJ 35 in Red Bank. From NJ 35, turn east onto Navesink River Road, just north of the Cooper Avenue bridge. Travel 2.8 miles and turn left onto unpaved Browns Dock Road. The park entrance is at the top of the hill.

For more information, contact the Environmental Education Center at (732) 872-2670, or the Monmouth County Park System, 805 Newman Springs Road, Lincroft, NJ 07738-1695; (732) 842-4000.

HENRY HUDSON TRAIL

The 9-mile Henry Hudson Trail occupies the former Central Railroad of New Jersey right-of-way between Aberdeen and the Middletown/Atlantic Highlands border. Along its course, the elevated rail bed and bridge crossing provide open views of stream corridors, tidal wetlands, and the Raritan Bay. It is an historic remnant of the late nineteenth and early twentieth centuries.

Hikers, bikers, and equestrians are welcome along the route. Traditionally, hikers yield to horses and bikers yield to both hikers and horses, but do not depend on it. Stay well to the right and do not walk abreast if bike traffic is heavy. For more information, contact the Monmouth County Park System, 805 Newman Springs Road, Lincroft, NJ 07738-1695; (732) 842-4000.

ISLAND BEACH STATE PARK

An undeveloped stretch of barrier beach and salt marsh on the north side of Barnegat Inlet, this 3,001-acre strip of unspoiled dune land has an almost impenetrable barrier of brier, holly, bayberry, and other shrubs between the fore dunes and the bay. Little grows above the height of the dunes, which shelter the vegetation from killing salt spray.

The 13 miles of trails include the beach for horseback riding, a paved bicycle path, and a canoe trail in Barnegat Bay. A recommended walk is the central paved road extending through the 8-mile length of the park, ending at a parking area. From there, 1.5 miles of beach lead to Barnegat Inlet, the passage to Barnegat Bay, and the tip of the park. Across Barnegat Inlet is Barnegat Lighthouse (172 feet), whose spiral staircase leads to views of the bay and the ocean. The lighthouse is accessible via NJ 72 east from the Garden State Parkway (Exit 63), across Barnegat Bay to Long Beach Island and the town of Ship Bottom. Turn north and drive 8.5 miles to the north end of Long Beach Island. The lighthouse is open May through October.

Island Beach State Park is off Exit 82 of the Garden State Parkway. From Exit 82, take NJ 37 east to NJ 35 south, and go 2 miles to the park entrance. A fee is collected from Memorial Day to Labor Day. For more information, contact Island Beach State Park, P.O. Box 37, Seaside Park, NJ 08752; (732) 793-0506.

MANASQUAN RESERVOIR

In 1990, Monmouth County opened this 1,086-acre recreation area. A 5-mile perimeter gravel trail offers hikers, bicyclists, and equestrians a scenic route around the 4-billion-gallon reservoir on the site of Timber Swamp Brook. This wide trail runs through young woods, wetlands, and grassy fields that border the reservoir. The wetlands are designated wildlife habitats and are off limits to visitors. Boardwalks and a bridge link all trail sections. The points on the trail where the shallow shoreline is easily accessible are good locations for viewing the waterfowl. Sitings have included many endangered and protected species.

In 1994, a visitor center opened, with a floating dock and launch area which is accessible to the handicapped. Boating, with some restrictions, is permitted. A boat rental and tackle/bait shop is on the lower level of the visitor center. Daily launch fees and seasonal passes are available for boats. The reservoir is closed to boating from December 1 to February 28. Stocked with bass, trout, various panfish species, and bullhead catfish, the reservoir is open for fishing year-round with a state license.

In winter, ice skating, ice-boating, and ice-fishing are permitted, depending on ice conditions. The perimeter trail serves as a 5-mile cross-country ski loop.

To reach the Manasquan Reservoir, take US 9 south from Freehold to Georgia Tavern Road. Use the jug handle for a left turn and travel 0.3 mile east to Windler Road. Turn right and continue 1.5 miles on Windler Road to the main entrance and a large parking area. For more information, call Manasquan Reservoir at (732) 919-0996, or the Monmouth County Park System at (732) 842-4000.

MONMOUTH BATTLEFIELD STATE PARK

Monmouth Battlefield State Park is the site of the longest battle fought during the Revolutionary War. Tramping through the gently rolling terrain of the former battlefield, hikers can almost hear the guns firing and the cries of the wounded as they sounded on that bloody June day during the Battle of Monmouth. The park has 4 miles of marked paths and a few unmarked ones. Some of the trails are multi-use for hikers, bikers, and horses.

The visitor center, located at the parking lot, contains battle displays, a gift shop, and restrooms. During the summer months, Revolutionary War encampments and battles are reenacted.

The Battle of Monmouth took place on June 28, 1778, as an effort to stop the British army retreat from Philadelphia to New York. George Washington sent 5,000 troops under General Charles Lee into Freehold to attack the rear guard of the British Army. General Lee encountered a stronger force than he had anticipated, and he retreated, leaving units stranded in the field. After encountering Lee, Washington sent him to the rear and took over full command. Americans reformed their lines as British and Hessian soldiers counterattacked. In the overwhelming heat of the afternoon, all fighting ceased except for an artillery duel. Gradually the Americans gained control. It was during this artillery battle that Mary Hays, known as "Molly Pitcher," carried water for the soldiers to quench their thirst and to cool the cannons. When her husband was fatally wounded by enemy fire, she took his position loading the cannon. The British continued their withdrawal, leaving the area after dark.

Who won at Monmouth is open to debate. Although the Americans succeeded in holding the blood-soaked terrain, the British wagon train reached Sandy Hook safely. But never again would the British Army engage George Washington and the main American Army. The training that Baron Friedrich von Steuben gave at Valley Forge had made the Continental Army the equal of the British regulars.

To reach Monmouth Battlefield State Park, take I-95 to the intersection of US 9 and NJ 33, and then take NJ 33 west 3 miles to the park entrance on the right. For more information, contact the park at 347 Freehold Road, Manapalan, NJ 07726; (732) 462-9616.

PORICY PARK

This 250-acre park is a good introduction to outdoor activities, as the 4-mile trail system takes visitors to a freshwater marsh, hardwood forest, pond, wet meadows, and fields. The fossil bed at Poricy Brook is what makes Poricy Park different from other nature preserves and historic sites. Not only can visitors dig for fossils, but they may also take them home. The fossils are approximately 72 million years old; most are shellfish. The park asks that visitors sift the sand and gravel in the stream bed and refrain from digging directly into the banks, which causes erosion. As the park frequently schedules programs at the fossil beds, it is advisable to call ahead.

Although the Township of Middletown owns the land and buildings, funding for the programs, professional staff, furnishings, and equipment are provided by the Poricy Park Citizens Committee. The site includes a restored Colonial house and barn dating to 1767.

From the Garden State Parkway, take Exit 114. Go 0.8 mile on Red Hill Road towards Middletown. Turn right on Balm Hollow/Oak Hill Road and go 2 miles to the park entrance on the right, immediately before the second set of railroad tracks. For more information, contact Poricy Park, P.O. Box 36, Middletown, NJ 07748; (732) 842-5966.

Sandy Hook　　　Shrewsbury River　　　Highlands

SANDY HOOK

This 6.5-mile sand spit, the nation's first urban park, boasts a rich history and varied habitats. Monstrous storms have wreaked havoc to Sandy Hook, ripping large parts of the spit away and sometimes creating islands that are later washed away. As a result, beaches have drastically changed in size and shape.

The park includes six miles of ocean beaches, the waters of Sandy Hook Bay, salt marshes, dunes, hiking trails, shorebird habitat, Historic Fort Hancock, and the Sandy Hook Lighthouse. This oldest lighthouse in the United States, built in 1764, lies 1.5 miles south of Sandy Hook's growing tip, the result of two centuries of littoral drift. On the 200th anniversary of its first lighting, the Sandy Hook Lighthouse was declared a National Historic Landmark. The now-automated lighthouse is not open to visitors. Fort Hancock was built in 1895 to protect New York Harbor as part of the coastal defense system. A camouflaged concrete wall hid guns that could fire on unsuspecting ships. In the 1950s, Nike missiles replaced the guns, which could disappear in the ramparts. The post was closed in 1974. The remote and deserted coastline was also a proving ground for military weapons between 1870 and 1919. Sandy Hook is a unit of Gateway National Recreation Area, created by Congress in 1972 to provide parkland around New York Harbor—the gateway through which millions of immigrants entered the New World.

Vegetation typical of barrier beaches thrives here: bayberry, beach plum, wild cherry, prickly pear, and poison ivy. A 60-acre stand of American holly, some of which is over three hundred years old, is accessible through guided tours. Sandy Hook is on the principal spring and fall migratory flyway and, as

NATURE CENTER (former COAST GUARD STATION), SANDY HOOK NATIONAL RECREATION AREA

a result, is an excellent place to watch for hawks, migratory shorebirds, and monarch butterflies.

The six miles of beaches attract hordes of sunbathers during the summer. However, the off-season visitor can use those same beaches for flying kites, walking, and fishing, or can cycle along the level roads unencumbered by heavy traffic. During spring and summer, several sections of beach are closed to protect nesting shorebirds.

The Spermaceti Cove Visitor Center offers ranger-led historical and natural interpretive programs. The Visitor Center is a former U.S. Life-Saving Station and features history and nature exhibits.

From the Spermaceti Cove Visitor Center, the one-mile Old Dune Trail meanders north through heather and bayberry to a portion of the holly forest. A natural history guide to the trail is available at the Visitor Center. Along the trail is a freshwater pond that harbors marsh hawks, turtles, and frogs. The trail eventually leads to a beach, then loops back toward Spermaceti Cove, completing its circuit. The 2-mile South Beach Dune Trail starts at Area F in the south of the park, and leads through dunes and holly forest. The Fisherman's Trail starts at the Area K lot, at the northern end of the park, and leads 1.5 miles to the tip of Sandy Hook at the ocean shore. An observation deck atop Battery Peck offers a view of the Manhattan skyline. Fort Hancock Historic District is located nearby at the northern end of Sandy Hook. Fort Hancock Museum and History House are open on weekends throughout the year, with extended hours during July and August.

To reach Sandy Hook, take the Garden State Parkway to Exit 117, and continue on NJ 36 east for 13.5 miles, following signs to the Gateway National Recreation Area entrance. There is a beach parking fee from Memorial Day to Labor Day. Public transportation is also available; New Jersey Transit's North Jersey Coast rail line goes to Red Bank, and New Jersey Transit bus

M24 continues to Highlands. For a schedule, phone (973) 762-5100. Bus transportation from New York City is via Academy Lines to Highlands; phone (212) 564-8484 for a schedule. Express Navigation goes between Pier 11 in Manhattan and Highlands; phone (800) BOAT-RIDE for the schedule. For more information about the Sandy Hook unit of the Gateway National Recreation Area, contact Superintendent, Sandy Hook Unit, Gateway NRA, P.O. Box 530, Fort Hancock, NJ 07732; (732) 872-5970.

TURKEY SWAMP

Turkey Swamp Park and Turkey Swamp Wildlife Management Area are on the northern edge of the Pine Barrens. The sandy and clay soils support scrub oak, white oak, pepperbush, huckleberries, and blueberries. Birders will find migrant songbirds, quail, grouse, and woodcock. To reach either the county park or the wildlife management area, take the Garden State Parkway to Exit 98 and continue on I-195 west. At Exit 22, turn right onto Jackson Mills Road, turn left onto Georgia Road, and follow signs to Turkey Swamp Park.

Turkey Swamp Park

Part of the Monmouth County Park System, 813-acre Turkey Swamp Park offers a variety of outdoor recreation activities. In addition to picnic facilities, boat rentals, ball fields, and fishing, there are 4 miles of marked trails. Ranging in length from 0.5 mile to 1.7 miles, these mostly level pathways cut through forests of pitch pine and oak. Seasonal camping is available on a first-come first-served basis. For more information, contact Turkey Swamp Park, 66 Gnomic Road, Freehold, NJ 07728; (732) 462-7286.

Turkey Swamp Wildlife Management Area

Adjacent to the county park, Turkey Swamp Wildlife Management Area includes 2,457 acres of upland pine oak, woodlands, lowlands, and swampy areas. Since there are no marked trails in Turkey Swamp Wildlife Management Area, users of the area should obtain the Adelphia USGS topographic quadrangle map. For more information, contact the New Jersey DEP, Division of Fish, Game and Wildlife, 501 East State Street, P.O. Box 400, Trenton, NJ 08625; (609) 292-2965.

TWELVE

CENTRAL JERSEY

ew Jersey has always been a
crossroads between present-day New York City and Philadelphia. Before the
Europeans settled in the area, the Native Americans developed routes across the
state which were adopted by the settlers who established farms in the area.
During the American Revolution, troops and supplies crossed the state many
times as the Continental Army engaged in nearly 100 battles and skirmishes. In
1809, the completed Easton Turnpike began serving as an artery of commerce.
Eleven years later, the Georgetown-Franklin Turnpike was completed. As more
and more goods needed to be moved, it was necessary to have more effective
transportation methods. Canals and then railroads became the preferred means
of transportation and brought prosperity into an agricultural economy.

In the second half of the twentieth century, superhighways cross the state,
but it is the state and county roads that ultimately lead residents and visitors to
interesting places to hike. Within Hunterdon, Mercer, and Somerset counties,
state, county, and municipal governments have set aside open space in order to
protect water resources and wildlife habitat, ensure suburban and rural ambi-
ance, and provide active and passive recreation. Hikers can avail themselves of
a wide range of hiking opportunities—rail trails, towpaths, ravines, wooded
hills, meadows, wetlands, and former farm fields. Small parks offer opportunities for fitness walking as well as wildlife observation. Wildlife management
areas beckon the more adventuresome who enjoy prowling through woods,

fields, and meadows (out of hunting season). Adaptive reuse has turned private estates, including vestiges of the gilded age, into educational centers, schools, and government offices, and at the same time the surrounding grounds have become protected open space.

Railroads

A network of railroads crisscrossing the northern part of the state was constructed during the latter half of the nineteenth century, linking formerly isolated communities. For the most part, the railroads brought coal from and iron to Pennsylvania, and carried supplies to villages and towns in Hunterdon and Morris counties. Passenger service was somewhat incidental, so when the mines closed down, it was not surprising that most of the rail lines eventually were abandoned. Although many of the lines were short, their sheer numbers attest to the impact iron and railroads once had on the area.

One line, the High Bridge Branch of the Central Railroad of New Jersey, ran from the town of High Bridge north to Hopatcong Junction, where it split into spurs that served iron mines at Hibernia, Mount Hope, Ogden, and elsewhere. Completed in 1876, passenger service was operated on the line until 1932, and freight service until the late 1970s. In 1980, the rails were removed from Bartley south to High Bridge, and the right-of-way was purchased by the Columbia Gas Company for use as a gas line and rail trail. Freight service is still operated on the northern portion of the line.

With so many abandoned lines in the northern part of the state, there are numerous opportunities to walk on the railbeds. The restored railbeds have paved or gravel surfaces which are suitable for cycling as well as walking. When the beds are not restored, the relatively level grades and obvious route provide a comfort level for those hikers wishing to try off-trail hiking. Some of the abandoned railbeds are on private property, and hikers should respect the rights of property owners and not trespass.

ASSUNPINK WILDLIFE MANAGEMENT AREA

Purchased under the Green Acres Program, the 5,600-acre Assunpink Wildlife Management Area includes man-made and natural lakes, wetlands, former farm fields, hedgerows, and mixed hardwood forests. The diverse habitats in the wildlife management area are home to a variety of wildlife, including deer, rabbits, squirrels, owls, and hawks. The three lakes are popular resting spots for migratory water fowl. Woods roads and mowed strips provide access to uplands and open fields.

To reach the Assunpink Wildlife Management Area, take Exit 11 (Imlaystown Road) from I-195. Go north on Imlaystown Road 2.6 miles to the parking lot at Assunpink Lake, then continue east about 0.5 mile on Clarksburg-Robbinsville Road to the headquarters. Since there are no marked trails in the Assunpink Wildlife Management Area, users of the area should obtain the Allentown and Roosevelt USGS topographic quadrangle maps. For more information, contact the New Jersey DEP, Division of Fish, Game and Wildlife, 501 East State Street, P.O. Box 400, Trenton, NJ 08625; (609) 292-2965.

CAPOOLONG CREEK
WILDLIFE MANAGEMENT AREA

Basically paralleling Capoolong Creek, the Capoolong Creek Wildlife Management Area follows the right-of way of the abandoned Pittstown Branch of the Lehigh Valley Railroad. The 3.7-mile rail trail follows the cinder railbed. Vegetation along the route includes hemlock, beech, and sycamore trees, honeysuckle, grapevines, and poison ivy.

To reach the Capoolong Creek Wildlife Management Area, take I-78 to Exit 15 (Clinton/Pittstown, NJ 173 east). At the end of the exit ramp, make a left onto County 513 south. To reach the southern end, go about 4 miles and turn left on Quakertown Road. The trail starts at the far end of the MCI Electric Company property, just after the road crosses a stream. Parking is available in Pittstown. To reach the northern end, go 0.6 mile and turn left (south) onto County 617 (Sydney Road). Go 1.4 miles, and turn left on Lower Landsdown Road for 0.5 mile. Turn right on Landsdown Road and quickly cross the railroad tracks, where the trail starts.

At the southern end on Quakertown Road, the rail trail passes, at 0.1 mile, the abandoned railroad station. At 0.8 mile, the trail reaches White Bridge Road. Here, the trail disappears, making it necessary for hikers to walk along the road. At 0.9 mile, the trail reappears and follows the creek closely. The trail comes to an iron bridge with ties at 1.3 miles and crosses Lower Kingtown Road. Hikers again must walk along the road to rejoin the trail at 1.9 miles. After crossing a tie bridge over a drainage gully at 2.3 miles, the trail crosses two roads and ends at active railroad tracks at 3.7 miles. For more information, contact the New Jersey DEP, Division of Fish, Game and Wildlife, 501 East State

Street, P.O. Box 400, Trenton, NJ 08625; (609) 292-2965.

CLINTON WILDLIFE MANAGEMENT AREA

This 1,115-acre wildlife management area surrounds most of Spruce Run Reservoir, with the exception of the day-use area of Spruce Run Recreation Area, which occupies two peninsulas jutting into the lake. Numerous woods roads and unmarked trails, which do not show on the High Bridge USGS topographic quadrangle map, crisscross the region with some actively farmed areas.

The section of the management area on the north side of Van Syckels Road offers approximately 2 miles of woods roads that are mowed to allow access to the area, which makes for very easy hiking. The hiker will pass through varying terrain and a combination of hardwood forest, consisting primarily of oak and ash, and open fields currently planted with corn. Access to this section is from the gravel parking area on either side of Van Syckels Road immediately after crossing Black Brook, approximately 0.2 mile after the entrance to Spruce Run.

It is possible to walk some sections of the shoreline of the reservoir, especially when the water level is low; however, other sections will remain impassable. Birders know the reservoir for its migratory waterfowl.

To reach the Clinton Wildlife Management Area, take Exit 17 (Clinton) from I-78, and go north on NJ 31 for 3.5 miles to the traffic light on Van Syckles Road. Make a left at the light and follow signs to Spruce Run Recreation Area. Continue 1.1 miles past the entrance of Spruce Run Recreation Area to the Clinton Wildlife Management Area office on the left. For more information, contact the New Jersey DEP, Division of Fish, Game and Wildlife, 501 East State Street, P.O. Box 400, Trenton, NJ 08625; (609) 292-2965.

DELAWARE AND RARITAN
CANAL STATE PARK

In the early part of the nineteenth century, people living in central New Jersey were isolated. The few roads that existed were at best difficult and at worst impassable. Rivers were not easily navigated, and railroads were in their infancy. A canal was seen as an effective means of transportation between Philadelphia and New York and a connection with the rest of the world. It took three years to build the 44-mile-long, 75-foot-wide, 7-foot-deep main canal and the 22-mile-long, 50-foot-

wide, 6-foot-deep feeder. Most of the workers were Irish immigrants, hired at very low pay to do the back-breaking work, mostly with hand tools.

Once completed, the Delaware and Raritan Canal became one of America's busiest navigational canals. Mule/horse- or steam-drawn tugs used it from 6 to 6 daily from early April until freeze. In 1871, its busiest year, total tonnage shipped surpassed the longer and more famous Erie Canal. With all the activity along the canal, it was necessary to impose a speed limit of 4 miles per hour to prevent damage to the canal banks.

To serve and be served by the canal boat operators, small commercial centers developed along the canal. The services offered were not limited to just stores. Canal boat operators, the majority of whom owned their own boats, could hire mules from barns at Bordentown, Griggstown, and New Brunswick. After the canal ceased operations, some of the towns remained, and they continue to offer services. In 1855, the Belvidere-Delaware Railroad was completed alongside the feeder canal and served as a wintertime supplement. But as railroads became a preferred mode of transportation, canals began to die. The D&R Canal ceased making a profit in 1892, although it continued to operate until 1933.

Once closed to navigation, both the main canal and the feeder were taken over by the State of New Jersey. After lock gates were removed and sluice gates installed, the canals became a source of water for farms, industry, and homes. As people began using the towpaths for walking, birding, and cycling and the canals for canoeing, they realized they were valuable resources. In 1974, 67 miles of canal and a narrow strip of land on both banks became a state park. The abandoned Belvidere-Delaware Railroad right-of-way was added to the park in the 1980s. The towpath of the main canal is open to the public from Mulberry Street just north of Trenton to Landing Lane Bridge in New Brunswick, but there is a gap where the canal crosses US 1. The Belvidere-Delaware railbed, which does not allow horses, is the trail alongside the feeder canal.

In 1998, the canals offer hikers, birders, canoeists, anglers, equestrians, cyclists, joggers, and picnickers the opportunity to enjoy the outdoors. There are more than 160 species of birds in the park, of which 90 are nesting. Turtles slide and frogs plop into the water at the first sound of danger. Wildflowers add color seasonally. Oak and maple trees form a canopy over the towpath in places. But regardless of what the vegetation along the towpath is, there seems to be an abundance of poison ivy.

At Princeton, the path follows the shore of Carnegie Lake, reaching, at three miles, a red mill and abundant water at Kingston. At five miles, the path reaches the Berrien House at Rockingham, just off County 518, where General George Washington drafted his farewell address.

A wide range of hikes is available, as there are small parking areas at nearly all road crossings providing access to the towpath. Users can easily keep track of how far they have been, since mileposts on the main canal indicate mileage to Trenton and to New Brunswick. The state-produced park map and state or county road maps provide information about access to the cross roads. From north of Blackwells Mills, a road on the east side of the canal heading toward the village of East Millstone provides an alternate route to Millstone. An alternate route to the feeder canal is the Delaware Canal in Pennsylvania. More complete descriptions of selected sections on both canals are avail-

able in books listed in "Selected Readings." For more information, including a brochure, contact the Delaware and Raritan Canal State Park, 625 Canal Road, Somerset, NJ 08873; (732) 873-3050.

DELAWARE CANAL STATE PARK

The Delaware Canal provided an economical means of transporting coal from the Upper Lehigh Valley to Philadelphia, where it could be shipped to New York and the eastern seaboard. The use of coal to fire iron furnaces reduced the depletion of forests in the rich hills of the Jersey Highlands. Although the towpath is in Pennsylvania, it provides an alternate route to the feeder canal of the Delaware and Raritan Canal. For more information, contact the Pennsylvania Department of Conservation and Natural Resources, Delaware Canal State Park, 11 Lodi Hill Road, Upper Black Eddy, PA 18972; (610) 982-5560.

FLEMINGTON GREENBELT

Hikers whose family members consider shopping a recreational activity have an alternative. Within walking distance of the outlet stores in Flemington are four small parks, none of which alone has enough trail mileage to keep a hiker busy. By combining the trails with road walks, the not-too-happy shopper can fill in what might otherwise be a boring time. The approximately 3.5-mile unmarked route is a loop and can be started at any point.

From Liberty Village, go north on Central Street and turn left onto Mine Street. Follow Mine Street past the main entrance to St. Magdalen Church and turn right on Shields Street, which becomes a country road. The Flemington water tower is on the right. Turn left on a footpath along the north end of a field, which leads to Mine Brook Park. Cross Mine Brook on a bridge, walk right on the park trail, and cross Capner Street to enter the Morales Nature Preserve. Wide trails within the preserve are marked with sign posts.

The trails begin just behind the kiosk with a trail map. Take the Main Trail as it wanders through the woods. After crossing the brook, walk up wooden steps and turn left on the Eagle Trail. Proceed uphill alongside the brook, entering an area with no understory. The edge of the path is delineated with rocks, so that you can hike straight uphill or switchback up to a bench. Continue to the right on the Meditation Trail. Those hikers who want a longer hike can take the left fork into Uplands Reserve. There, an old paved road leads to mowed paths along the edges of fields.

The Meditation Trail ends at the Main Trail, which should be followed back to the entrance. Turn left on Capner Street to walk along the Reading-Fleming Middle School perimeter fence to Tuccamirgan Park. Proceed on a trail to Bonnell Street. The rear entrance to the parking lot at St. Magdalen Church is across the street. To return to Liberty Village, either turn left, staying on Bonnell Street, turn right on Park Street, right on Central Street and right on Mine Street, or walk through the church property to make a left on Mine Street.

INSTITUTE WOODS

The Woods encompass an area which was once farmed but has grown up at various times over the last two-and-a-half centuries to establish woodland of diverse age and content. It was founded as a part of (and is adjacent to) the Institute for Advanced Study in Princeton, perhaps best known as the intellectual home of Albert Einstein. Within the 589 acres, some four miles of generally flat trails and cinder paths crisscross the abandoned fields on which the campus was built, providing a haven for walkers, birds, strolling scholars deep in thought, and scientists studying the Woods themselves. Since the Woods and the adjacent Rogers Refuge are considered the best place in New Jersey for observing the spring migration of warblers and other songbirds, expect to find crowds in early to mid-May.

A booklet, *The Woods at the Institute for Advanced Study*, written by a Princeton University biologist, is available at the Reception Desk in Fuld Hall, the main building of the Institute. This quirky but informative brochure details the forest succession which resulted in the present variety of trees growing in the area, providing an overview, informative guided walk, map, tree identification key, and scientific references.

To reach the Woods, take NJ 27 to a left fork onto Mercer Road, just before the intersection with US 206. Turn left onto Olden Lane and drive to the end, where parking is available. The main cinder path starts from a point near the base of the turn-around at the end of the road. For more information, contact the Institute for Advanced Study, Olden Lane, Princeton, NJ 08540; (609) 734-8000.

KEN LOCKWOOD GORGE

This 260-acre wildlife management area is managed primarily for hunting and fishing. Towering hemlocks lining the steep walls of the Ken Lockwood Gorge provide shade and contribute to a sense of isolation. A 2.5-mile stretch of the South Branch of the Raritan River flows through the gorge, cascading over boulders, spilling over small waterfalls, and pouring into quiet pools. From April to November, fly fishermen test their skills in the stream, reported to be one of the best trout fishing streams in the region. Hikers can enjoy a stroll along the unpaved access road as it parallels the river. For those people not wishing to walk the whole distance, there are numerous pull-out places to park cars.

A shuttle hike of 5.5 miles is possible if one car is left in the village of High Bridge and another vehicle driven to the north end of the gorge. After walking 2.5 miles along the road in the gorge, hikers can reach the other car in High Bridge via the Columbia Trail of South Branch Reservation, which crosses the river on a high trestle.

To reach Ken Lockwood Wildlife Management Area, take I-78 to Exit 17 (NJ 31), and continue north on NJ 31 into High Bridge. Turn right and follow County 513 as it zig-zags through the village and past Voorhees State Park. After milepost 20, turn right onto County 512. After crossing the bridge, make an immediate right turn onto River Road and enter the gorge. Public transportation is available to High Bridge via weekday commuter service on the NJ Transit Raritan Valley Line. For more information, contact the New Jersey DEP, Division of Fish, Game and Wildlife, P.O. Box 400, Trenton, NJ 08625; (609) 292-2965.

MOUNTAIN LAKES NATURE PRESERVE

This natural area located just outside downtown Princeton is a favorite for family walks, bird watching, and fishing. Originally part of King George III's land grant to William Penn, it was farmed through the eighteenth century before being developed by an ice company in the nineteenth century. At that time, the brooks were dammed to form the three lakes that now grace the park. A network of several miles of trails makes two main loops through the 70 acres of predominantly wooded land, with areas of wetlands. The parking lot is located just off US 206 in Princeton, on Mountain Avenue. For more information, contact Mountain Lakes Nature Preserve, P.O. Box 374, Princeton, NJ 08540; (609) 924-8720.

MUSCONETCONG RIVER RESERVATION

Rising in Lake Hopatcong in Morris County, the Musconetcong River flows 44 miles to the Delaware River. It is a trout stream, with forests buffeting large segments. In its lower reaches, the river slices through a deep limestone valley, shadowed by 1,000-foot ridges. Two sections of the reservation in Hunterdon County are protected as part of the Hunterdon County park system. The Musconetcong Gorge section and the Point Mountain section each have about 5 miles of blazed hiking trails. For more information about both sections, contact the Hunterdon County Park System, 1020 Highway 31, Lebanon, NJ 08833; (908) 782-1158.

Musconetcong Gorge Section

Bisected by two creeks, the Musconetcong Gorge Section is a heavily wooded 379-acre tract that slopes down to the Musconetcong River. Limited hunting by permit is permitted in this area. Charcoal landings, stone foundations, and long-abandoned water pipelines give evidence of man's activities in years past. The trail system is comprised of a marked nature trail, an abandoned railroad, and a ridge trail. Although the trail mileages are short, the terrain is steep and rocky. Hikers should be aware that the trails lead downhill from the parking area; therefore, the return trip is uphill. Fortunately, connections between the upper and lower trails make possible hikes of 2, 3, or 5 miles.

From the parking area, walk around the guardrail and go downhill, following the orange trail markers. Within 0.2 mile, the sounds of the road and the Warren Glen paper mill disappear and the predominant sound is Gas Line Creek, as it twists into the gorge. Cross the bridge over the stream and continue on the white-blazed trail which leads into the forest. Upon reaching the service road, turn right and head uphill for about 50 feet. At the junction with the Waterfall Trail (white), turn right. Once again the creek can be heard. Follow the creek upstream and pass a circular foundation used as a cistern. Double back to the left and proceed up the switchback to rejoin the service road. Continue on the service road, crossing some seeps and reaching Gas Line Creek.

For the two-mile hike, continue across the creek and, in about 75 feet, reach a white-blazed trail on the right. Follow the trail along the rocky slope, back down to the gas pipeline. Bear right and follow the clearing, then go left, back to the sign at the beginning of the nature trail.

For the three- or five-mile circular hike, climb the stairs on the embankment to ascend the ridge, strewn with rocks ranging in size from baseball to box car. Midway along the ridge is the high point on the circular hike, about 300 feet above the level of the gorge. For the three-mile hike, at the trail junction near the high point, go left downhill. There are several flat, cleared areas known as charcoal landings where, in the eighteenth and nineteenth centuries, trees were burned for charcoal. The trail descends, sometimes steeply, to reach the Railroad Trail, an abandoned rail bed. Turn left to return to the orange-blazed trail and ascend to the parking area.

At the junction at the high point mentioned above, for the five-mile loop, continue straight along the Ridge Trail, heading downhill. Pine Creek is the midpoint of the hike. As the trail descends, it comes closer to the ridge line, offering a glimpse through the trees. After making two sharp turns, it descends to Pine Creek. A left turn onto the Railroad Trail, an abandoned rail bed, leads back to the orange-blazed trail and the ascent to the parking area.

To reach the Musconetcong Gorge Section, take I-78 to Exit 6 (Bloomsbury). Take NJ 173 west to its junction with Warren County 639 toward Warren Glen. At the junction with Hunterdon County 519, go south, cross the Musconetcong River, and turn left onto unpaved Dennis Road. Park in the gravel turnout at a curve in the road. The preserve is on both sides of County 519.

Point Mountain Section

The Point Mountain section is approximately 15 miles upstream from the Gorge section in the northwest corner of the county. It offers river access, a mature forest, and mowed paths through cornfields. The 935-foot-high summit of Point Mountain offers sweeping views of small towns, fertile farmland, and the Musconetcong River valley. The trails are marked throughout with orange squares on trees and wooden posts in the open fields.

To reach the Point Mountain section, take Exit 17 (Clinton) of I-78 and go north on NJ 31 to Washington. Take NJ 57 east approximately 4 miles to the traffic light at Point Mountain Road. Turn right and head south, down a hill and across a bridge. Parking is available on pullouts on either side of the road, just after crossing the river. Additional parking is available on Penwell Road at the northern end of the Point Mountain section, just east of the river and NJ 57.

ROUND VALLEY

Located south of Lebanon in the northern portion of Hunterdon County, Cushetunk Mountain is a horseshoe-shaped ridge which encircles the reservoir in the Round Valley Recreation Area. It is comprised of traprock, similar to the diabase of the Palisades of the Hudson, and part of the same outflows of Triassic time. The rocks of this curving ridge had their origin in an intrusion of diabase between strata of the Brunswick shales and sandstones of the Triassic Period. They were eventually exposed by erosion, which wore down the softer shales above and around and left the harder igneous material standing 800 feet above sea level and 400 feet above the surrounding Hunterdon countryside.

The Cushetunk ridge, never having been glaciated as were the Palisades, has more residual soil than the latter. A second growth of hardwood covers most of its upper portion. The region is attractive in both spring and fall, when the dogwood trees are most colorful. There are views eastward over the plain of the Raritan Valley, bordered on the south by similar traprock ridges, which are also a southwestward extension of the Palisades intrusion. Half a mile west of the south limb of the Cushetunk horseshoe, in abandoned limestone quarries, are the remains of the kilns where the rock was burned to convert it to lime. The rock has an unusual blue color, possibly due to its manganese content. Four miles north of Round Valley Reservoir, a smaller horseshoe of diabase shows a curious topography. The Brunswick shales of the interior valley are open, while the contact with the traprock and border conglomerates is generally indicated by the forest that covers the ridge.

Cushetunk Mountain Nature Preserve

Adjacent to Round Valley Recreation Area is the 363-acre Cushetunk Mountain Nature Preserve. Two short, unmarked trails from the parking lot connect to the crest of Cushetunk Mountain and provide 180-degree views overlooking the nearby hills and valleys to the north as well as seasonal views of Round Valley Reservoir to the south. One trail goes directly to the ridge top. The other follows a wooden-pole power line east to steel-supported high tension wires and turns right into the woods. Both trails connect with the Round Valley Trail described below.

To reach the Cushetunk Mountain Nature Preserve, take Exit 20A (Lebanon) from I-78 west and turn right onto NJ 22 east. Turn right onto County 523 south and then right onto Railroad Avenue. Cross the railroad tracks and turn left onto Old Mountain Road. Parking is on left, just after crossing the tracks. Public transportation is available via weekday commuter service to Whitehouse Station on the NJ Transit Raritan Valley Line and entails a two-mile walk along Railroad Avenue. For more information, contact the Hunterdon County Park System, 1020 Highway 31, Lebanon, NJ 08833; (908) 782-1158.

Round Valley Recreation Area

New Jersey has developed a comprehensive recreation area here, with hiking, swimming, camping, picnicking, boating, and other facilities in its three-mile-long, two-mile-wide reservoir and 400-foot hills. Round Valley has 116 wilderness campsites spread over some 3 miles of the south and east shores of the reservoirs. This backcountry camping area is accessible only by walking or boating. The wooded sites, many of them near the water, are available from April 1 to October 31 with a permit from headquarters.

To reach Round Valley Recreation Area, take Exit 20A (Lebanon) from I-78 west. Go to US 22 and turn right. In 0.8 mile take the jug handle turn for the recreation area. The park entrance and headquarters are on County 629 (Lebanon-Stanton Road). Public transportation is available to Lebanon via weekday commuter service on the NJ Transit Raritan Valley Line and entails a three-mile walk from the Lebanon railroad station. From the train station, hikers should turn right on Cherry Street (County 629) and then left onto Lebanon-Stanton Road to the park entrance. For more information about the recreation area, contact the Round Valley Recreation Area, Box 45-D, Lebanon-Stanton Road, Lebanon, NJ 08833; (908) 236-6355.

Round Valley Trail   *Length: 9 miles Blaze: unmarked*
This combination hiking-bridle trail nearly encircles the reservoir on the Cushetunk ridge and passes the backcountry camping area. The trail, which begins at the main parking lot at the west end of the reservoir on Lebanon-Stanton Road, was originally planned to encircle the reservoir completely, but the restricted areas at the dam have prevented that. As of 1998, hikers must retrace their steps to return to the parking area.

The trail itself is marked only by an occasional footprint or horseshoe sign, but it is well defined. It starts from the southwest corner of the parking area and climbs a small rise to give a view of the sparkling, deep-blue reservoir surrounded by hills. Continuing on through open fields into a patch of woods, the trail crosses a paved private road and climbs a hill to reveal views south. The trail goes down a steep slope on the west side of one of the dams and within sight of the road.

Entering the woods to follow the ridge line, the trail dips down to near lake level, where the campsites are. Viewpoints have been cleared and feature small log benches that make ideal lunch spots. The trail continues on the ridge through dense forests, with some steep ups and downs and rough places, for 3.0 miles past the camping area, before terminating at 6.0 miles at a fence with a locked gate. Another three miles of ridge trail may be opened seasonally, but hikers should check first with park officials.

Pine Tree Trail *Length: 0.7 mile Blaze: unmarked*
This well-worn fisherman's path starts across the entry road from the camping parking lot. With short ups and downs, it follows the west shore of the reservoir, with views of the reservoir. The return to the parking area is via the same route.

SIX MILE RUN STATE PARK

Named for a river, Six Mile Run State Park is undeveloped parkland, consisting of farmlands and deciduous forest. In the early 1970s, the state purchased 2,869 acres south and east of Millstone to order to create a reservoir. Alternate sites were identified in 1989 and the then-governor Thomas H. Kean decided that area would become a state park. In 1998, some of the land is leased for agricultural use. Woods and farm roads are throughout the area, but as of 1998 they are not marked.

Users of Six Mile Run State Park should obtain the Monmouth Junction USGS topographic quadrangle map. For more information, contact the Delaware and Raritan Canal State Park, 625 Canal Road, Somerset, NJ 08873; (732) 873-3050.

SOURLAND MOUNTAIN

A 10-mile-by-4-mile-long traprock ridge known as Sourland Mountain rises from the red sandstone plain and runs southwest of Somerville towards the Delaware River. This ridge was formed when geological forces turned a basaltic intrusion on end, and then softer layers of rock eroded away. Heavily forested with some rough, rocky terrain, the ridge is high enough to permit a view of Manhattan skyscrapers. It is quite evident when driving west from US 206 on County 514.

The exact origin of the name is not known. It might have been derived from the German word *sauerland*, meaning land that is not sweet. The land in the area is rocky and acidic. The name could also refer to the sorrel or red-brown color of the soil on the plains adjacent to the mountain. On some records the name Sowerland is used.

Whatever the origin of the name, Sourland Mountain has remained mainly undeveloped because the land has never been worth much agriculturally or commercially, and it is far from major thoroughfares. Its relative isolation has resulted in the area serving as a retreat for many people, including Charles Lindbergh, whose child was kidnapped there. However, its lack of development brought some people in the area to seek its preservation. Since 1989, the Sourland Regional Citizens Planning Council has pressed for its protection, which has proved to be difficult as the mountain is located in three counties — Hunterdon, Mercer and Somerset.

Northern Stony Brook Greenway

Located along the ridge of Sourland Mountain, this 295-acre tract of privately owned land straddles the Hunterdon/Mercer county line. Northern Stony Brook Greenway is the headwaters for Stony Brook and is protected through easements by the Delaware & Raritan Greenway, Inc. This regional land conservancy is protecting and preserving land along the Delaware and Raritan Canal and its tributary streams. A hike along the three miles of trails takes one through woodlands in varying stages of maturity, wetlands, and open meadows.

Begin at the yellow trail just to the left of the Greenway sign in the parking area. The yellow trail proceeds through mature forest of northern red oak, shagbark hickory, tulip, white ash, and walnut trees, with spice bush, viburnum, and sassafras as the understory. Bear left at the Y junction and follow the orange trail. After crossing two stone walls, the orange trail descends to a wetland. This heavily forested area has not been actively cut since the early 1920s.

The orange trail ends at the junction with the yellow trail. Continue on the yellow trail, passing a spring, where box and snapping turtles can sometimes be seen. Generally wandering in a southwesterly direction, the yellow trail encounters a former farm road and turns right. Leave the yellow trail at the junction with the blue trail and ascend, via the blue trail, through large boulders to the top of the hill. After reaching a meadow, the blue trail skirts a corner and enters a new-growth wooded area. After crossing stone walls, it reaches another former

Cattail

farm road and ends at the junction with the yellow trail. The parking area is straight ahead.

A right turn on the yellow trail heads southeast, crossing a large meadow on the left and an overgrown one on the right. In early spring, woodcocks may be seen in their mating flights. Turning southwest, the yellow trail passes the stone foundations of the original farm site along the former farm road. The trail bends left alongside another meadow carpeted with wildflowers in the spring and summer. The blue trail, which was the route followed earlier on the hike, is on the right. Stay on the yellow trail, retracing your route between the blue and the orange trails. Once past one end of the orange trail, en route to the parking area, one will pass through some wet areas and ascend a hill on a meandering course through a mature forest.

To reach Northern Stony Brook Greenway, take US 202/NJ 31 south from Flemington to the jug handle turn for Wertsville Road (County 602) east and proceed 3.3 miles to Rileyville Road (County 607). Turn right, and in just under 2 miles, turn right again on Mountain Road. The parking area is on the left, 0.6 mile from the intersection. For more information, contact the Delaware and Raritan Greenway Project, 570 Mercer Road, Princeton, NJ 08540; (609) 924-4646.

Sourland Mountain Nature Preserve

The third edition of the *New York Walk Book,* published in 1951, suggested a walk on Sourland Mountain along country roads north of Hopewell. In 1998, those wishing to visit the area will find Sourland Mountain Nature Preserve an alternative to a six-mile road walk. Known as Pero Hill, this area was a source of large boulders which were crushed to obtain railroad ballast, concrete aggregate, and surfacing for road beds. From the small parking area, a one-mile woods road leads into the 273-acre hardwood forest. A loop off the trail provides some variation in the return route. Hunting is by permit only.

To reach the reservation, take US 202/NJ 31 south from Flemington to the jug handle turn for Wertsville Road (County 602) east and proceed 3.3 miles to Rileyville Road (County 607). Turn right and continue 1.9 miles to the park entrance on the left. Follow the gravel road straight ahead to the parking area. For more information, contact the Hunterdon County Park System, 1020 Highway 31, Lebanon, NJ 08833; (908) 782-1158.

Sourland Mountain Preserve

The largest of the three open spaces on Sourland Mountain is the over-2,000-acre Sourland Mountain Preserve, a Somerset County park. The preserve contains nested loop and connecting trails through a mature hardwood forest of primarily oak, beech, and tulip trees. Volunteers from the Sourland Regional Citizens Planning Council, Boy Scout Troop 46, and the federal Youth Conservation Corps built the trails.

The Pondside Trail (circle) is an easy 0.5-mile loop trail over level to gently sloping terrain. Another easy trail, the Maple Flats Trail (triangle), loops 1.1 miles further into the preserve. Rising and descending moderately to the ridge, the Ridge Trail (rectangle) covers 3.3 miles. An unmarked connecting trail shortcuts a portion of the Ridge Trail.

In dry season, when posted as appropriate, mountain bikes and horses can use the trails. The parking lot and trailhead are located on East Mountain Road, 0.6 mile south of NJ 514 (Amwell Road), off US 206 near Somerville. For more information, including a trail map, contact the Somerset County Park Commission, P.O. Box 5327, North Branch, NJ 08876; (908) 722-1200.

SOUTH BRANCH RESERVATION

Along the South Branch of the Raritan River are a series of Hunterdon County parks. Although each one has a unique name, such as Deer Path Park or Echo Hill, collectively they are administered as the South Branch Reservation. Some sections are picnic or fishing areas, while others offer walking opportunities. The Columbia Section is the most interesting to hikers. For more information, contact the Hunterdon County Park System, 1020 Highway 31, Lebanon, NJ 08833; (908) 782-1158.

Columbia Trail   *Length: 7 miles Blaze: unmarked*
Following the route of the former High Bridge Branch of the Central Railroad of New Jersey, the Columbia Trail parallels the South Branch of the Raritan River for

much of its length. To reach the trail in High Bridge, take I-78 to Exit 17 (Clinton), continue north on NJ 31, and turn right onto County 513. Public transportation is available to High Bridge via weekday commuter service on the NJ Transit Raritan Valley Line and entails a four-block walk from the station.

The trail begins at the Borough of Commons Public Parking on Main Street just north of the center of High Bridge. Although the trail is not officially open because of bridges that may be unsafe, walkers and cyclists nonetheless use the trail. With private property on both sides of the right-of-way, trail users are asked to stay on the path. The many access points have limited parking at most road crossings or places where local roads come close to the trail.

About 0.3 mile from the beginning of the trail, there is a waterfall visible on the right. The trail passes soon passes Lake Solitude (created by a dam) on the right and begins to parallel the South Branch of the Raritan River. At 1.0 mile, there is an active Boy Scout camp down a steep embankment on the right. Entering the Ken Lockwood Wildlife Management Area, large silver maples line the path before it reaches the High Bridge trestle at 3.0 miles. In 1998, the trestle is marked with "No Trespassing" signs.

The Columbia Trail crosses Hoffman's Crossing Road, reaching the former railroad station in Califon at 5.0 miles. Converted to a museum by the Califon Historical Society in 1970, the station is open on a very limited basis. The trail passes the Califon Fire Company buildings and ends, at 7.0 miles, at the junction of Vernoy and Valley Brook roads, where there is parking. County 513 is about 0.5 mile left on Vernoy Road. The trail north from the junction of Vernoy and Valley Brook roads into Morris County is part of the Highlands Trail (teal diamond). See Chapter 14, "Long Distance Trails," for a complete description of the trail in Morris County.

For more information about the Hunterdon County section, contact the Hunterdon County Park System, 1020 Highway 31, Lebanon, NJ 08833; (908) 782-1158. For information about the Morris County section, contact the Morris County Park Commission, P.O. Box 1295, Morristown, NJ 07962; (973) 326-7600.

SPRUCE RUN RECREATION AREA

Occupying a pair of peninsulas jutting into Spruce Run Reservoir, the 1,910-acre Spruce Run Recreation Area is typical of most of the day-use areas found in many of New Jersey's state parks and forests. A park office and visitor center await the visitor immediately upon entering the recreation area, a quick right off the entrance road. There is a seasonal parking fee for the beach area and bathhouse complex. Further down the peninsula is the overnight camping area, which is by permit only. Camping is permitted April 1 to October 31.

Like the Clinton Wildlife Management Area, which is adjacent to the recreation area and surrounds the rest of the reservoir, there are no marked trails, except that a segment of the Highlands Trail (teal diamond) is proposed. However, the hiker can ramble through the hardwood forest and explore the shoreline, with views to the south and west across the reservoir. Birders like the area, as the diverse habitat attracts a wide variety of migratory waterfowl.

To reach Spruce Run Recreation Area, take I-78 to Exit 17 (Clinton), and go north on NJ 31 for 3.5 miles to the traffic light at Van Syckles Road. Make a left at the light and follow signs to Spruce Run Recreation Area. The entrance is 1.4 miles ahead on the left. For more information, contact Spruce Run Recreation Area, 1 Van Syckles Road, Clinton, NJ 08809-1053; (908) 638-8572.

TEETERTOWN RAVINE NATURE PRESERVE

Named after John Teeter, the builder of a nearby mill complex (c. 1810), the 147-acre Teertertown Ravine Nature Preserve is one of the most significant natural areas in Hunterdon County. A narrow dirt road surrounded by dense woods leads into a ravine along a twisting stream, with its waters cascading over rocks. The steep sides of the ravine, with its large boulders and rock outcroppings, contribute to the sense of solitude. Several varieties of ferns are under the mature tulip, black birch, maple, beech, and oak trees. Evidence of a lime kiln and iron forge have been found in the area. Within the preserve are areas that were quarried around 1900. Teeter's house and mill are a private residence. The three blazed trails in the preserve are open to hiking, mountain biking, horseback riding, and cross-country skiing.

To reach Teetertown Ravine Nature Preserve, take NJ 31 to High Bridge and continue on County 513 north 6.8 miles to Sliker Road. In 1.8 miles, turn right on Teetertown Road, and in 0.9 mile turn left on Hollowbrook Road. The ravine is 0.1 mile from the junction. For more information, contact the Hunterdon County Park System, 1020 Highway 31, Lebanon, NJ 08833; (908) 782-1158.

UNION FORGE NATURE PRESERVE

Perched on a hillside overlooking Spruce Run Reservoir, this 95-acre Hunterdon County Park contains a hardwood forest of oak, ash, and maple that is predominant in the area. A segment of the Highlands Trail (teal diamond) will pass through the preserve; the remaining trails consist of overgrown woods roads that are not easily navigated due to the dense vegetation and hilly terrain. A compass and tick protection are a must when exploring this nature preserve.

To reach Union Forge Nature Preserve, take I-78 to Exit 17 (Clinton), and go north on NJ 31 for 3.5 miles to the traffic light at Van Syckles Road. Make a left at the light and park in the gravel parking area immediately on the left. Access to the nature preserve is across Van Syckles Road, on the north side, next to the "Union Forge Nature Preserve" sign. For more information, contact the Hunterdon County Park System, 1020 Highway 31, Lebanon, NJ 08833; (908) 782-1158.

UPLANDS RESERVE

The Uplands Reserve is an undeveloped 101-acre Hunterdon County park. Located on a hilltop just north of Flemington, it is the former estate of Judge Edward Large. The name Uplands refers to the geographic area on the eastern rim of the Hunterdon Plateau. The open fields and hardwood forest of the preserve offer wildlife observation and birding opportunities. As of 1998, there are only unmarked roads up the mountain and mowed swatches along the edges of former farm fields. At one point in the estate, a former road passes by old growth and stately oak trees.

The Reserve is reached either via trail from Morales Nature Preserve (see Flemington Greenbelt) or from the end of Altamont Road. From the center of Flemington, go north on North Main Street, which becomes Thatchers Hill Road (County 617), and then continue about 1 mile to Altamont Road on the left. For more information, contact the Hunterdon County Park System, 1020 Highway 31, Lebanon, NJ 08833; (908) 782-1158.

VOORHEES STATE PARK

Situated in the rolling hills of Hunterdon County, Voorhees State Park was the home of Foster M. Voorhees, a former governor of New Jersey. In 1929, he donated his 325-acre farm "Hill Acres" to become a state park. During the Great Depression, the Civilian Conservation Corps (CCC) developed the park's picnic sites, parking areas, roads, and trails. In 1998, it encompasses over 600 acres, with year-round camping facilities, an observatory, and five trails that meander along varying terrain through a mixed hardwood forest. A segment of the Highlands Trail (teal diamond) traverses the park.

To reach Voorhees State Park, take I-78 to Exit 17 (Clinton), go north on NJ 31 for 2.1 miles, then turn right on County 513, and go 1.2 miles to High Bridge. Continue north on County 513 for 2 miles to the park entrance on the left. Public transportation is available to High Bridge via weekday commuter service on the NJ Transit Raritan Valley Line and entails a two-mile road walk to the family campground. For more information, contact Voorhees State Park, 251 County Road 513, Glen Gardner, NJ 08826; (908) 638-6969.

WASHINGTON CROSSING STATE PARK

Established in 1912, Washington Crossing State Park is the site where the Continental Army landed after crossing the Delaware River on Christmas night 1776. Originally the park contained 100 acres, but it has grown to 900, of which 500 were purchased through the Green Acres program. A portion of the park is a 140-acre natural area which contains fields in various stages of secondary succession and a mixed hardwood forest. With 13 miles of hiking trails, there are plenty of places to walk in the park. In winter, when conditions are favorable, these trails may be used for cross-country skiing or snowshoeing.

Other facilities in the park are a visitor center, interpretive center, Ferry House, open-air theater, picnic grove, and group campsites.

To reach the park, take NJ 29 north from Trenton to County 546. A right turn onto County 546 leads to the park entrance and Visitor Center. A left turn onto County 546 and then a right onto River Road leads to parking lots near the approximate site of the crossing. There is a seasonal entrance fee. For more information, contact Washington Crossing State Park, 355 Washington Crossing/Penn Road, Titusville, NJ 08560; (609) 737-0623.

WOODFIELD RESERVATION

This 100-acre reservation near Princeton is owned by Princeton Township. Approximately half of the reservation was made available for public use by Mrs. John P. Poe in 1964 and subsequently purchased by the township in 1997. It is a mix of dry hardwood forest and wetland. There is a full understory of shrubs, ferns, and wildflowers. The woods are home to a wide range of birds and attract migrant songbirds. The two unmarked hiking trails cross small streams to reach Council Rock, which overlooks a boulder basin, and Tent Rock, a large boulder. These boulders are the result of weathering and erosion, and were not deposited by glaciers.

To reach Woodfield Reservation from the junction of US 206 and NJ 27 in Princeton, go south on US 206 and turn right at the traffic light at Elm Street. At 0.6 mile, the name changes to The Great Road. Bear right at the Y junction onto Old Great Road. The parking area, with a trail map, is across from the Tenacre Foundation. A gravel drive leads to the parking area. For more information, contact Princeton Township at (609) 921-7077.

THIRTEEN

THE PINE BARRENS

ascinating and forbidding
are ways to describe the strange, wild beauty of the New Jersey Pine Barrens. A
unique block of wilderness close to the urban areas of New York and Philadelphia, the region is a broad expanse of relatively level land covering approximately 1.7 million acres. Roughly eighty miles long and thirty miles wide, it
lies on the coastal plain and extends into nine counties in southern New Jersey.
The region is entirely unglaciated, with few hills and no rock outcroppings.

A person flying over this area or driving its long straight highways is likely
to think of the Pine Barrens as wasteland. Pine forests, sometimes scorched or
scrubby, cover vast sandy stretches with little sign of habitation, crops, or livestock. But this remarkable physiographic and biologic province is far from
being botanically barren. Temperature maps for the winter and spring months
show that it has a climate nearly as mild as that of Virginia and the Carolinas,
200 to 400 miles farther south.

This wild and primitive region claimed the attention of early naturalists
and became especially well known for unusual plants. To botanists, the Pine
Barrens or Pinelands, as they are also known, are a natural wilderness recov-
ered from its early clear-cutting by lumbermen and charcoal burners. A number
of areas have become major botanical meccas, and many have historical and senti-
mental value as well. The combination of natural history and human interest associated with these places gives them an intellectual aura and educational value that

has demanded preservation.

Underlying the whole region beneath the mats of vegetation and layers of sand are great aquifers. This tremendous water resource, estimated at more than seventeen trillion gallons, influenced Joseph Wharton (industrialist and founder of the Wharton School of Finance and Commerce at the University of Pennsylvania) to acquire nearly 100,000 acres in the late 1800s. Wharton estimated that the water from his holdings would furnish nearby cities with up to 300 million gallons daily. In 1905, however, New Jersey passed a law that gave the state control of the export of its waters, and Wharton could not carry out his plan. Subsequent laws have replaced the 1905 law, but the state retains control over its waters, and a 1981 law specifically restricts removal of water from the Pinelands.

The trend has been for slow, but continuous, development which has eaten away at the edge of the Pine Barrens. Uncontrolled development could have a negative effect not only on the surface environment, but also on the quality and yield of the aquifer beneath the Pinelands, the largest potential source of fresh water in the state. The disturbance that would be caused by industry, housing developments, and highways is incalculable.

Fortunately, legislation has recognized the value of the Pine Barrens and has attempted to control development of the area. In 1978, the federal government established the Pinelands National Reserve and called for the State of New Jersey to adopt a comprehensive plan for the region. In 1979, New Jersey adopted the Pinelands Protection Act, which specified a framework for the plan. The Pine Barrens are divided into seven management areas, each accommodating a particular class of land use: Preservation Area, Protection Area, Agricultural Production Area, Rural Development Area, Regional Growth Area, Pinelands Towns, and Military and Federal Installations.

The two largest management areas are the Preservation Area and the Protection Area. The Preservation Area, covering about 370,000 acres in the heart of the Pine Barrens, preserves a large, contiguous tract of land in its natural state and promotes compatible agricultural, horticultural, and recreational uses. The Protection Area, covering about 790,000 acres extending through much of the state east and south of the Preservation Area, preserves the essential character of the existing Pinelands environment, while accommodating needed development in an orderly way. Preserved open space in the Pine Barrens includes state forests and parks, county parks, wildlife management areas, natural areas, and wild river areas, all of which are managed in accordance with the uses for each area.

Other statutes regulating the Pine Barrens continue to move through the state and federal legislatures. However, not all of the laws are favorable. It is too much to hope that the Pine Barrens are safe from all unwise exploitation. Yet an awareness of their great value offers hope that the essential character of the Pine Barrens can be preserved and protected.

Human activities in the Pinelands are generally in keeping with the area's natural aspect and condition. Forest management practices, such as selective harvesting of timber in special plots, experimental planting, and controlled burning to combat wildfire and maintain the dominance of the pines, have little effect on the Pine Barrens as a whole. The culture of cranberries and blueberries contributes to the appeal of the area, which has been used for berry growing for almost 100 years.

Hikers, canoeists, campers, hunters, fishermen, birders, nature students, history buffs, and solitude seekers can find opportunities to pursue their interests. Some sites offer opportunities to glimpse life in the Pinelands, visit nature centers, or walk along bogs. Other places are for sportsmen and, as such, are managed for hunting or fishing. The wildlife management areas (WMA) often have multiple access points, such as the numerous sand roads which lead off of paved country roads. With no main entry point, the diamond shaped WMA signs posted along the roads are the easiest way to find the areas.

A bewildering web of sand roads interlaces the thousands of acres of forests and cedar swamps of the Pine Barrens. Every now and then along these roads, ghost towns appear with one or two structures—vague reminders of a flourishing past. Few of these routes are marked, but to the hiker who knows how to use a map and compass, there are many opportunities for exploration, ranging from a few hours to many days. The miles of marked trails are few in comparison with the miles of sand roads, and include the Batona Trail, short nature walks in the state parks, state forests, and wildlife management areas, and trail networks in Belleplain State Forest and Wells Mills County Park. The Batona Trail is the longest hiking trail, running 49.5 miles through Lebanon, Wharton, and Bass River state forests.

With many rivers in the area, it is not surprising that there are ample opportunities for canoeing. The principal streams are several branches of Rancocas Creek, the Great Egg Harbor, Toms, and Metedeconk rivers, Westecunck, Oyster, and Cedar creeks, and the Mullica River and its tributaries (Wading, Bass, and Batsto rivers, and Nescochague and Landing creeks). The Oswego River and Tulpehocken Creek flow into the Wading River. The popular canoe routes are on the bigger streams, with stretches of the Oswego, Wading, Batsto, and Mullica rivers being most frequently used. A number of campsites are available to canoeists and hikers on the major streams and hiking trails.

History

The first white people to enter the Pinelands of southern New Jersey undoubtedly followed the trails of the Lenni Lenape that led to the shell fisheries on the coast. The peculiar wildness of the region, empty of human life, must have impressed these early explorers, accustomed to the massive deciduous forest and the grass meadows of the uplands, and the river valleys and coastal marshes where an occasional Native American village could be found. Although these trails through the pines represented a long day's journey, there is no evidence of any permanent Native American camp or village within the area. The Native Americans apparently held the deep Pinelands in a certain awe and avoided them as much as possible.

From the earliest Colonial period, the people of New Jersey have used the region for whatever profitable ventures it afforded. First to move in were the loggers, who clear-cut the forests. Pine and cedar lumber moved steadily to shipyards and nearby towns for years before, during, and after the Revolution. Roads to the coastal communities followed the loggers and charcoal burners, and hostelries were established at a number of places along the sand roads. Bog iron was discovered in the Pine Barrens, and forges and furnaces were built on the major streams and their tributaries. Iron proved a fairly profitable venture for a generation or so, but the bog iron works were forced to rely on iron ore of uncertain quality and charcoal of limited availability for fueling their forges. Shortly after the mid-nineteenth century, the Jersey iron industry practically disappeared, overwhelmed by competition from the Pennsylvania furnaces, with their superior ore and coal fuel.

Glassmaking, using the fine silica sands of certain areas, followed the iron era and flourished for a time. A few large glassworks still prosper on the southern edge of the Pine Barrens, around Glassboro. Paper mills were built on several of the streams, with salt hay used for fiber, but they, too, were short-lived. The ruins of a paper mill and its community can be seen at Harrisville.

The gathering and drying of sphagnum moss for sale to nurseries and for packing and insulating is an industry that has disappeared in many sections. In former days, local inhabitants augmented the family income by gathering laurel, mistletoe, arbutus, and medicinal herbs for sale in Philadelphia and other cities. In a few localities, as in the vicinity of Tabernacle and Indian Mills, considerable truck farming still exists.

By the start of the twentieth century, extensive acreage of cut-over white cedar swamps had been cleared for cranberry growing, while large tracts of

drier ground were used for blueberry production, continuing to the present day. Cranberrying has expanded to some extent. Construction of dikes allowed blueberry fields to be converted to cranberry bogs. These two industries are the only substantial and profitable ones active in the Pinelands.

Aside from the berry growing, the Pine Barrens have been put to little productive or consumptive use. Both individuals and land promoters made many attempts to settle the area with homes and farms. Most were complete failures, resulting in property abandonment, tax sales, removal of names from assessment lists, selling and reselling, subdividing, and a general confusion of ownership. Clear titles were often difficult to obtain. The land appeared worthless to many hopeful owners, and the attempt to populate the uninhabited Pinelands slowed to a halt. In the 1990s, retirement villages have been built, increasing the population, and providing jobs which help the local economy.

Where the ironworks once stood, nature has practically obliterated all traces of once-busy communities. Ghost towns dot the Pine Barrens, with only the remains of a structure or two, as vague reminders of the places where people once lived and worked. A number of the ponds that were built to power saw-mills and gristmills and to furnish water for other purposes still remain. The shores of these ponds, such as the ones at Harrisville and Martha, provide fertile grounds for Pine Barrens flora. Likewise, abandoned cranberry bogs and old clearings have become ideal propagation grounds for the characteristic growth of the Pinelands.

Natural History

The unusual soil and water acidity and large areas of sand have truly made the New Jersey Pine Barrens an "island" habitat for several species of plant and animal life not found in other parts of the state. As an outdoor laboratory and museum for biologists and ecologists, the Pinelands have no equal in the state. Approximately 30 percent of the land in New Jersey is part of the Pine Barrens.

The vegetation, in general, is the flora that has occupied this area since prehistoric days. Existing essentially as it did in its original state, it provides rare opportunities for plant research. Some sites are in the protected state lands within the Pine Barrens, but there are other sites of equal ecological significance, currently privately owned, that should be protected from disturbance. The pine and oak areas are among the last of these biologically important types. Ecologists look to the Pine Barrens, with its oak interludes, as a significant segment of a continent-wide biological reserve.

The white sandy soil of the Pine Barrens, developed on what is known to geologists as the Cohansey formation, is largely infertile. With the exception of blueberry and cranberry culture and isolated truck farms, it is not suited to commercial agriculture. The natural forest covering the bulk of the region is predominantly pitch pine, with scattered stands of shortleaf pine. In no other region in North America is the pitch pine the dominant tree over such an extended area. Oaks of several species are common where the pines have been removed, and oak becomes the climax type where firmly established. In the swamps and along the streams, southern white cedar, swamp magnolia, and sweet magnolia are common, with sour gum, red maple, and gray birch on somewhat drier soils nearby.

The forest understory and thicket consist of a variety of woody shrubs and sub-shrubs such as blueberries, huckleberries, sweet pepperbush, buttonbush, winterberries, chokeberries, poison sumac, shadbush, greenbriers, and Virginia creeper. There is also an abundance of sweet fern, sand myrtle, sheep laurel, *hudsonia*, bearberries, viburnum, and azalea. Well over a hundred species of herbaceous plants, some exceedingly rare, are found in the bogs, wooded swamps, and dry woods, and along the roadsides. In areas of fire-ravaged woodland, the underbrush is often very dense and furnishes protection for the young pitch pines that sprout profusely from the burnt stumps of the parent trees.

The cranberry bogs were established in cut-over cedar swamps. Where cranberry growing has been abandoned, the bogs have gradually changed to savannah types, with grasses, other herbaceous plants, and seedling deciduous trees and shrubs moving in. Where conditions have been favorable, a few pines have entered the bog edges.

The white cedar swamps still in existence approach their primeval condition and appearance in every way, except in size of trees. The straight trunks of the southern, or Atlantic, white cedar grow in thick stands, rising from the soggy ground where their buttress roots are matted with sphagnum mosses. Shade-tolerant ferns, vines, and shrubs thrive in the dark and humid surroundings, and a few moisture-loving flowers find a home in the brandy-colored cedar water. The mossy hummocks and fallen logs also carry their little colorful gardens of interesting plant life. There is little animal life in these gloomy but intriguing morasses. A few birds call, and the occasional track of a raccoon or fox may be found.

In the east-central part of the region, north and northeast of Bass River State Forest and Penn State Forest, there is a tract of about 15,000 acres popularly known as the Plains. This tract supports a growth of unusually scrubby oak and pine that scarcely reaches an average height of 4 feet. Scientists have published several theories accounting for this stunted forest, the consensus pointing to a combination of factors: fires, infertility, exposure, and aridity. Yet a fairly heavy ground cover, mostly heath types, with a generous mixture of herbaceous plants, grows under the trees. Typical of Plains flora are carpets of the Conrad crowberry and the bearberry, both reminiscent of the cold barrens of the North. In spite of repeated fires that have swept the Plains since before white settlement, an interesting variety of plant life continues to thrive there.

Where underbrush furnishes browse and protection and the savannahs support desirable grasses, white-tailed deer are plentiful. The local herds do not seem to have been reduced to any appreciable extent by the heavy hunting. Deer may be seen on almost any excursion into the woods. Other mammals in the area include gray fox, skunk, raccoon, rabbit, beaver, opossum, muskrat, and otter. Smaller mammals include mink, weasel, a few species of mice, red squirrel, gray squirrel, common mole, shrews, and little brown bats. More than 80 species of birds are known to breed in the Pine Barrens.

There are thirteen types of frogs and toads, nine types of salamanders, three varieties of lizards, eighteen kinds of snakes, and ten species of turtles that live in the Pine Barrens. Two of the frog species are rare: the Pine Barrens tree frog and the carpenter, or sphagnum, frog. The former has its principal habitat here, and is known elsewhere only in isolated colonies in the South. The carpenter frog lives in cool, mossy bogs in places other than New Jersey, but nowhere is it a common species. It is undoubtedly the peculiarly acid waters of the habitat that have localized these two amphibians.

Forest fires are a critical part of the ecology of the Pinelands because, without them, new growth cannot occur. The state's program of controlled burning utilizes controlled fire to clear forest underbrush that, if it were allowed to accumulate, could make wild fires much more dangerous. As part of its forest management program, the state maintains a network of fire-cuts—paths bulldozed through the underbrush every few hundred

Muskrat

feet. On days that are cool and not too dry, fires are set along roads and fire-cuts on the side from which the wind is coming. With these downwind barriers keeping it from running with the wind, the fire backs slowly into the wind, with flames only a few inches high, clearing out the debris on the forest floor but doing no damage to trees or larger shrubs. Winter is the best time to see these burns. Even when it is controlled, fire in the Pine Barrens is an eerie sight.

In April 1995, a massive forest fire burned over 20,000 acres in the Pine Barrens. The Garden State Parkway was closed because of the proximity of the fire and intense smoke, and nearby residents were evacuated. Fortunately, with modern firefighting techniques of back fires and bulldozed fire breaks, there were no lives lost. Evidence of the fire can be easily seen in the Greenwood Wildlife Management Area along County 539. Blackened trees reaching upward are reminders of how powerful a fire is. By 1998, the understory had returned, a confirmation of nature's power of regrowth.

BASS RIVER STATE FOREST

Bass River State Forest covers 25,434 acres to the southeast of the Wharton State Forest. Forest headquarters is at Lake Absegami, where there are also camping areas, a beach, cabins, shelters, and lean-tos for rent, and a short nature trail that traverses a cedar swamp.

Five loop walking trails vary in length from 1.0 to 3.3 miles. With map and compass, it is possible to hike any number of circular routes over the sand roads in the area. A circular hike of about ten miles to Munion Field and back leads through typical Pine Barrens forests, with stands of oak and cedar as well as pine, and passes through private lands where timber has been heavily harvested.

From northern New Jersey, take Exit 52 (New Gretna) of the Garden State Parkway and turn right onto County 654 (East Green Street), following the signs to Bass River State Forest. Bear right at the Y junction, and right at the stop sign onto Stage Road. The state forest headquarters is about a mile on the left. From southern New Jersey, take Exit 50 (New Gretna, US 9) of the Garden State Parkway to New Gretna and turn left onto County 679. After 1.5 miles, bear right onto County 654. At the junction with Stage Road, turn right and follow the signs to the campground. For more information, contact Bass River State Forest, P.O. Box 118, New Gretna, NJ 08224; (609) 296-1114.

BATONA TRAIL

Extending 49.5 miles through the heart of the Pine Barrens, the Batona Trail (pink) is the longest blazed hiking trail in southern New Jersey. It starts from Bass River State Forest and goes through Wharton State Forest and Lebanon State Forest to Ong's Hat on Buddtown Road, 1.5 miles northwest of Four Mile Circle. The trail was established in 1961 by the Batona (Back to Nature) Hiking Club of Philadelphia, and is still maintained by that group. To pierce the genuine wilderness of the area, the Batona Trail avoids the sand roads as much as possible. About 20 percent of the trail's treadway is soft sand, which makes for slower-than-expected progress in parts of this generally level trail.

Good starting points for trips on the trail are the Lebanon State Forest Headquarters and the Batsto Visitor Center. Permits, trail maps, and information may be obtained there, as well as at the Atsion Ranger Station and the Bass River Forest Office. Camping without a permit is illegal in the state forests. There are three campsites in an 18-mile stretch along the northern half of the trail. Paved roads cross the trail in a number of places, making possible a variety of trips. A New Jersey DEP map for the Batona Trail is available. For more information about the Batona Trail, contact either Wharton State Forest, RD #9, Hammondton, NJ 08037; (609)561-0024, or Lebanon State Forest, P.O. Box 215, New Lisbon, NJ 08064; (609)726-1191.

Batona Trail   *Length: 49.5 miles Blaze: pink*
The Batona Trail begins near the junction of Coal Road and Stage Road, near Lake Absegami, in the Bass River State Forest. It parallels Stage Road before turning north to cross Martha Road and Oswego Road. It loops around to return to Martha Road going west, which it follows to Martha Bridge at 6.7 miles, entering Wharton State Forest en route. It reaches County 679 at 8.0 miles and Evans Bridge on County 563 at 8.7 miles.

From the Evans Bridge parking area, which is also a take-out for canoe trips on the Wading River, the Batona Trail runs generally west, and at 9.2 miles reaches Batsto Village, the restored iron town where the headquarters of Wharton State Forest is located. Camping is possible at nearby Buttonwood Hill, which is not directly on the trail, but is accessible by car. From Batsto, the trail proceeds north, generally following the Batsto River and playing tag with Goodwater Road (a sand road) that also parallels the eastern bank of the stream. The trail passes Quaker Bridge 6.1 miles from Batsto, at a point where several sand roads converge to cross the river. From here, the trail follows a sand road for 0.1 mile, then veers northeast through the woods. At 7.1 miles from Batsto, an 0.2-mile spur heads north along the river to the Lower Forge Camp. This camp is also used on canoe trips on the Batsto River, and is not accessible by car.

Twelve miles from Batsto, the Batona Trail crosses railroad tracks to reach the Carranza Memorial, on Carranza Road, 0.2 mile west of the trail crossing. It is a monument to the Mexican pilot Emilio Carranza, whose plane crashed here in 1928 while he was returning to Mexico City after a goodwill flight to New York. Half a mile to the north is the Batona Camp, which can be crowded and noisy, since it is accessible by paved and sand roads. Leaving the camp, the trail turns eastward on the south side of Skit Branch and then crosses Skit Branch Stream about a mile farther on. The trail goes up and down over several hummocks, then reaches the fire tower on Apple Pie Hill, which is the highest point on the trail and provides a view over the Pine Barrens.

For the next 6 miles, the trail continues on a northeasterly course, generally on sand roads, crossing several paved roads before reaching NJ 72 and Lebanon State Forest. The Batona Trail turns northwest through the forest, generally paralleling NJ 72, past Pakim Pond and the site of the Lebanon Glass Works. The trail comes within 0.1 mile of forest headquarters, about 27 miles from Batsto. A mile later, Deep Hollow Pond is reached on the way to the trail's northernmost point at Carpenter Spring. The trail turns southwesterly, passing through some oak-pine forests. The Batona Trail ends at Ong's Hat on Buddtown Road (NJ 72), 40.3 miles from Batsto and 49.5 miles from the terminus at Stage Road in the Bass River State Forest.

BELLEPLAIN STATE FOREST

Located in the southern Pine Barrens, Belleplain State Forest contains over 13,000 acres of lowland hardwood swamps, former agricultural areas, stands of cedar, plantations of evergreens, and marshes. Established in 1928, the state forest is used for public recreation, timber production, wildlife management, and water conservation. In the 1930s, there were three Civilian Conservation Corps camps on the property. In addition to constructing the nature center and the maintenance buildings, the corps created much of the road system, bridges, and dams and improved vast tracts of fields and forest through silvicultural techniques.

Hunting, trapping, and fishing are permitted within the forest, subject to New Jersey's fish and game laws. Wildlife includes deer, grouse, squirrel, rabbit, raccoon, fox, and various waterfowl.

Motorized routes, multi-use trails, and the abandoned railroad bed of the former Pennsylvania-Reading Seashore Lines criss-cross the state forest. East Creek trail goes 6.5 miles around Lake Nummy, named in honor of the chief of the Kechemeches, the last to rule in the Cape May area. Pickle Pond Trail is about a mile long. There are two nature walks that are accessible to the disabled and approximately 10 miles of additional marked paths.

To reach Belleplain State Forest, take Exit 17 (Woodbine/Sea Isle City) off the Garden State Parkway. Bear right, then turn right onto US 9 for 0.6 mile. After a left turn onto County 550, go 6.3 miles to Woodbine, where County 550 makes a left and then a right. From here, it is 1.4 miles to the state forest, with the entrance road on the left. Once inside the state forest, turn right at the first intersection to reach Lake Nummy and the nature center. For more information, contact Belleplain State Forest, County Route 550, P.O. Box 450, Woodbine, NJ 08270; (609) 861-2404.

COLLIERS MILLS WILDLIFE MANAGEMENT AREA

Covering more than 12,000 acres, the Colliers Mills Wildlife Management Area is comprised of pitch pine and scrub oak forests, white cedar swamps, fields, impoundment lakes, and a few areas of deciduous forest. A main sand road leads past lakes, through the heart of the area, and exits on the other side. Other sand roads interlace the area, including some which restrict vehicles. The size of the wildlife management area invites exploration and solitude; however, in some areas, heavy greenbrier undergrowth prevents bushwhacking.

Colliers Mills Wildlife Management Area is a good place to hear the Pine Barrens tree frogs in the late spring and summer. Rabbits, squirrels, foxes, grouse, deer, mallards, black ducks, wood ducks, teals, and quail are the principal wildlife residents. Hunters heavily use the area in the fall hunting season, but a portion is set aside as a wildlife refuge.

To reach Colliers Mills Wildlife Management Area, take Exit 16A (Six Flags) of I-95 and turn right onto County 537. Go 3.4 miles and turn left on Hawkin Road. The office is on the left, with a main sand road into the area shortly after. Visitors to the area should obtain the Casswood and Lakehurst USGS topographic quadrangle maps. For more information, contact New Jersey DEP, Division of Fish, Game and Wildlife, P.O. Box 400, Trenton, NJ 08625; (609) 292-2965.

DOUBLE TROUBLE STATE PARK

Unfortunately, there is only speculation about how Double Trouble State Park was named. But it is not just an intriguing name that should draw visitors. Located a few miles south of Toms River, the 5,000-acre park is a captivating blend of natural and cultural history. Productive cranberry bogs, a sawmill, a 1.5-mile hiking trail, and a restored village are on what once was a thriving nineteenth century lumbering operation. Along the upper reaches of Cedar Creek is a typical white cedar swamp. A sawmill, pickers' cottages, a cranberry sorting and packing house, a general store, and a one-room schoolhouse built in 1890 are open to visitors.

To reach Double Trouble State Park from northern New Jersey, take Exit 80 of the Garden State Parkway. Turn left onto Double Trouble Road and drive to the end, where the park entrance is straight ahead. From southern New Jersey, take Exit 81 of the Garden State Parkway. Turn left at the end of the ramp onto the access road and then make an immediate left at the light to follow signs to Garden State Parkway south. Go back onto the parkway and follow the directions from Exit 80 above. For more information about the park, contact Double Trouble State Park, P.O. Box 175, Bayville, NJ 08721; (908) 341-6662.

GREENWOOD FOREST/PASADENA WILDLIFE MANAGEMENT AREA

The Greenwood Forest/Pasadena Wildlife Management Area stretches for miles along County 539 in Ocean County and its size offers days, not just hours, of exploration. The almost 28,000 acres contain forests of pitch pine and scrub oak in uplands areas and white cedar swamps in the lowlands. Its fields are managed for wildlife, with hedgerows and plantings of wildlife food and cover crops. In 1998, blackened trees are reminders of the April 1995 fire which swept through the Pinelands.

Sand roads lead into the vast interior. For those not wishing to venture too far, there is a boardwalk at Webb's Mill Bog Cedar Swamp for observation of native plants and animals. Sundew, St. Johnswort, cranberry, curly-grass fern, orchids, dwarf huckleberry, and leatherleaf grow on sphagnum moss hummocks. At slightly higher elevations, pine, clammy azalea, sheep laurel, inkberry, and swamp magnolias surround the bog. Uplands vegetation includes golden heather, sand myrtle, bearberry, scrub oak, and bayberry. The boardwalk is also an ideal place for viewing reptiles and amphibians. During late spring evenings, a chorus of Pine Barrens tree frogs may be heard.

To reach Greenwood Forest/Pasadena Wildlife Management Area, turn north at the intersection of NJ 72 and County 539. Sand roads leave from both sides of the road into the interior. To reach the boardwalk at Webb's Mill Branch, drive 6.5 miles from the intersection of NJ 72 and County 539 and park by the bridge, where the boardwalk is visible. Hikers wishing to explore the area should obtain the Keswick Grove, Whiting, Woodmansie, and Brookville USGS topographic quadrangle maps. For more information, contact New Jersey DEP, Division of Fish, Game and Wildlife, P.O. Box 400, Trenton, NJ 08625; (609) 292-2965.

LEBANON STATE FOREST

Lebanon State Forest covers 31,965 acres in the northern Pinelands and offers many days' worth of exploration. It is named for the Lebanon Glass Works that, between 1851 and 1867, was a thriving manufacturer of window glass and bottles. When the wood supply was exhausted, the industry collapsed, and the small town it supported was abandoned. The state began acquiring the property in 1908. Over the years, as the acreage expanded, so did the recreation opportunities. In 1998, the state forest has something for the most active or passive of outdoor enthusiasts, as there are opportunities to hike, camp, bicycle, bird, horseback ride, picnic, and swim. A handicapped accessible trail is near Pakim Pond.

There is no shortage of cedar swamps in Lebanon State Forest, and a portion of the state forest is designated the Cedar Swamp Natural Area. Tall Atlantic white cedar crowd together with dense vegetation at their base—orchids,

Lebanon Forest, near Glass Works

sundews, pitcher plants, and curly grass ferns. A portion of the Batona Trail (pink) goes through this area. Along the gravel road, it is accessible to the handicapped.

Within Lebanon State Forest is Whitesbog Village, an historic site open to the public. Here, at the turn of the twentieth century, J. J. White established a large cranberry plantation. Although also known as the place that cultivated the first successful blueberry crops, there is birding at Whitesbog, with over 200 species of birds. A chain of sand roads connects the 3,000 acres of bogs, fields, wetlands, and forests. The state leases portions of the state forest to commercial growers. Hunting is allowed, so users of the area should take precautions in the fall or visit the area on Sundays, when hunting is not permitted. An annual festival is held in June, with Pinelands bluegrass music, ecological tours, and blueberry and cranberry foods.

The Lebanon State Forest headquarters is a starting point for hikes that use the Batona Trail (pink). Directly across the road from the office, a blue-blazed trail leads 0.1 mile to a junction with the Batona Trail. In order not to miss the turn on the return trip, hikers should walk a few steps, turn, and then note what the intersection looks like. A right turn at the trail junction leads 4.0 miles northwest to the terminus of the Batona Trail at Ong's Hat on Buddtown Road and passes stands of pine, oak, and cedar. A left turn at the intersection leads, in about three miles, to Pakim Pond, with picnic tables, camping facilities, swimming, and guided nature walks. There is a cedar swamp just on the other side of the dam. An alternative is to start hikes at Pakim Pond, named for the Lenape word for cranberry.

To reach the office at Lebanon State Forest, take Exit 88 (NJ 70 west) of the Garden State Parkway to NJ 70. Follow NJ 70 to Four Mile Circle (the junction of NJ 70 and NJ 72) and take NJ 72 east. At the one-mile marker, turn left, and take the first right. The office is on the left. To reach Pakim Pond from Four Mile Circle, take NJ 72 east and turn left onto Buzzard Hill Road at the three-mile marker, cross Shinns Road, and go 0.5 mile to the picnic facilities at Pakim Pond.

To reach Whitesbog Village, take Exit 88 (NJ 70 west) of the Garden State Parkway. Follow NJ 70 west and turn right onto County 530. At just one mile, turn onto the paved portion of Whitesbog Road and follow the road a short distance to the town of Whitesbog. For birding, turn right at the stop sign and stay to the right as you go through the town until you reach a large reservoir on the left and cranberry bogs on the right. This area offers the best birding opportunities. Visitors to Lebanon State Forest who wish to use the sand roads should obtain the Browns Mills, Chatsworth, Whiting, and Woodmansie USGS topographic quadrangle maps or the New Jersey DEP Lebanon State Forest map. For more information, contact Lebanon State Forest, P.O. Box 215, New Lisbon, NJ 08318; (609) 726-1191.

MANCHESTER WILDLIFE MANAGEMENT AREA

Located in Ocean County, the Manchester Wildlife Management Area contains 2,376 acres, which include white cedar swamps. The uplands of pitch pine and scrub oak provide habitat for deer, grouse, rabbit, and quail. Even though the area is rimmed with private homes, once away on the sand roads, there is only a hint or two of human intrusion. In spring and summer, the beauty of bog flowers and the fragrance of sun-warmed pines and cedars is apparent. Autumn brings a colorful palette, while winter offers a stark, and sometimes snow-streaked loneliness.

To reach the Manchester Wildlife Management Area, take NJ 70 to the junction with either Beckertown Road or County 539 and turn north. Sand roads lead off the paved roads into the interior. Private properties line the edges of the paved roads, so hikers should take care not to trespass. Hikers wishing to use the area should obtain the Cassville, Keswick Grove, and Whiting USGS topographic quadrangle maps. For more information, contact New Jersey DEP, Division of Fish, Game and Wildlife, P.O. Box 400, Trenton, NJ 08625; (609) 292-2965.

PENN STATE FOREST

A prime attraction of the 3,366-acre Penn State Forest is Oswego Lake, whose water, because of the iron and the cedar in the Pine Barrens, is the color of tea. Stretching out northeast from the lake, the forest is interlaced with sand roads that can be hiked in many combinations. In the center of the forest is Bear Swamp Hill, where there is parking and the foundation of a fire tower that was knocked down in an airplane crash in 1971.

In Penn State Forest, as in other sections in the Pine Barrens, activity by military aircraft is quite noticeable. Fort Dix, McGuire Air Force Base, and Lakehurst Naval Air Station form a huge presence in the northern part of the Pine Barrens. About four miles east of Oswego Lake is the U.S. Navy Target Area at Warren Grove, and it is common in the Pine Barrens to see fighters and bombers practice here. The area around the target installation, just west of County 539, is one of the best places to see the Plains, the bizarre pygmy forests in which full-grown trees are less than 4 feet tall.

To reach Penn State Forest, take County 563 and turn east onto Chatsworth-New Gretna Road for 3.2 miles to Lake Oswego. This intersection is 1.4 miles north of the junction with County 679. The parking area is on the right, just over the bridge. Visitors to Penn State Forest should obtain the Oswego and Woodmansie USGS topographic quadrangle maps or the New Jersey DEP Penn State Forest map. For more information, contact Penn State Forest, P.O. Box 118, New Gretna, NJ 08224; (609) 296-1114.

RANCOCAS STATE PARK

Located on the western edge of the Pine Barrens, the 1,249-acre Rancocas State Park is a mix of extensive lowlands, upland forest, overgrown fields, and freshwater streams and marshes. The New Jersey Audubon Society operates the Rancocas Nature Center, which is housed in a 130-year-old farm house. The center and 120 acres are leased from the state of New Jersey.

Mowed trails cross the fields, providing chances to view a variety of plants, some of which were introduced by early European settlers. Self-guided nature trails inform visitors about Inner Coastal Plain vegetation. Wildlife in the area includes house wrens, chickadees, tree swallows, a variety of ducks, gray squirrels, red squirrels, raccoons, and an occasional great horned owl.

To reach Rancocas State Park, take Exit 44A from I-295, and go east on Rancocas Road for 1.5 miles to the Rancocas Nature Center entrance on the right-hand side of the road. For more information about the nature center, contact Rancocas Nature Center, 794 Rancocas Road, Mt. Holly, NJ 08060; (609) 261-2495. For information about the state park, contact Lebanon State Forest, P.O. Box 215, New Lisbon, NJ 08318; (609) 726-1191.

STAFFORD FORGE WILDLIFE MANAGEMENT AREA

Easily reached via the Garden State Parkway, the 7,288-acre Stafford Forge Wildlife Management Area is used by hikers, birders, hunters, and fishermen. Access is via sand roads, some of which go the length of the wildlife management area. Dense underbrush and pitch pines make bushwhacking through some of the terrain extremely difficult. Both birds and birders alike find the series of four ponds along dammed Westecunk Creek attractive. Sand roads go along both sides of the southernmost and largest pond. It is possible to cross the dikes between the ponds on foot. There are numerous sand roads leading away from the ponds.

Wildlife found in the area include deer, rabbit, quail, bobwhite, tundra swan, purple martin, and wood duck. Hunters frequent the area in the fall, so hikers should take precautions during that season or visit the area on Sundays, when hunting is prohibited.

To reach Stafford Forge Wildlife Management Area, take Exit 58 (Tuckerton/Warren Grove) of the Garden State Parkway and turn right onto County 539. Proceed 0.3 mile and turn right onto County 606 (Forge Road). The southernmost of the ponds is at 1.3 miles along the left side of Forge Road. Hikers wishing to use the area should ob-

Pitch pine

tain the West Creek and Oswego Lake USGS topographic quadrangle maps. For more information, contact New Jersey DEP, Division of Fish, Game and Wildlife, P.O. Box 400, Trenton, NJ 08625; (609) 292-2965.

WELLS MILLS COUNTY PARK

The land in what is now Wells Mills County Park has had a productive past. The abundance of Atlantic white cedar on the property prompted James Wells, in the latter part of the eighteenth century, to build a sawmill and dam Oyster Creek for water power. Cedar is a strong, rot-resistant wood, a characteristic that the ship and boat industry sought. Shipments of lumber milled at the site reached ports along the Atlantic coast. The mill passed through several owners and was eventually purchased by Christopher Estlow and his sons. It was Tilden Estlow, a grandson, who added moss gathering, shingle making, lumbering, and clay gathering to the site's products. The clay was hauled to a Trenton factory where it was made into pottery and china. The site was purchased for private recreational purposes in 1936 and eventually, in the late 1970s, became public open space.

In 1998, the 810-acre park offers a nature center, observation deck, canoe rental, and fishing on the mill pond. Ten miles of marked trails lead visitors through pine-oak forests, Atlantic white cedar swamps, freshwater bogs, and maple gum swamps. Trails in the park include those designated for tree identification, nature, mountain bikes, and the visually impaired. Mountain bikes are permitted only on the trail designated for that use. A portion of three co-aligned trails leads briefly into an adjacent Girl Scout Camp, and users are asked to stay on the trail. A trail map is available at the information kiosk and the visitors center.

From northern New Jersey, take Exit 67 of the Garden State Parkway and go west on County 554 to NJ 72. Stay on NJ 72 west briefly and make the next right turn, following signs. The park is on the right at 2.5 miles. From southern New Jersey, take Exit 69 of the Garden State Parkway and go west on County 532. Park signs are on the left after about 1.5 miles. For more information, contact Wells Mills County Park, Box 905, Wells Mills Road, Waretown, NJ 08758; (609) 971-3085.

WHARTON STATE FOREST

Located in heart of the Pine Barrens, Wharton State Forest is well known as a canoeist's paradise with narrow, twisting streams gently flowing through the cedar, pine, and oak forests. For those who prefer to explore drier routes, there is a network of 500 miles of sand roads and trails in the 109,771-acre tract, enough mileage to keep a hiker busy for weeks. The central part of the forest is farther from a paved road than any other place in New Jersey. The state forest is the largest tract of public land administered by the State of New Jersey.

What is now Wharton State Forest once played an important role in the industrial development of the United States. Bog ore and the ready supply of trees and water resulted in the building of iron furnaces and sawmills. Between 1766 and 1876, the business and property were sold many times. The last owner was Joseph Wharton who, before he died in 1909, purchased more land, established a cranberry industry, and tried unsuccessfully to divert the water supply to Camden and Philadelphia. In 1954-55, the state purchased the forest as recreation and watershed lands. Aside from the recreation facilities at Batsto and Atsion, the property has remained undeveloped. Within the state forest are Batsto and Oswego River natural areas, and Batsto and Whitesbog villages.

A principal community of the iron days, Batsto Village was established in 1765, a few miles from the salt reaches of the lower Mullica River. Although fire and neglect have left their destructive marks, the core of the village has remained. Protection and restoration by the state have resulted in an authentic early Pine Barrens village. Some of the 33 historic buildings and structures are open to visitors: the "big house" where the master lived, several workers' cottages, the general store and post office, a sawmill, a gristmill, and a number of other old buildings.

Batsto Village is located is located on County 542 at the southern edge of Wharton State Forest. The visitor center has maps and books for sale, including books on the history of Batsto and the other iron towns in the area. A two-mile nature trail offers a glimpse of pitcher plants, sphagnum moss, and British soldiers (a lichen with a red head). Nearby, the Batona Trail (pink) can be combined with sand roads for a variety of hikes.

A 12-mile circular hike from Batsto Village begins by following village trails up the east side of Batsto Lake. A few short spurs dead-end at the lake, with views of the lake. The lake becomes shallower toward the north, more filled with grasses and trees, grading off at the sides into cedar swamp. Along here are dozens of tree stumps left by the beavers that live around the lake. The path runs along the shore of the lake, following a fire-cut and a sand road. After skirting the lake for its full length of about a mile, the path meets the

Batona Trail (pink), which comes from the south, having crossed Washington Pike at the fire tower a few hundred yards northeast of Batsto. The circular route continues on the Batona Trail (pink) for about 6 miles to a convergence of four sand roads into a single sand road that crosses the Batsto River on Quaker Bridge. This spot was the site of a tavern on the stage route from Philadelphia to Tuckerton. The route proceeds across the bridge and turns left on the first sand road on the west side of the Batsto River. It heads back south to Batsto Village.

Another hike from Batsto is to Atsion, about 10 miles northwest. Atsion is the site of another Pine Barrens iron town, with a manor house and several other buildings still standing, though none of the buildings are open to the public. Several routes over sand roads connect Atsion and Batsto, including the section of the Batona Trail between Batsto and Quaker Bridge. Atsion has an office, a campground, and cabins at Atsion Lake, and can be reached by car from US 206. The area between Atsion and Batsto is on the Atsion USGS topographic quadrangle map.

Hiking is also possible in the southeast area of Wharton State Forest, around

Evans Bridge on County 563. West of Evans Bridge, sand roads lead several miles to Washington, the site of a former Pine Barrens town, where a stone ruin stands in the middle of the woods. Southeast of Evans Bridge are the ruins of Harrisville on the Oswego River, where a paper mill once stood, and a little farther upriver is the site of Martha, an iron town of which almost no traces remain. A variety of plants grow near the ponds at Harrisville and Martha.

There are many access points to Wharton State Forest. To reach Batsto, follow the signs from Exit 52 of the Garden State Parkway. Access to Evans Bridge is via County 563, where there is parking at Evans Bridge, or from County 679, where there is room for several cars to park along the road at Harrisville. Hikers wishing to use the area should obtain the Atsion, Chatsworth, Greenbank, Hammonton, Indian Mills, Jenkins, or Medford Lakes USGS topographic quadrangle maps. The New Jersey DEP Wharton State Forest map is available at the park office. For more information, contact Wharton State Forest, Batsto, RD #9, Hammonton, NJ 08037; (609) 561-0024.

WHITING WILDLIFE MANAGEMENT AREA

Tucked behind retirement villages, the Whiting Wildlife Management Area contains 1,200 acres of protected open space. The sand road leading from the entrance has numerous sand roads branching off from it to nooks and crannies that harbor a variety of wildlife. Some areas are managed as open fields, while others are mixed forest of pine, oak, and blueberry. A short distance into the property, there is a sense of isolation, as the dense vegetation muffles the nearby sounds of civilization.

To reach the Whiting Wildlife Management Area, take NJ 70 west past Lakehurst to the traffic light at Manchester Road. Turn left and go 0.6 mile to Wrangle Brook Road. The wildlife management area is one mile on the left at a sharp turn in the road. Hikers wishing to use the area should obtain the Keswick Grove USGS topographic quadrangle map. For more information, contact New Jersey DEP, Division of Fish, Game and Wildlife, P.O. Box 400, Trenton, NJ 08625; (609) 292-2965.

FOURTEEN

LONG DISTANCE TRAILS

ost trails that cannot be walked comfortably from end to end in one day are considered long distance trails. These trails, which span multiple chapters within this book or the *New York Walk Book*, can be completed by hiking one section at a time or by backpacking several sections in a longer hike. Hikers need to plan for transportation at the end point. Alternatively, hikers can cover a segment of the trail and then hike back to the starting point the same way they came or on a different trail, if one is available.

The New York area boasts two premier long distance trails—the Appalachian Trail and the Long Path. Both trails have separate guidebooks, so only selected sections are described here. As of 1998, another long distance trail is growing. Ninety-five miles of the Highlands Trail are open and blazed. Eventually, it will go from Storm King Mountain on the Hudson River to the Delaware River. Long distance trails that are contained within a single region are described in the relevant chapter of this book. The Batona Trail is an example.

APPALACHIAN NATIONAL SCENIC TRAIL

The Appalachian Trail, known by hikers as the AT, runs from Springer Mountain in Georgia to Mount Katahdin in Maine, a distance of about 2,150 miles. In the New York area, it runs from the Delaware Water Gap to Connecticut. In general, it follows the spine of the Appalachian Mountains and seemingly goes over every mountain along the way.

Benton MacKaye, a regional planner, first proposed the trail in the *Journal of the American Institute of Architects* in 1921, in an article entitled "An Appalachian Trail: A Project in Regional Planning." He foresaw the large concentration of an urban population along the east coast and their need to retreat to nature for spiritual renewal.

The first section of the Appalachian Trail was built by volunteers from the New York-New Jersey Trail Conference in 1922-23, from the Bear Mountain Bridge to the Ramapo River south of Arden in Bear Mountain-Harriman State Parks. The following year they completed the section from Arden to Greenwood Lake. The entire trail from Georgia to Maine was completed in 1937;

however, much of it was on private land and subject to interruptions as landowners changed. In 1968 Congress passed the National Trails System Act, which designated the Appalachian Trail and the Pacific Crest Trail as the first official National Scenic Trails. As of 1998, there are twenty National Scenic and Historic Trails. Additional provisions of the Act included assigning responsibility for the National Scenic Trails to the National Park Service and the U.S. Forest Service, acquiring rights-of-way for the trail where it is outside federal or state lands, and protecting the trails from incompatible uses—specifically, limiting the Appalachian Trail to primarily foot traffic. Funding for land purchases first became available through amendments to the Act in 1978. In 1982, New Jersey became the first state to acquire a complete corridor on protected lands.

In 1984, the U.S. Department of the Interior signed an agreement with the Appalachian Trail Conference (formed in 1925) to manage the trail and the newly purchased corridor. The Appalachian Trail Conference delegates its responsibilities to trail clubs along the length of the trail. In this area, the New York-New Jersey Trail Conference has responsibility for the 162 miles in New York and New Jersey. This cooperative agreement among national, state, and local governments and volunteers serves as a model for efficient use of resources in an era of declining budgets. In 1998, only 33 miles of trail remain unprotected, with the year 2000 the target date for protecting the whole trail.

Every year, several hundred people *thru-hike* the Appalachian Trail—that is, they hike it continuously from end to end—generally taking from five to seven months to complete it. Many other people complete the trail over several years or decades, doing it a section at a time.

The *Appalachian Trail Guide to New York-New Jersey* and similar guides for other states describe the trail in great detail, with comments about trail features every few tenths of a mile. These guides are revised every three to five years. The *Appalachian Trail Data Book*, published by the Appalachian Trail Conference, is revised yearly and covers the whole trail in less than a hundred pages. It lists only major features along the trail, such as road crossings, shelters, rivers, and mountain tops. The trail is uniformly marked with a 2"x 6" white-painted, vertical blaze. Most major road crossings are well marked, and the basic trail route appears even on most commercial road maps, although not always accurately.

Hikes along the Appalachian Trail in New Jersey

From the Delaware Water Gap, where the Appalachian Trail crosses the Delaware River from Pennsylvania, the Appalachian Trail proceeds north along the Kittatinny Ridge, paralleling the Delaware River. At High Point State Park it turns east and follows the New York-New Jersey line to a ridge above Greenwood Lake, where it enters New York. The entire New Jersey section is 74 miles long. The following five hikes are typical of the area. See the *Appalachian Trail Guide to New York-New Jersey* for more details about the AT in New Jersey.

Sunfish Pond
Length: 9 miles Blazes: various

The hike along the AT to Sunfish Pond covers one of the most heavily used portions of the entire AT. To avoid crowds, start hiking in the early morning hours on weekends, or hike on a weekday.

Sunfish Pond is a gem of a glacial lake that was a rallying point in the 1960s and 1970s for the environmental movement. Repeated pilgrimages to the pond saved it from almost-certain destruction by New Jersey's public utilities. The fight to save Sunfish Pond also led to the eventual deauthorization of the Tocks Island Dam project and the preservation of the Delaware as a National Wild and Scenic River. Now beavers reside here.

The hike begins at the Dunnfield Creek AT parking lot on I-80. The trail follows Dunnfield Creek uphill on a woods road, passing the Blue Dot (blue)

WEST PACHUNK MOUNTAIN SHAWANGUNK SLIDE SAN

springtime
hillside

Ver

and Dunnfield Creek (green) trails at 0.4 mile, where the AT takes the left fork. At 1.5 miles, the Beulahland Trail (yellow) begins on the left, while the un-marked Holly Springs Trail starts to the right. The Douglas Trail (blue) to the left is reached at 3.1 miles, at the junction with another woods road and the site of a backpacker campsite. The southern end of Sunfish Pond is reached at 3.7 miles. One may loop around the pond by taking the Sunfish Pond Fire Road to the right. After 0.5 mile, follow the Turquoise Trail to the left to return to the AT in 0.4 mile at the northern end of the pond. Turn left on the AT to walk along the boulder-lined western shore of Sunfish Pond and return to the parking area where the hike started.

Kittatinny Ridge *Length: 10.2 miles Blazes: various*
This challenging loop hike passes through a variety of ecosystems, and encoun-ters some fascinating man-made features. It begins on the Coppermines Trail (red). Parking is 7.8 miles north of I-80 on Old Mine Road. The trail ascends steeply along a hemlock ravine to the top of Kittatinny Ridge (an 800-foot gain in elevation). Hikers should take time along the way to explore the various entrances to nineteenth-century copper mines. These mines yielded little cop-per but were a highly effective scheme to fleece naive investors of their cash. At 1.6 miles, the Coppermines Trail reaches the AT. Take it left (north) along the

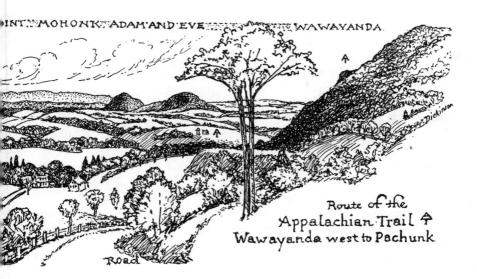

INT MOHONK ADAM AND EVE WAWAYANDA

Route of the
Appalachian Trail
Wawayanda west to Pachunk

Kittatinny Ridge, with views from the ledges. The Rattlesnake Swamp Trail (orange) is passed on the left and, at about 4 miles into the hike, the Catfish Fire Tower is reached. In 0.6 mile, the route intersects the Rattlesnake Swamp Trail a second time. This time, the orange blazes should be followed to the left in a loop down off the ridge, through a swamp where fern fiddleheads rise out of the forest floor in the spring. Skirting Catfish Pond (at the edge of AMC's Camp Mohican), the hike now ascends on the Rattlesnake Swamp Trail back up to the AT. The return route is via the AT and Coppermines Trail to the parking area trailhead.

High Point State Park *Length: 7–9 miles Blazes: various*
An open ridgetop walk along the AT combines with a shaded valley walk along the Iris Trail to make a pleasant loop hike. It begins at the High Point AT parking lot on the south side of NJ 23, near the park office. The AT heads south, passing almost immediately by the start of the Iris Trail (red) on the left. The AT soon ascends to the Kittatinny Ridge and offers a number of views, the first one looking west over Sawmill Lake. A further ascent leads to another view west to the Pocono Mountains. At 2.5 miles, there is a view east over Lake Rutherford from Dutch Shoe Rock. The AT now reaches the Iris Trail

(red) and forms a rough figure-eight, with the Iris Trail crossing the AT twice, once at 3.3 miles and again at 4.6 miles into the hike. Walkers can loop back to the NJ 23 parking lot at either point. The Iris Trail descends from the ridgetop into a heavily forested valley. It follows a shady woods road, parallels the shore of Lake Rutherford, and reconnects with the AT just short of the NJ 23 parking lot.

Wawayanda State Park   *Length: 6.2 miles Blazes: various*
This relatively easy, two-car hike begins at the Wawayanda State Park office located just west of the park entrance off Warwick Turnpike. The hike begins by heading north on the Hoeferlin Trail (blue), behind the park office, and, at 0.3 mile, intersects the AT. A left turn onto the AT leads south along a woods road that once provided a primary access to the top of Wawayanda Mountain. The AT passes through second-growth forest, which has healed the damage caused by the intense farming, grazing, logging, and iron mining activities that left Wawayanda Mountain denuded of trees in the nineteenth century. Just below and to the right of the Wawayanda AT shelter, at 0.5 mile, is a shallow iron ore test pit. Iron mines can be found throughout the park, though none are immediately visible from the AT. The AT crosses many stone walls, which testify to the mountain's agricultural past. At 2.5 miles, the trail skirts the edge of the High Breeze Farm, a nineteenth-century subsistence farmstead listed on the State and National Register of Historic Places. The farm buildings are being restored, but are closed to the public. Panoramic views of Mounts Adam and Eve, the Shawangunks, and the Catskills can be seen from High Breeze's hillside fields. At 4.6 miles, the AT reaches the top of the Wawayanda escarpment. The rock here is Precambrian, some of the oldest on the entire AT. The trail descends briefly and reaches a 0.1-mile-long blue-blazed trail leading off to the right to Pinwheel's Vista. Views of Vernon Valley, High Point Monument, and the Kittatinny Ridge reward hikers. On the short blue-blazed trail, an immense gray limestone glacial erratic is visible to the left on the return hike. The hike continues down the mountain on the AT on a series of more than four hundred stone steps and switchbacks constructed by New York-New Jersey Trail Conference and Appalachian Trail Conference crews in the early 1990s. The hike ends at the NJ 94 parking area.

Greenwood Lake Loop   *Length: 14 miles Blazes: various*
This ridgetop hike begins in New York state, but extends into New Jersey. The starting point is the AT crossing of NY 17A, where parking is available. The

hike begins by heading south through thick woods. After about 2 easy miles, the AT opens out onto the magnificent "sidewalks" of Mount Peter/Bearfort Mountain. These long, upturned ledges are made of Devonian puddingstone, a conglomerate mix of vividly colored red sandstone and red-and-white quartz pebbles and chips. The trail follows these ledges 5.9 miles south from the starting point into New Jersey. The ledges give views of Greenwood Lake far below, and Sterling Ridge across the valley. On a clear day, the skyscrapers of Manhattan can be seen glinting in the late afternoon sun. To complete the loop, hikers should turn left on the State Line Trail (blue). After 0.2 mile, the trail intersects with the Ernest Walter Trail (yellow). Hikers should turn right on the Ernest Walter Trail and follow it past Surprise Lake, a glacial pond. The hiking route then loops back and intersects the AT again. To reach the starting point on NY 17A, hikers should turn right and follow the AT back along the cliffs.

LONG PATH

When Vincent and Paul Schaefer originally conceived the idea of the Long Path in the 1930s as New York's version of the justly famous Long Trail in Vermont, they had a unique vision. The trail would consist of an unmarked route through backcountry and wilderness corridors loosely linking points of interest. The Long Path (LP) obtained its name from Raymond Torrey's weekly column, "The Long Brown Path," in the *New York Post*. Torrey was one of the founders of the New York-New Jersey Trail Conference in 1920. The Schaefers' idea, nurtured by Torrey, gained momentum, and in the 1930s construction of the trail in the area of the Palisades was begun. With the death of Torrey in 1938, the initial burst of energy faded, and it was not until the 1960s that Robert Jessen and Michael Warren took up the challenge and began laying out the Long Path that currently exists.

The Long Path System comprises about 300 miles of trail, making it longer than Vermont's Long Trail—and more mileage is on the way. While the business of building trails has not changed appreciably since the Long Path's beginnings, contemporary legal hurdles make bridging streams and moving boulders seem like child's play. Nonetheless, many dedicated members of the hiking community are willing to work at not only protecting what is already there, but proposing improvements and additions. Thus, the Long Path represents a living trail system, one whose size and shape are ever changing, one that responds to environmental challenges and takes advantage of emerging opportunities. Since the fifth edition of the *New York Walk Book* was published, more than 100 miles of new trail have been added to the Long Path, and countless relocations have improved the hiking experience in established areas.

New Jersey Palisades

Length: 12.7 miles Blaze: turquoise

From the George Washington Bridge, the LP follows the level cliff-top of the Palisades north. It is generally fairly level walking with frequent views over the Hudson River. The viewpoints are excellent places for watching thousands of migrating hawks each fall. The trail offers examples of a mixed oak forest, where five different species of oak (red, white, black, scarlet, and chestnut) dominate the woods. The Long Path has readily available public transportation via the Red and Tan Lines 9 and 9A buses. See chapter 4, "The Palisades," for details and the history of the area. See the *Guide to the Long Path* for details of the rest of the trail in New York. Hikers should note that in New Jersey, the LP's proximity to roads means that the sound of traffic is frequently present.

The most scenic approach to this section of the LP is on foot across the George Washington Bridge. An alternative route is by bus to Bridge Plaza in Fort Lee, New Jersey. The Long Path begins on Hudson Terrace at the foot of the stairs leading up to the pedestrian walkway across the George Washington Bridge.

From the bridge, a wide, level path swings toward the cliff. Lower Manhattan can be viewed from the farthest projecting cliff near the bridge tower. A quarter-mile farther along is a view of one of the best of the southern rock faces. At the last of several signs for "Trail to River," the Carpenters Trail descends to the Shore Trail (white).

The route passes a mounted cannon, the walls of several former estates, and, at 1.4 miles, the entrance to William O. Allison Park. This park is maintained by the Palisades Interstate Park Commission and is open most of the year. Past the campus of St. Peters College, the LP swings to the shoulder of the Palisades Interstate Parkway and enters a small woodland near Allison Park, the site of the Palisades Mountain House, built in 1869. At Palisade Avenue, at 2.1 miles, the LP passes the foot trail to the shore that, for part of the way, follows the sidewalk along the road.

Continuing northward, the path soon traverses the former Dana estate, with an exotic oriental pine that stands near the parkway. In the woodland beyond is a rock promontory, High Tom, with views north and down to Undercliff Grove and the old cemetery. At 3.2 miles, the trail crosses Rockefeller Lookout, with views of Spuyten Duyvil and the northern tip of Manhattan.

After passing the ruins of the Cadgene estate, the LP follows undulating terrain through woodland to a meadow and depression, Devils Hole. The slight rise beyond is Clinton Point, a favorite viewpoint from the time of the first settlers. Few heights along the Palisades give a more striking effect from above of a prow overhanging the water. At 5.1 miles, the trail crosses the road into Greenbrook Sanctuary, a restricted nature preserve, protecting native species. The route continues north along the fence with a few short, steep stretches. At the end of the fence, at 6.0 miles, the Huyler Landing Trail (red) joins from the shore below. A half-mile later the LP reaches Alpine Lookout. The best viewpoint is from the pinnacle just south of the main area.

The path reenters the woods, passes several foundations, and reaches views of the Alpine Boat Basin far below. Shortly, an underpass under the parkway leads to Closter Dock Road, 7.5 miles from the bridge. To reach the shore, hikers continue on the LP for several minutes more and then descend on a broad and well-shaded path. At 8.3 miles, the LP passes the Administration Building of the New Jersey Section of the Palisades Interstate Park, the former Oltman House, with limited parking. Soon, a tower west of the parkway comes into view on the site of the first FM radio station, built by Major Edwin Armstrong, the radio pioneer.

The LP reenters woodland, where in winter and early spring, 300-foot ice columns form where the water plunges over the cliff. Skirting a quarter-mile-long retreat in the cliff edge, the path then swings past Bombay Hook. Eventually the route leads over broad, flat, embedded rocks, ending at abandoned Ruckman Road (10.0 miles) at the edge of the cliff, here 520 feet high. No part of the Palisades has better scenery.

The trail crosses Ruckman Road, bearing left at the fork. The woods road to the right leads to a projection overlooking Forest View. On the main woods road, exotic plants from the former Burnet estate occasionally appear. Upon reaching a well-used woods road, the path turns toward the cliff edge. The route to the left leads over a bridge to the entrance to Boy Scouts' Camp Alpine, and a bus stop on US 9W for the Red and Tan Lines 9 and 9A buses.

Heading northward, the trail descends and crosses the brook from Maistand (Cornlot) Hollow. The stairway on the right continues down to Forest View at the shore. The trail continues up another stairway and swings right along a park road to State Line Lookout (Point Lookout), which has parking. Woods roads once used as bridle paths provide a variety of cross-country ski trails leading from the parking area.

Inwood Park   *Fort Tryon*
                                  Riversi

Beyond the snack bar at 11.3 miles, the LP continues through a picnic area and then along a wide woods road near the cliff. At 11.9 miles, the LP reaches the NJ-NY state line, marked by a fence and a 6-foot-high monument erected in 1882. The path descends near the cliff edge, through a gate to High Gutter Point. This name recalls the early wood-burning river steamers that docked at a wooden chute on the bank for their fuel. There are views of Hook Mountain, the mile-long pier at Piermont, and Tappan Zee. A staircase of natural stone leads down, often steeply, into Skunk Hollow with hemlocks and waterfalls. At the end of the steps at 12.2 miles, the Shore Trail (white) starts to the right. Part of this area is the Lamont Sanctuary, and beyond was the site of an early African-American community, now long since disappeared. When the stream is crossed, the trail on the right leads to the former Italian Garden at the shore. The LP goes left to US 9W, where the Red and Tan Lines 9 and 9A buses stop at the Lamont-Doherty Earth Observatory entrance, 12.7 miles from the George Washington Bridge.

HIGHLANDS TRAIL

The Highlands Trail highlights the natural beauty of the New Jersey and New York Highlands region, and draws the public's attention to this endangered resource. It is a cooperative effort of the New York-New Jersey Trail Conference, conservation organizations, state and local governments, and local businesses. When completed, it will extend over 150 miles from Storm King Mountain on the Hudson River in New York south to Phillipsburg, New Jersey, on the Delaware River. The route will connect major scenic attractions in both states. Ultimately, a network of trails including alternate routes and multi-use paths is envisioned. Camping is not permitted along the Highlands Trail. Thru-hiking

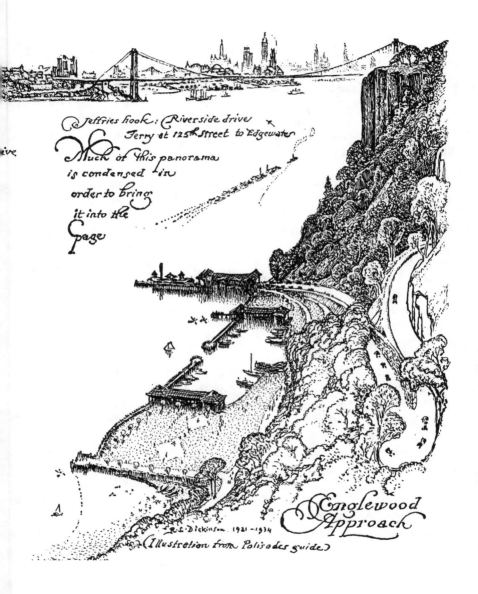

Jeffries hook : Riverside drive
Ferry at 125th Street to Edgewater

Much of this panorama
is condensed in
order to bring
it into the
page

Englewood
Approach

R.L. Dickinson 1921-1924
(Illustration from Palisades guide)

opportunities will depend on the establishment of bed-and-breakfast facilities along the route that will be willing to cater to hikers.

Sections of the Highlands Trail

The Highlands Trail is a combination of co-alignment on established trails, new trails, and road walking. The co-aligned routes bear both blazes, except for the Sterling Ridge and Allis trails, which have plastic Highlands Trail logos at critical points. Hikers must pay attention at intersections and turns, as the Highlands Trail often leaves one trail to join another. See individual trail descriptions for more details of the co-aligned trails. As of 1998, the trail route has been established through Sterling Forest, the Wyanokies, the Pequannock Watershed, and Mahlon Dickerson Reservation; however, south of Mahlon Dickerson Reservation, although the overall route is known, its exact location within a park will depend on receipt of permission from state or county officials and how quickly volunteers of the New York-New Jersey Trail Conference can build the trail. The publicly owned properties it will eventually pass through include Schooley's Mountain, Columbia Trail, Voorhees State Park, Union Forge Nature Preserve, Spruce Run Recreation Area, Clinton Wildlife Management area, and the Musconetcong Gorge section of Musconetcong River Reservation. Before hiking the Highlands Trail in this area, contact the New York-New Jersey Trail Conference for information.

County 511 to Otter Hole   *Length: 13.0 miles Blaze: teal diamond*
To reach the northern end of this section of the Highlands Trail, take County 511 to Hewitt. The trail starts at a brook crossing just south of the parking area at the junction of County 511 and East Shore Road. Public transportation is via NJ Transit bus 197. The southern end of the section is accessible from Glenwild Avenue which can be reached from I-287 by taking Exit 53 west to Bloomingdale. Take County 694 (Main Street) 1.4 miles through Bloomingdale, bear right as it becomes Hamburg Turnpike, and shortly turn right at the Y junction onto Glenwild Avenue toward West Milford. After 3.2 miles, there is a parking area on the right side of the road. In addition to the parking available at each end of this section, cars may be parked at the end of Lake Rickonda Road, along Stonetown Road, and at the Weis Ecology Center on Snake Den Road East, which is off of West Brook Road.

The Highlands Trail in this section is routed onto parts of existing trails. Where it is co-aligned, the trail is marked with both blazes. There are planned relocations from Windbeam Mountain to Wyanokie High Point, so watch for changes in this area. Going south from County 511, the Highlands Trail follows the Hewitt-Butler Trail (blue) and turns left, at 0.9 mile, onto the Horse Pond Mountain Trail (white) at its northern end. At 1.2 miles, the Hewitt-Butler Trail rejoins the Horse Pond Mountain Trail from the right, only to leave again to the right at 1.4 miles under a power line. At 3.0 miles, the Horse Pond Mountain and Highlands trails meet the Stonetown Circular Trail (red triangle on white). Here, the Horse Pond Mountain Trail ends. The Highlands Trail turns left on the Stonetown Circular Trail (red triangle on white), reaching Lake Rickonda Road at 4.7 miles. Continuing along the road, both trails turn left onto Stonetown Road at 4.9 miles, and go another 0.3 mile to White Road. The trails turn right on White Road and go to the end of the road, where they enter the woods. Going over Board, Bear, and Windbeam mountains, they reach Stonetown Road, for the second time, at 8.3 miles, where the Highlands Trail turns left. Parking for one or two cars is available along the road at a gate to the watershed property (which must not be blocked) a few yards north on Stonetown Road.

The Highlands Trail follows Stonetown Road for 0.2 mile, then turns right onto West Brook Road for 0.5 mile. It turns left on Snake Den Road East for 0.6 mile, reaching the Weis Ecology Center, with parking, at 9.9 miles. Just before the parking area is reached, the Wyanokie Circular Trail, in the counterclockwise direction, joins the road and Highlands Trail until it splits off to the right in 0.2 mile. Shortly, Snake Den Road East becomes unpaved and the Hewitt-Butler Trail joins from the right. Now following the Hewitt-Butler Trail for 0.3 mile, the Highlands Trail turns left (south) and joins the Mine Trail (yellow on white) for 0.1 mile before splitting off to the right. At 10.5 miles, the Macopin Trail (white) begins to the right. In another 0.2 mile, almost at the top of Wyanokie High Point (10.7 miles), the Wyanokie Circular Trail joins from the left. All three trails continue for 0.2 mile until the Wyanokie Circular Trail splits off to the right. The Hewitt-Butler and Highlands trails continue ahead, passing on the left the northern end of the Carris Hill Trail (yellow). At 12.1 miles, the two trails reach the Post Brook Trail (white), which goes off to the left as the joint trails make a sharp right turn.

At 12.4 miles, the Wyanokie Crest Trail (yellow) comes in from the right and joins the Highlands and Hewitt-Butler trails for 0.1 mile before leaving to the left. At 13.0 miles, the trail reaches the Otter Hole Trail (green). Parking is available 0.1 mile straight ahead, where the Hewitt-Butler Trail crosses Glenwild Avenue.

Otter Hole to Echo Lake Road   *Length: 6.3 miles Blaze: teal diamond*

The northern end of the section is accessible from Glenwild Avenue, which can be reached from I-287 by taking Exit 53 west to Bloomingdale. Take County 694 (Main Street) 1.4 miles through Bloomingdale, bear right as it becomes Hamburg Turnpike, and shortly turn right at the Y junction onto Glenwild Avenue toward West Milford. After 3.2 miles on Glenwild Avenue, the parking area for the northern trailhead is on the right. The southern trailhead is in the parking lot at the Newark Watershed CDC Office on Echo Lake Road, which is reached from I-287 by taking Exit 52 and proceeding west to Butler on NJ 23. It is 7.6 miles to Echo Lake Road, then right 1.1 miles to the parking lot.

From the parking area on Glenwild Avenue, proceed north for 0.1 mile on the Hewitt-Butler Trail (blue), crossing a large stream. Here, the Highlands Trail continues its southbound trek by going north on the Otter Hole Trail (green), which begins to the left. At 0.4 mile, the Highlands Trail leaves the Otter Hole Trail and turns left onto the Wyanokie Crest Trail (yellow), which crosses the Otter Hole Trail here. Together, the Highlands and Wyanokie Crest trails ascend Buck Mountain, where there are several viewpoints. The first two viewpoints are from the east to the southeast, with the Manhattan skyline in the distance. There is a brief rock scramble to the top after the second view. The third viewpoint is from the southeast to the west. Leaving the Wyanokie Crest Trail at 0.9 mile, the Highlands Trail descends to Otter Hole Road at 1.3 miles, where it turns right and passes many houses in the next 0.7 mile of road walking. It crosses the outlet between two lakes and then turns left onto Crescent Road at 1.5 miles. After a right turn at a T junction, the Highlands Trail follows Newton Terrace to Algonquin Way. At the end of the road at 2.0 miles, the Highlands Trail enters the open hardwood forest on a woods road.

Almost immediately, the Highlands Trail turns left off the woods road and gently climbs uphill. Over the next 0.5 mile, the Highlands Trail crosses or joins several woods roads. At 2.7 miles, the Highlands Trail crosses a major woods road and becomes a narrow trail. It descends until it meets a woods road at 3.0 miles and then crosses the outlet of a wetland. At 3.2 miles, the trail reaches a large rock outcrop with a seasonal view and then begins a steep descent. Just after crossing a dirt road at 3.3 miles, it enters the Pequannock Watershed property and passes through acres of ground pine. At 3.9 miles, the Highlands Trail reaches Macopin Road where it jogs to the right, turns left off the road, and enters a pine forest at 4.0 miles. In another 0.8 mile, it reaches the shore of Echo Lake where it meets the Echo Lake East Trail (white) at a

T junction. Going left along the lake for a little over a mile, it reaches Echo Lake Road at 6.0 miles. The trail follows Echo Lake Road as it rounds the south end of the lake, and turns right on a driveway to reach the watershed office at 6.3 miles, where there is parking.

Hiking along this section of the Highlands Trail between Macopin Road and the Pequannock Watershed requires a permit. Contact NWCDC by mail at P.O. Box 319, Newfoundland, NJ 07435, or in person at their office at 223 Echo Lake Road, West Milford, NJ 07480; (973) 697-2850.

Echo Lake Road to Clinton Road   *Length: 7.2 miles Blaze: teal diamond*
To reach either end of this section of the Highlands Trail from I-287, take Exit 52 and proceed west on NJ 23 towards Butler. Access to the northern trailhead is via Echo Lake Road (7.6 miles west of I-287), which leads 1.1 miles north to the parking lot at the Newark Watershed CDC Office. Access to the southern trailhead is via Clinton Road (9.8 miles west of I-287), which leads 4.8 miles north to parking area P4.

From the parking lot at the Newark Watershed CDC office on Echo Lake Road, the Highlands Trail heads west. It passes the gatehouse for the dam and a nature trail at the west end of the dam where it turns north to follow the west shore of Echo Lake on the Echo Lake West Trail (white). Heading north, the two trails pass through occasional laurel groves and conglomerate rocks with large white quartz pebbles. At the north end of the lake at 1.9 miles, the Echo Lake West Trail (white) ends, and the Highlands Trail goes up Kanouse Mountain. At a T junction with Kanouse Road (dirt), the Highlands Trail turns right and follows the road for 0.1 mile. It then turns left and descends through heavy laurel growth and hemlock trees. The trail crosses Gould Road at 3.1 miles, a power line at 3.9 miles, and Union Valley Road at 4.1 miles.

From Union Valley Road, the Highlands Trail climbs steeply to a viewpoint to the south and east, and 100 yards later it reaches the Hanks East Trail (white). It turns right on the Hanks East Trail for 100 yards and then turns left, reaching the Hanks West Trail (blue/white) in 0.1 mile. It follows the Hanks West Trail briefly to the left, and then turns right to reach the Bearfort Fire Tower at 5.3 miles. The Highlands Trail turns right at the cement pillar just south of the tower and joins the Fire Tower West Trail (yellow) at a T junction in 50 feet. It follows the Fire Tower West Trail to the left along a rocky ridge, reaching a view of Cedar Pond to the west, and then, at 6.1 miles, follows the Two Brooks Trail (white) to the right. The trail crosses two major brooks, with

bridges at 6.3 and 6.7 miles and a minor stream in between. After the second bridge, the trails descend steeply to Mossmans Brook, which they follow until reaching Clinton Road. Here the Two Brooks Trail ends, while the Highlands Trail turns left and almost immediately crosses Mossmans Brook on the road bridge. It reaches the entrance to parking lot P4 at 7.2 miles.

Hiking along this section of the Highlands Trail in the Pequannock Watershed requires a permit. Contact NWCDC by mail at P.O. Box 319, Newfoundland, NJ 07435, or in person at their office at 223 Echo Lake Road, West Milford, NJ 07480; (973) 697-2850.

Clinton Road to NJ 23   *Length: 6.5 miles Blaze: teal diamond*
To reach this section of the Highlands Trail from I-287, take Exit 52 and proceed west on NJ 23 towards Butler. From the Clinton Road exit on NJ 23 (9.8 miles west of I-287), it is 4.8 miles north to parking area P4 and access to the

north end. Access from the south is at the junction of NJ 23 and Canistear Road (13.1 miles west of I-287), where parking is available.

At the P4 parking area on Clinton Road, the Highlands Trail joins the Clinton West Trail (white). The trails ascend the ridge through an open hardwood forest littered with rocks. They pass, at 0.3 mile, a blue trail which connects with the Bearfort Waters/Clinton Trail (yellow). At 0.8 mile, the trails begin a gradual descent, and they reach a view of the Clinton Reservoir at 1.3 miles. The trails cross the Buckabear Pond Trail (red triangle on white) at 1.5 miles, continue down the ridge and, at 1.8 miles, pass a large boulder on the right. At 2.0 miles, they pass another view of the reservoir accessible via a herd path.

The trails gradually descend the ridge, then turn and become a woods road at 2.3 miles. They contour their way down to reach the reservoir at 2.7 miles and continue along the shore. They meet the west end of the Buckabear Pond Trail (red triangle on white) and turn left to cross a dam between Clinton Reservoir and Buckabear Pond. In 1998, beaver activity determined the water level in the pond. On the far side of the dam, at 2.9 miles, the trails turn left. To the right is the southern end of the Bearfort Waters/Clinton Trail (yellow).

The trails parallel the shoreline, join a woods road at 3.3 miles, and then cross a stream. At 3.7 miles, the Clinton West Trail continues straight ahead while the Highlands Trail turns right off the woods road. This area was heavily farmed, as evidenced by many stone walls, with some piled high while others are low and wide. At 4.0 miles, the trail crosses an old farm road between two stone walls. It turns right on Lud Day Road at 4.5 miles and then jogs off it to the left. The trail ascends the ridge, with a stand of planted pines off to the left, reaches the top at 4.7 miles, and begins to descend. At 4.9 miles, it turns left on a woods road and then in 50 yards turns right. Continuing to descend, the Highlands Trail passes a hemlock grove at 5.3 miles and heads towards Dunker Pond. At 5.4 miles, the trail turns to parallel the narrow, rocky gorge which drains the pond. On one side, large rocks covered with lichen, moss, and ferns tumble down to the woods road, while vertical slabs form the other side. The trail crosses the rushing water, turns right onto a woods road, and begins a steady climb of about 300 feet. At 5.7 miles, the Highlands Trail reaches the top, passing several large rocks before beginning its descent. Reaching Canistear Road at 6.5 miles, the trail turns left and goes through a narrow railroad underpass. Parking is available at the parking lot at the corner of Canistear Road and NJ 23.

Hiking along this section of the Highlands Trail in the Pequannock Watershed requires a permit. Contact NWCDC by mail at P.O. Box 319, Newfoundland, NJ 07435, or in person at their office at 223 Echo Lake Road, West Milford, NJ 07480; (973) 697-2850.

NJ 23 to Weldon Road *Length: 11.5 miles Blaze: teal diamond*

To reach this section of the Highlands Trail from I-287, take Exit 52 and proceed west on NJ 23 towards Butler. Access at the north is at the parking area at the junction of NJ 23 and Canistear Road (13.1 miles west of I-287). The south end of the section is reached by continuing west 1.5 miles on NJ 23 to Holland Mountain Road, which is a left turn shortly after NJ 23 becomes a non-divided highway. Go south for about 3.7 miles to Ridge Road, turn left for less than 0.2 mile to Russia Road, then proceed about 1.4 miles south to Weldon Road. The entrance to the picnic area parking lot is on the right at 1.9 miles.

This section of the Highlands Trail is remarkably free from visible intrusions of civilization. From the parking lot on Canistear Road just north of NJ 23, the Highlands Trail crosses NJ 23 and heads east along the road shoulder. At 0.3 mile, the trail crosses the Pequannock River on a bridge, immediately turns right into the woods, and enters the Pequannock Watershed (permit required). For Pequannock Watershed permits, contact NWCDC by mail at P.O. Box 319, Newfoundland, NJ 07435, or in person at their office at 223 Echo Lake Road, West Milford NJ 07480; (973) 697-2850.

The footpath is through open deciduous forest, reaching a view of the Oak Ridge Reservoir at 1.8 miles. Leaving the viewpoint, the trail descends the ridge, reaches a woods road at 2.3 miles, turns right, and, in 250 feet, turns right off the road. The trail ascends Green Pond Ridge, reaching a seasonal view at 2.7 miles. Descending the ridge, the trail turns on and off numerous woods roads, so hikers are advised to watch for turns.

At 3.8 miles, the Highlands Trail crosses Holland Mountain Road and again begins to follow woods roads. After crossing two streams, the trail crosses Rock Lodge Road at 4.6 miles and begins a gentle ascent. At 4.8 miles, it skirts a glacial erratic on the right. The trail descends and, at 5.0 miles, turns right on Rock Lodge Road, leaving the watershed property. Following Rock Lodge Road, the trail reaches a Y junction at 5.2 miles. Here, the Highlands Trail takes the left fork, staying on Rock Lodge Road. When the pavement ends at 5.3 miles, the trail continues on Rock Lodge Road, now a woods road. The Highlands Trail reaches a major and confusing intersection at 5.5 miles; here, the trail proceeds straight ahead. After following the rutted, sometime muddy, unpaved Rock Ledge Road for another mile, the Highlands Trail, at 6.5 miles, takes a sharp left onto a woods road.

The Highlands Trail then ascends along the woods road, with detours off muddy sections. It descends to reach Ryker Lake at 7.2 miles, where a side trail leads right, down to a point along the shore. At the far end of the lake, the trail bears left off the woods road and descends to reach Russia Brook at 7.8 miles. The Russia Brook crossing may be difficult at high water, but there is an old bridge well downstream to the left. The trail crosses Glen Ridge Road, enters the Paulist Fathers' property at 7.9 miles, and crosses a power line. On a series of ascents and descents over small hills, the Highlands Trail joins and leaves paint-blazed woods roads. Stay on the Highlands Trail and do not follow these other marked trails where they diverge from it.

At 9.6 miles, the Highlands Trail turns left off a woods road and passes a glacial erratic on the right. It reaches Sparta Mountain Road at 10.0 miles and turns right. The trail turns left off the road and enters Mahlon Dickerson Reservation, where there is a multi-use trail system. The Highlands Trail almost immediately comes to a T junction and turns left to join the Pine Swamp Loop (white). The two trails pass a yellow trail to the right at 10.2 miles, the Boulder Trail (green) to the right at 10.7 miles, a blue trail to the left at 11.0 miles, and unmarked woods roads. At 11.3 miles, at a major junction, the Highlands Trail turns left, while the Pine Swamp Loop continues straight ahead. The Highlands Trail reaches the picnic area parking lot at 11.4 miles, and 0.1 mile later reaches Weldon Road.

Weldon Road to Saffin Pond   *Length: 3.2 miles Blaze: teal diamond*
To reach either end of the trail, take I-80 to Exit 34B (NJ 15 North, Jefferson, Sparta). For the southern end, follow NJ 15 north for 4.7 miles, and exit right at the Weldon Road/Milton Oak Ridge turnoff. Follow Weldon Road north for 3.1 miles to Saffin Pond and turn right into the parking area. The northern end begins 1.3 miles further along Weldon Road, on the left in the picnic parking area. Alternatively, see the driving instructions in the previous section to reach the picnic area from NJ 23.

From just to the right of the bulletin board in the picnic area parking lot of Mahlon Dickerson Reservation, the Highlands Trail follows a narrow path which crosses Weldon Road in 0.1 mile. In another 0.3 mile, the Highlands Trail reaches Headley Overlook, with a view to the east and south. It follows the edge of the cliffs, passing a very narrow angle view at 0.5 mile and a broad view at 0.6 mile, with Lake Hopatcong visible in the distance to the south. From here it descends, crossing a yellow-blazed woods road at 0.7 mile and a stream at 1.0 mile. It crosses another stream at 1.3 miles on a wooden bridge and yet another stream at 1.4 miles. The northern end of the Beaver Brook Trail is reached at 1.5 miles. Here, the Highlands Trail bears right as the Beaver Brook Trail starts straight ahead. Another stream is crossed at 1.7 miles as the trail swings around to the west and eventually north. It joins and leaves a number of woods roads before reaching the dam at Saffin Pond at 2.8 miles. There are a several picnic tables near the dam. As of 1998, the exact route to continue south from this point is not finalized. To reach the parking area at the southern end of the section, continue by following the east shore of the pond and cross an inlet brook on a wooden bridge at 3.1 miles.

Stephens State Park to US 46   *Length: 3.1 miles Blaze: teal diamond*
To reach the northern end of this section, take Exit 25 north from I-80 and follow the signs to Waterloo Village (about 2.5 miles). Continue for another 3.9 miles on Waterloo Road to Waterloo Valley Road. Turn left, cross the Musconetcong River on a bridge, and turn right almost immediately into the Upper Picnic Area parking lot. The southern end of this section on US 46 is reached by continuing on Waterloo Road (which becomes Willow Grove Road) for 2.5 miles to US 46 in Hackettstown. Take US 46 east 2.7 miles from the Willow Grove Road intersection to Naughright Road. The trail crossing is on the westbound lanes 0.2 mile west of this intersection, with parking available on the south side of US 46 about 0.1 mile east of the intersection.

Going through five gates which are usually closed to cars, the Highlands Trail follows the park roads through the Upper Picnic Area, the main area where the ranger station is located, and the Lower Picnic Area. After the last picnic table at 0.6 mile, the trail narrows and follows the Musconetcong River until it bears left at a Y junction at 1.0 mile. Then it angles up the hill on an old road to a small ravine formed by a stream at 1.2 miles. The trail crosses the stream and continues to ascend steeply, then more gradually, to a broad summit at 1.5 miles.

The Highlands Trail continues across the thinly-wooded hilltop with low-growing vegetation, including may apples, jack-in-the-pulpits, and brambles. It descends to a stand of evergreens and reaches a gravel water company road at 1.7 miles, where the trail enters Hackettstown Municipal Utilities

Authority property. This watershed property alternates between planted ever-greens and hardwood forests. The Highlands Trail crosses the gravel road again and passes under a power line at 2.0 miles. After ascending a hill, the trail goes down a straight row through evergreens, with straight, evenly-spaced columns stretching in either direction. Emerging from the stand, the Highlands Trail turns right and descends to cross a stream at the bottom of a gorge at 2.3 miles.

After angling up the side of the gorge on an old road, the Highlands Trail takes a sharp left near the top. Coming to an old well or cistern, the trail turns right and descends toward US 46, crossing two streams to reach the road at 2.8 miles. Follow US 46 to the left on the narrow shoulder to Naughright Road at 3.1 miles.

Long Valley to Califon   *Length: 6.0 miles Blaze: teal diamond*
In the center of Long Valley, NJ 24 makes a turn to the north. From here, the Highlands Trail heads south, following the Columbia Trail along the aban-doned High Bridge Branch rail bed, which now accommodates an underground natural gas line. There is ample parking at this end of the trail 0.1 mile north of the center of town. The Califon end of the trail is reached by following County 513 for 5.6 miles south from Long Valley to County 512 and turning right 0.7 mile into Califon.

The trail parallels County 513 and the South Branch of the Raritan River. Shortly after leaving the trailhead at Schooley's Mountain Road (NJ 24), the 12-foot-wide cinder-based trail enters a deciduous forest. Occasional wetlands are visible between the trail and the river as it meanders through the Schooley's Mountain piedmont. At 0.7 mile, it crosses a dirt road with a 5 mph speed limit to the west and 8 mph toward County 513. A few farms are visible along this stretch during the winter. At 1.5 miles, the trail crosses a bridge over a feeder branch to the river, which is 200 feet to the east. The poison ivy growing along the sides poses no threat to hikers who stay on the trail.

The Highlands Trail crosses Middle Valley Road at 2.6 miles, and then passes a group of houses and a collection of 1950 to 1970 vintage cars. At 2.9 miles, the trail crosses the river and then crosses West Mill Road (County 513) at 3.6 miles, where there is parking for a few cars. The rail bed disappears temporarily, so hikers must follow the road and turn left just before a fence. Skirting a tree nursery, the trail follows the fence to where the rail bed resumes and turns right. The Highlands Trail now passes through a mix of farmlands and woodlands. At 4.2 miles, where, the trail crosses Valley Brook Road and the Morris-Hunterdon county line, it enters a Hunterdon County Park which protects the right-of-way. It briefly meets the river at 4.6 miles and crosses Vernoy Road, then parallels it for 0.2 mile along the banks of the South Branch before reentering the forest. At 5.3 miles, the trail again skirts Vernoy Road and occasional backyards as it approaches the Borough of Califon.

After reaching Main Street at 5.9 miles, the trail follows Railroad Avenue and passes the firehouse. This section ends at Academy Street (County 512), at the former railroad station which is now the Califon Historical Society Museum. Here is an opportunity to see rails and ties—the only place on this section of the Highlands Trail. There is ample parking near the museum.

FURTHER READING

This list of books is meant to be a starting point for those people wishing more information. Many of these books, particularly the trail guides, have frequent revisions, so be sure you use the latest versions. For historical information, consult local history rooms in public libraries.

Backcountry Ethics

Hampton, Bruce and David Cole. *Soft Paths: How to Enjoy the Wilderness Without Harming It.* Harrisburg, PA: Stackpole Books, 1988.

Hodgson, Michael. *The Basic Essentials of Minimizing Impact on the Wilderness.* Merrillville, IN: ICS Books, 1991.

Waterman, Laura and Guy Waterman. *Backwoods Ethics: Environmental Issues for Hikers and Campers.* Woodstock, VT: The Countryman Press, Inc., 1993. 2nd rev.

———. *Wilderness Ethics: Preserving the Spirit of Wilderness.* Woodstock, VT: The Countryman Press, Inc., 1993.

Flora and Fauna

Barbour, Spider and Anita Barbour. *Wild Flora of the Northeast.* Woodstock, NY: Overlook Press, 1995.

Boyle, William J, Jr. *A Guide to Bird Finding in New Jersey.* New Brunswick, NJ: Rutgers University Press, 1986.

Cobb, Boughton. *A Field Guide to Ferns and Their Related Families: Northeastern and Central North America.* Boston, MA: Houghton Mifflin Company, 1975.

Conant, Roger. *A Field Guide to Reptiles and Amphibians of Eastern and Central North America.* Boston, MA: Houghton Mifflin Company, 1991. 3rd ed.

Fadala, Sam. *Basic Projects in Wildlife Watching: Learn More about Wild Birds and Animals through Your Own First-hand Experience.* Harrisburg, PA: Stackpole Books, 1989.

Forrest, Louise R. *Field Guide to Tracking Animals in Snow.* Harrisburg, PA: Stackpole Books, 1988.

Held, Patricia Contreras. *A Field Guide to New Jersey Nature Centers.* New Brunswick, NJ: Rutgers University Press, 1988.

Krieger, Louis C. *The Mushroom Handbook.* Mineola, NY: Dover Publications, 1967.

Miller, Dorcas S. *Berry Finder: A Guide to Native Plants with Fleshy Fruits.* Berkeley, CA: Nature Study Guild, 1986.

Murie, Olaus J. *Field Guide to Animal Tracks.* Boston, MA: Houghton Mifflin Company, 1975.

Niering, William A. *Wetlands.* Audubon Society Nature Guides. New York: Alfred A. Knopf, 1985.

Peterson, Roger Tory. *A Completely New Guide to All the Birds of Eastern and Central North America.* Boston, MA: Houghton Mifflin Company, 1980. 4th rev/en ed.

Petrides, George A. *A Field Guide to Eastern Trees.* Boston, MA: Houghton Mifflin Company, 1988.

Robbins, Chandler S., Bertel Brunn, and Herbert S. Zim. *Birds of North America.* New York: Golden Press, 1983.

Robichaud-Collins, Beryl and Karl Anderson. *Plant Communities of New Jersey: A Study of Landscape Diversity.* New Brunswick, NJ: Rutgers University Press, 1994.

Stalter, R. *Barrier Island Botany for the United States.* Dubuque, IA: William C. Brown, 1993.

Stanne, Stephen P., Roger G. Panetta, and Brian E. Forist. *The Hudson: An Illustrated Guide to the Living River.* New Brunswick, New Jersey: Rutgers University Press, 1996.

Stokes, Donald W. and Lillian Q. Stokes. *A Guide to Animal Tracking and Behavior.* Boston, MA: Little, Brown and Company, 1987.

Sutton, Ann and Myron Sutton. *Eastern Forests.* Audubon Society Nature Guides. New York: Alfred A. Knopf, 1985.

Food

Angier, Bradford. *Field Guide to Edible Wild Plants.* Magnolia, MA: Peter Smith, 1992.

Jacobson, Cliff. *Cooking in the Outdoors: The Basic Essentials.* Merrillville, IN: ICS Books, 1989.

Prater, Yvonne and Ruth Dyar Mendenhall. *Gorp, Glop and Glue Stew: Favorite Foods from 165 Outdoor Experts.* Seattle, WA: The Mountaineers, 1981.

Richard, Sukey, Donna Orr, and Claudia Lindholm (ed.). *NOLS Cookery*. Harrisburg, PA.: Stackpole, 1991. 3rd ed.
Viehman, John (ed.). *Trailside's Trail Food*. Emmaus, PA: Rodale Press, 1993.
Weiss, John. *The Outdoor Chef's Bible*. New York: Doubleday, 1995.

Geology

The American Geological Institute Staff. *Dictionary of Geological Terms*. New York: Anchor Press/Doubleday, 1984. 3rd rev. ed.
Chew, V. Collins. *Underfoot: A Geologic Guide to the Appalachian Trail*. Harpers Ferry, WV: Appalachian Trail Conference, 1993. 2nd ed.
Geological Highway Map of Northeastern Region (Map No. 10, United States Geological Highway Map Series, National Bicentennial Edition). The American Association of Petroleum Geologists, P.O. Box 979, Tulsa, OK 74101. 1976.
Isachsen, Yngvar W. et al. *Geology of New York: A Simplified Account*. New York State Museum Education Leaflet Series No. 28. New York State Museum Science Center, Cultural Education Center, Albany, NY 12230. 1991.
Wyckoff, Jerome. *Rock Scenery of the Hudson Highlands and Palisades*. Lake George, NY: Adirondack Mountain Club, 1971.

Health

Auerbach, M.D., Paul S. *Medicine For The Outdoors: A Guide to Emergency Medical Procedures and First Aid for Wilderness Travelers*. Boston, MA: Little, Brown and Company, 1986.
Forgey, William W. *First-Aid for the Outdoors: The Basic Essentials*. Merrillville, IN: ICS Books, 1988.
———. *Wilderness Medicine*. Merrillville, IN: ICS Books, 1987. 3rd ed.
Rosen, Albert P. *Health Hints for Hikers*. New York: New York-New Jersey Trail Conference, 1994.
Wilkerson, James (ed.). *Medicine for Mountaineering and Other Wilderness Activities*. Seattle, WA: The Mountaineers, 1992. 4th ed.

Hiking and Camping

Angier, Bradford. *How To Stay Alive in the Woods*. Magnolia, MA: Peter Smith, 1983.
Churchill, James E. *The Basic Essentials of Survival*. Merrillville, IN: ICS Books, 1989.

Evans, Jeremy. *Camping and Survival*. New York: Crestwood/MacMillan, 1992.

Fletcher, Colin. *The Complete Walker III*. New York: Alfred A. Knopf, Inc., 1984. Rev/en 3rd ed.

Frazine, Richard. *The Barefoot Hiker*. Berkeley, CA: Ten Speed Press, 1993.

Getchell, Annie. *The Essential Outdoor Gear Manual*. New York: McGraw-Hill, 1995.

Goll, John. *The Camper's Pocket Handbook. A Backcountry Traveler's Companion*. Merrillville, IN: ICS Books, 1992.

Jacobson, Cliff. *The Basic Essentials of Camping*. Merrillville, IN: ICS Books, 1988.

————. *The Basic Essentials of Trailside Shelters and Emergency Shelters*. Merrillville, IN: ICS Books, 1992.

Kuntzleman, Charles T. *Complete Book of Walking*. New York: Pocket Books, 1992.

Logue, Victoria. *Backpacking in the Nineties: Tips, Techniques and Secrets*. Birmingham, AL: Menasha Ridge Press, 1993.

Meyer, Kathleen. *How to Shit in the Woods*. Berkeley, CA: Ten Speed Press, 1989.

Roberts, Harry. *Backpacking: The Basic Essentials*. Merrillville, IN: ICS Books, 1989.

Ross, Cindy and Todd Gladfelter. *A Hiker's Companion: Twelve Thousand Miles of Trail-tested Wisdom*. Seattle, WA: The Mountaineers, 1993.

Seaborg, Eric and Ellen Dudley. *Hiking and Backpacking*. Champaign, IL: Human Kinetics, 1994.

Sierra Club, San Diego Chapter Staff. *Wilderness Basics: The Complete Handbook for Hikers and Backpackers*. Seattle, WA: The Mountaineers, 1992.

Sumner, Louise Lindgren. *Sew and Repair Your Outdoor Gear*. Seattle, WA: The Mountaineers, 1988.

The Ten Essentials for Travel in the Outdoors. Seattle, WA: The Mountaineers, 1993.

Townsend, Chris. *The Backpacker's Handbook*. New York: McGraw-Hill, Inc., 1992.

Viehman, John (ed.) *Trailside's Hints and Tips for Outdoor Adventure*. Emmaus, PA: Rodale Press, 1993.

Hiking and Camping - Children

Euser, Barbara J. *Take 'em Along: Sharing the Wilderness with Your Children*. Boulder, CO: Cordillera Press. Inc., 1987.

Foster, Lynne. *Take a Hike! The Sierra Club Kid's Guide to Hiking and Backpacking*. Boston, MA: Little, Brown and Company, 1991.

Silverman, Goldie. *Backpacking with Babies and Small Children*. Berkeley, CA: Wilderness Press, 1986.

Sisson, Edith A. *Nature with Children of All Ages: Adventures for Exploring, Learning and Enjoying the World around Us*. New York: Prentice Hall Press, 1982.

Zatz, Arline and Joel. *Best Hikes with Children in New Jersey*. Seattle, WA: The Mountaineers, 1992.

Hiking and Camping - Map and Compass

Baynes, John. *How Maps are Made*. New York: Facts on File, Inc., 1987.

Fleming, June. *Staying Found: The Complete Map and Compass Handbook*. Seattle, WA: The Mountaineers, 1994. 2nd ed.

Jacobson, Cliff. *Map and Compass: The Basic Essentials*. Merrillville, IN: ICS Books, 1988.

Kjellstrom, Bjorn. *Be Expert with Map and Compass*. Greenwich, CT: Macmillan, Inc., 1976, new rev. ed.

Randall, Glenn. *The Outward Bound Map and Compass Book*. New York: Lyons and Burford Publishers, 1989.

Hiking and Camping - Winter

Conover, Garrett and Alexandra Conover. *Snow Walker's Companion: Winter Trail Skills from the Far North*. Camden, ME: Ragged Mountain Press/International Marine Publishing Company, 1994.

Dunn, John M. *Winterwise: A Backpacker's Guide*. Lake George, NY: Adirondack Mountain Club, 1989.

Gorman, Stephen. *Winter Camping*. Boston, MA: Appalachian Mountain Club Books, 1991.

Prater, Gene. *Snow-shoeing*. Seattle, WA: The Mountaineers, 1988.

Randall, Glenn. *Cold Comfort: Keeping Warm in the Outdoors*. New York: Lyons and Burford, 1987.

Weiss, Hal. *Secrets of Warmth*. Seattle, WA: Cloudcap, 1992. 2nd ed.

History

Albert, Richard C. *Damming the Delaware: The Rise and Fall of Tocks Island Dam*. University Park, PA: Penn State University Press, 1988.

Carmer, Carl. *The Hudson*. Bronx, NY: Fordham, 1989.

Cavanaugh, Cam. *Saving the Great Swamp: The People, the Power Brokers and an Urban Wilderness*. Frenchtown, NJ: Columbia Publishing Company, 1978.

Cohen, David S. *The Ramapo Mountain People*. New Brunswick, NJ: Rutgers University Press, 1986.

Cottrell, Alden T. *The Story of Ringwood Manor*. Ringwood Manor Administrative Committee, North Jersey Highlands Historical Society, P.O. Box 248, Ringwood, NJ 07456, 1988.

Garvey, Edward B. *Appalachian Hiker*. Oakton, VA: Appalachian Books, 1978.

Haagensen, Alice M. *Palisades and Snedens Landing from the Beginning of History to the Turn of the Twentieth Century*. Irvington, NY: Pilgrimage Publishing, 1986.

Mack, Arthur C. *The Palisades of the Hudson*. New York: Walking News, Inc., 1982.

Ransom, James M. *Vanishing Ironworks of the Ramapos*. New Brunswick, NJ: Rutgers University Press, 1966.

Serraro, John. *The Wild Palisades of the Hudson*. Upper Saddle River, NJ: Lind Publications, 1986.

Thomas, Lester S. *The Pine Barrens of New Jersey*. New Jersey Department of Environmental Protection, CN 404, Trenton, NJ 08625. 1983.

Wilson, Harold F. *The Story of the Jersey Shore*. Princeton, NJ: D. Van Nostrand Company, 1964.

Trail Guides

Brown, Michael P. *New Jersey Parks, Forests and Natural Areas. A Guide*. New Brunswick, NJ: Rutgers University Press, 1992.

Chazin, Daniel D. (ed.) *Appalachian Trail Data Book*. Harpers Ferry, WV: Appalachian Trail Conference, issued annually.

Dann, Kevin and Gordon Miller. *Thirty Walks in New Jersey*. New Brunswick, NJ: Rutgers University Press, 1992.

Drotar, David Lee. *Hiking the U.S.A.: A Sourcebook for Maps, Guidebooks, Inspiration*. Washington, DC: Stone Wall Press, 1991.

Guide to the Long Path. New York: New York-New Jersey Trail Conference, 1996. 4th ed.

Harrison, Marina and Lucy D. Rosenfeld. *A Walker's Guidebook: Serendipitous Outings near New York City including a Section for Birders.* New York: Kesend Publishing, 1988.

Lenik, Edward. *Iron Mine Trails.* New York: New York-New Jersey Trail Conference, 1996.

Lippman, Helen and Patricia Reardon. *Enjoying New Jersey Outdoors: A Year-Round Guide to Outdoor Recreation in the Garden State and Nearby.* New Brunswick, NJ: Rutgers State University, 1991.

Miskowski, Nick. *Hiking Guide to Delaware Water Gap National Recreation Area.* New York: New York-New Jersey Trail Conference, 1994. 2nd ed.

New York-New Jersey Trail Conference. *Appalachian Trail Guide to New York-New Jersey.* Harpers Ferry, WV: Appalachian Trail Conference, 1998. 14th ed.

————. *Day Walker.* New York: New York-New Jersey Trail Conference, 2nd ed. forthcoming.

————. *New York Walk Book.* New York: New York-New Jersey Trail Conference, 1998. 6th ed.

Scheller, William G. *Country Walks Near New York.* Boston, MA: Appalachian Mountain Club Books, 1986. 2nd ed.

Scofield, Bruce. *Circuit Hikes in Northern New Jersey.* New York: New York-New Jersey Trail Conference, 1995. 4th ed.

Scofield, Bruce, Stella J. Green, and H. Neil Zimmerman. *Fifty Hikes in New Jersey: Walks, Hikes and Backpacking Trips from the Kittatinnies to Cape May.* Woodstock, VT: Backcountry Publications, 1997. 2nd ed.

Turco, Peggy. *Walks and Rambles in Orange and Ulster Counties.* Woodstock, VT: Backcountry Publications, 1996.

Wood, Robert S. *Dayhiker.* Berkeley, CA: Ten Speed Press, 1991.

Zatz, Arline. *New Jersey's Special Places: Scenic, Historic and Cultural Treasures in the Garden State.* Woodstock, VT: The Countryman Press, 1994. 2nd rev. ed.

INDEX

Page numbers in **bold** refer to trail descriptions.
Page numbers in *italics* refer to illustrations.

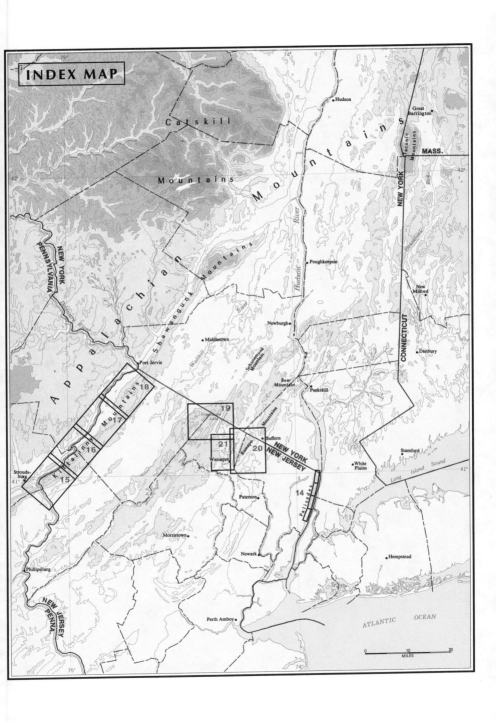

INDEX MAP

LEGEND

———————— Marked Trail

    (B) Blue   (BL) Black   (BR) Brown   (G) Green

    (W) White   (Y) Yellow   (R) Red   (O) Orange

— — — — — Unmarked Trail or Woods Road

——— — — ——— State Boundary

——— — — ——— County Boundary

═══════════ Highway

———————— Main Road

———————— Secondary Road

P   Parking

KO   Keep Out

★   Viewpoint

S   Shelter

◉   Tower

⚒   Mine

⚔   Quarry or Pit

•   Spring or Well

〰   Marsh

•*1423*   Spot Height in Feet
(contours every 100 feet, except in the Catskills)

+ + + + + Railroad

+ + + + Abandoned Railroad

— · — — — · — Powerline

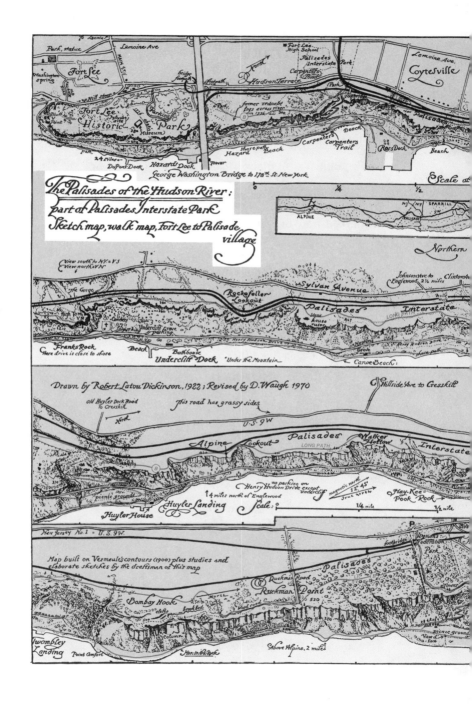

The Palisades of the Hudson River:
part of Palisades Interstate Park
Sketch map, walk map, Fort Lee to Palisade
village

Drawn by Robert Latou Dickinson, 1922; Revised by D. Waugh 1970

Map built on Vermeule's contours (1900) plus studies and
elaborate sketches by the draftsman of this map

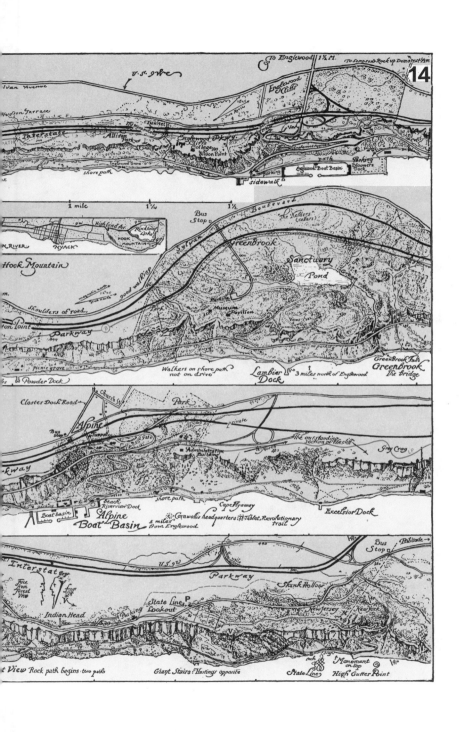

14

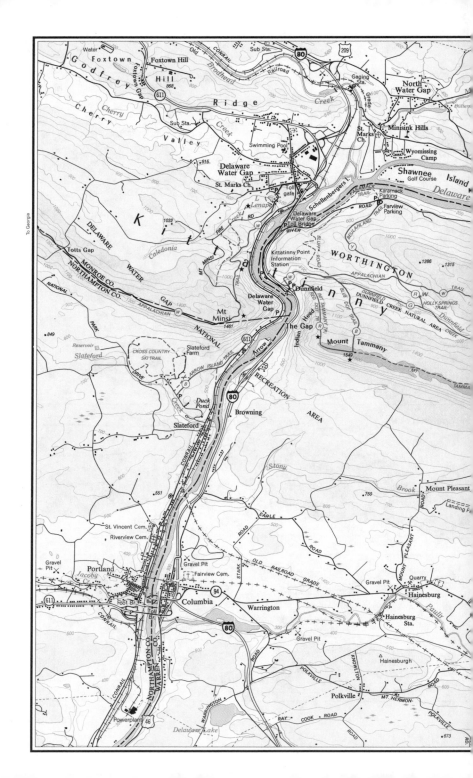

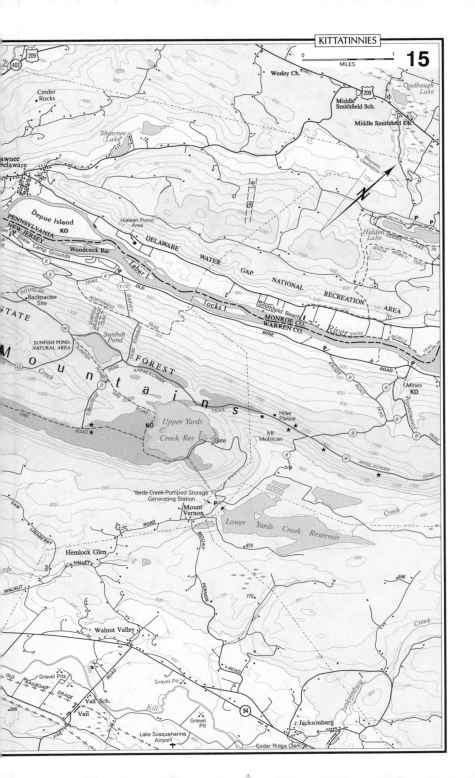

0   1
MILES

Wesley Ch.

Coolbaugh Lake

Cinder Rocks

Middle Smithfield Sch.

Middle Smithfield Ch.

Shawnee Lake

Shawnee Delaware

Magnetic Declination

N

Depue Island
KO

Hialeah Picnic Area

Hidden Lake

HIDDEN LAKE TR

PENNSYLVANIA
NEW JERSEY
KO

Woodcock Bar

State Camp Grounds

DELAWARE

WATER

GAP

NATIONAL

RECREATION

AREA

SNOW MOBILE TRAIL

Labar I.

OLD

B

Y/O

P

DOUGLAS

Backpacker Site

NORTHWEST

SUNRISE BRANCH TRAIL

GARVEY

TRAIL

Tocks I.

Smithfield Beach

MONROE CO.
WARREN CO.

River

SNOW

MOBILE

TRAIL

STATE

SUNFISH POND NATURAL AREA

Sunfish Pond

Mountains

FOREST

APPALACHIAN

KAISER

ROAD

P

P

Mines
KO

COPPERMINES

TRAIL

Creek

TURQUOISE

FIRE

ROAD

FIRE

ROAD

SUNFISH POND TRAIL

KO

Upper Yards Creek Res

Gate

TRAIL

Hiller Plaque

Mt Mohican

B

APPALACHIAN

TRAIL

B

W

Yards Creek Pumped Storage Generating Station

Mount Vernon

P

Lower

Yards

Creek

Reservoir

Creek

SAM

LINABERRY

RD.

MOUNT

VERNON

Hemlock Glen

VALLEY

WALNUT

ROAD

870

846

775

Creek

Walnut Valley

ROAD

Gravel Pits

OLD

RAILROAD

GRADE

Gravel Pit

Vail Sch.

Vail

645

94

VAIL

Gravel Pit

Kill

Lake Susquehanna Airport

Jacksonburg

Jacksonburg

Cedar Ridge Cem.

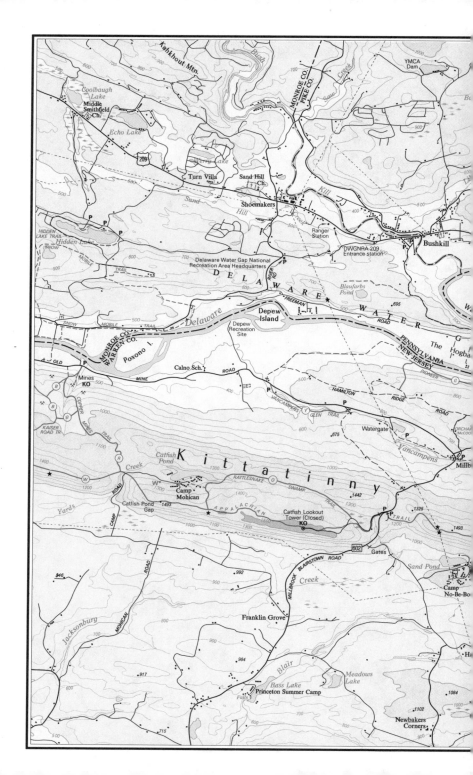

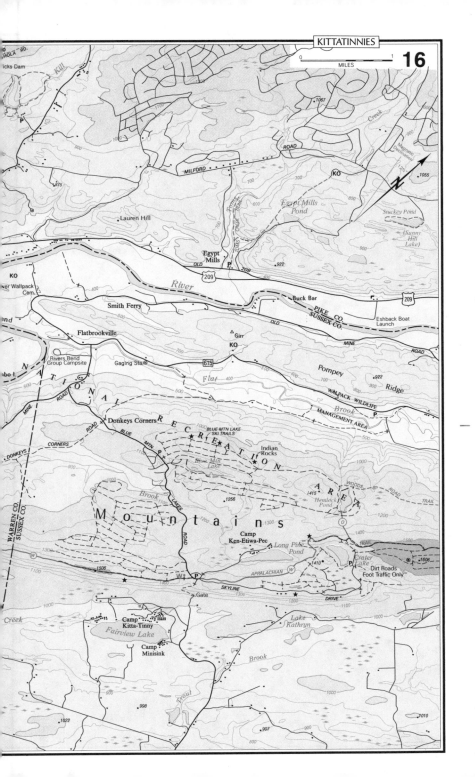

icks Dam

P

Kill

1700

1067

ROAD

MILFORD

700

700

KO

1055

575

Egypt Mills
Pond

800

Magnetic
Declination

126°

Lauren Hill

900

Snuckey Pond

(Sunny
Hill
Lake)

Egypt
Mills

OLD

209

P

209

400

922

KO

er Wallpack
Cem.

River

400

400

Buck Bar

209

Smith Ferry

500

OLD

PIKE CO.
SUSSEX CO.

Eshback Boat
Launch

end

500

Flatbrookville

Girr

MINE

ROAD

KO

615

Rivers Bend
Group Campsite

Gaging Sta.

Flat

400

Pompey

922

Ridge

mbo I

N
A
T
I
O
N
A
L

ROAD

MINE

500

500

500

700

900

900

WALPACK WILDLIFE

Brook

MANAGEMENT AREA

P

500

R
E
C
R
E
A
T
I
O
N

Donkeys Corners

CORNERS

BLUE

BLUE MTN LAKE
SKI TRAILS

500

DONKEYS

ROAD

MTN

P

Blue Mtn
Lake

Indian
Rocks

1000

A
R
E
A

1000

1256

1415

Hemlock
Pond

WOODS

ROAD

TRAIL

1200

WARREN CO.
SUSSEX CO.

Brook

900

1100

LAKES

ROAD

1300

1500

Camp
Ken-Etiwa-Pec

Long Pine
Pond

1400

TRAIL

1500

1606

W

1309

1506

1100

W

P

APPALACHIAN

W

1410

Crater
Lake

P

Dirt Roads
Foot Traffic Only

1600

1000

Gate

SKYLINE

1500

DRIVE

1800

1100

1000

Creek

Camp
Kitta-Tinny

Fairview Lake

Lake
Kathryn

Camp
Minisink

Brook

1000

998

Trout

1022

907

2010

900

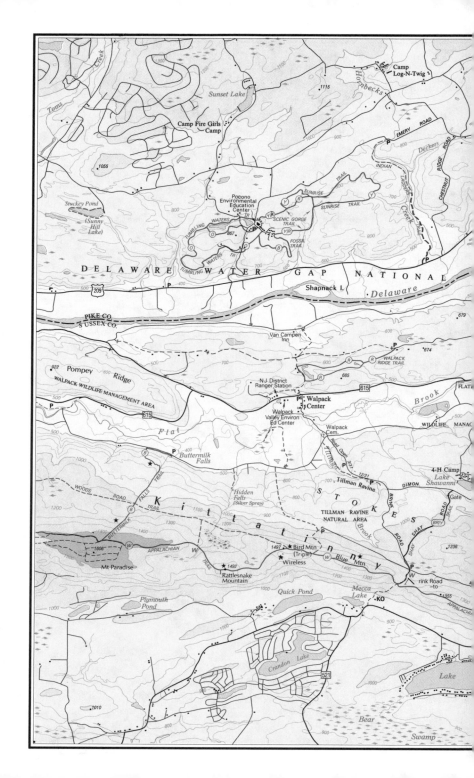

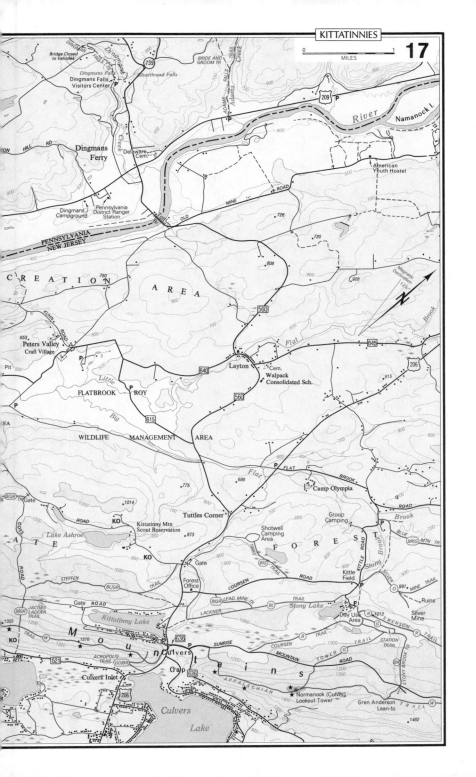

0   MILES   1

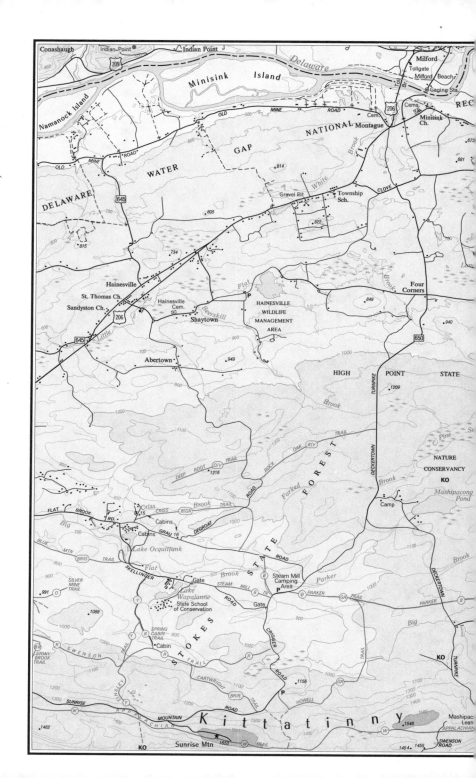

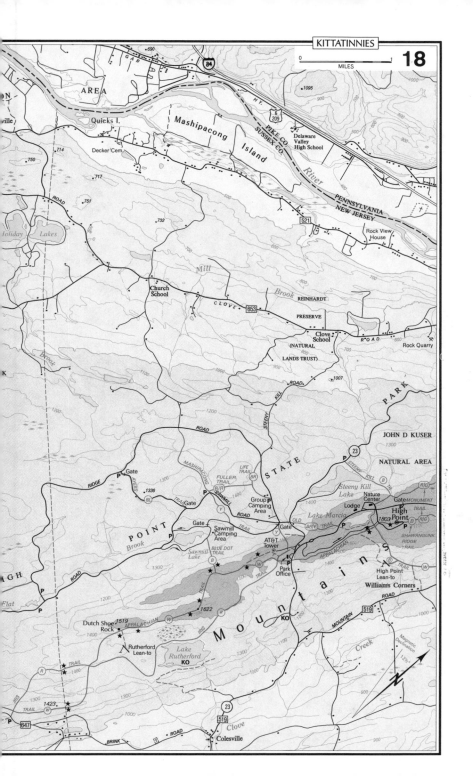

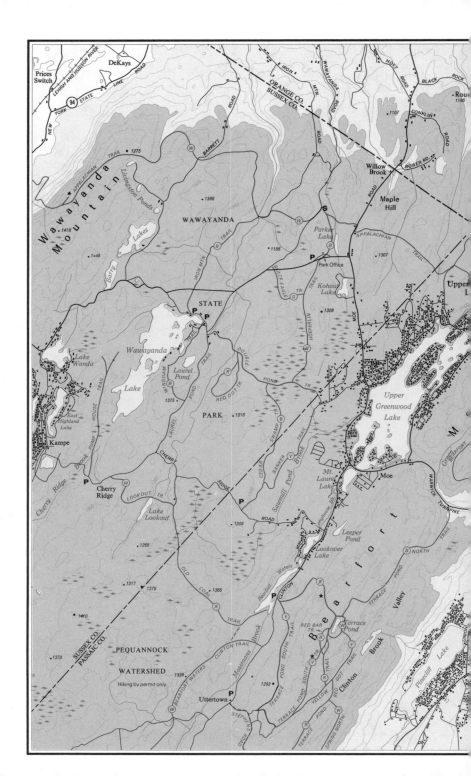

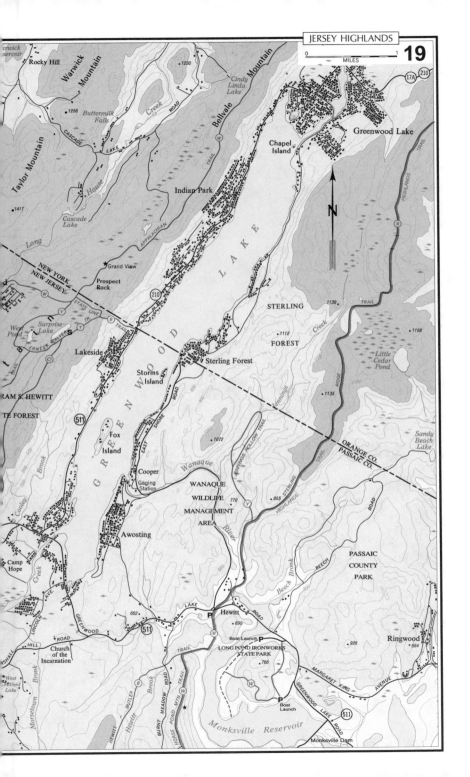

Warwick
Reservoir

Rocky Hill

Warwick Mountain

•1230

Cindy Linda Lake

Bellvale Mountain

17A 210

•1258

Buttermilk Falls

Creek

Chapel Island

Greenwood Lake

CASCADE

LAKE

House

Taylor Mountain

Indian Park

APPALACHIAN

TRAIL

•1417

Cascade Lake

Long

Grand View

N

NEW YORK
NEW JERSEY

Prospect Rock

STATE LINE

210

STERLING

•1139

TRAIL

Surprise Lake

West Pond

ERNEST WALTER

FOREST

•1112

Creek

•1158

Little Cedar Pond

Lakeside

Sterling Forest

•1135

HIGHLANDS

TRAIL

RAM S. HEWITT
TE FOREST

Storms Island

Brook

511

Fox Island

EAST SHORE ROAD

•1072

Wanaque

JENNINGS HOLLOW TRAIL

RIDGE

TRAIL

Sandy Beach Lake

Cooper
Gaging Station

WANAQUE

WILDLIFE

MANAGEMENT

AREA

River

770

•855

STERLING

HIGHLANDS

ORANGE CO.
PASSAIC CO.

Cooley

Awosting

PASSAIC

COUNTY

PARK

BEECH

ROAD

Brook

Camp Hope

Creek

Beech

•926

LINCOLN

662

LAKE

Hewitt

511

690

Ringwood
•684

GREENWOOD

ROAD

Church of the Incarnation

MARSHALL HILL

West Milford Lake

Morsetown

Brook

HEWITT

BUTLER

BROOK

HORSE POND MTN. TRAIL

Boat Launch

LONG POND IRONWORKS
STATE PARK

•766

Boat Launch

Monksville Reservoir

MARGARET KING

AVENUE

511

GREENWOOD LAKE ROAD

Monksville Dam

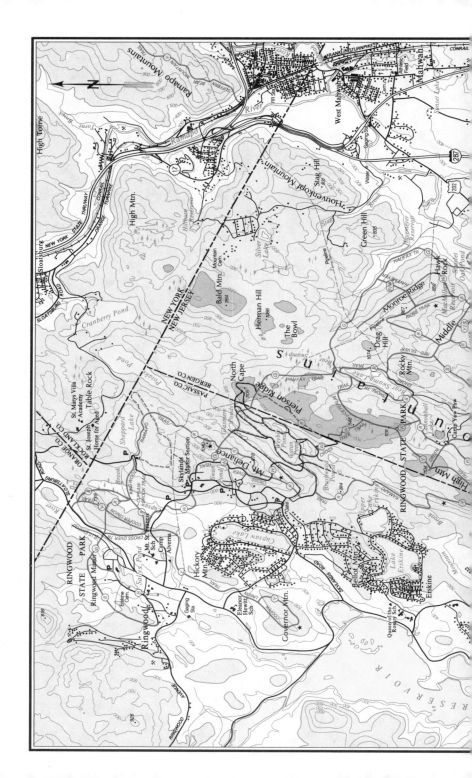

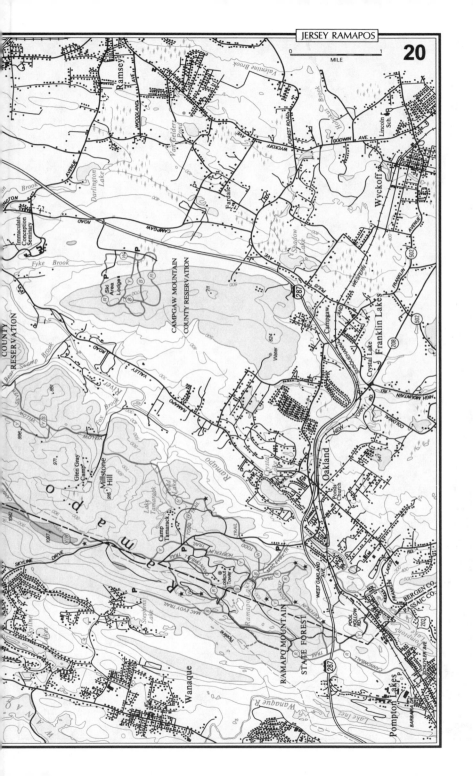

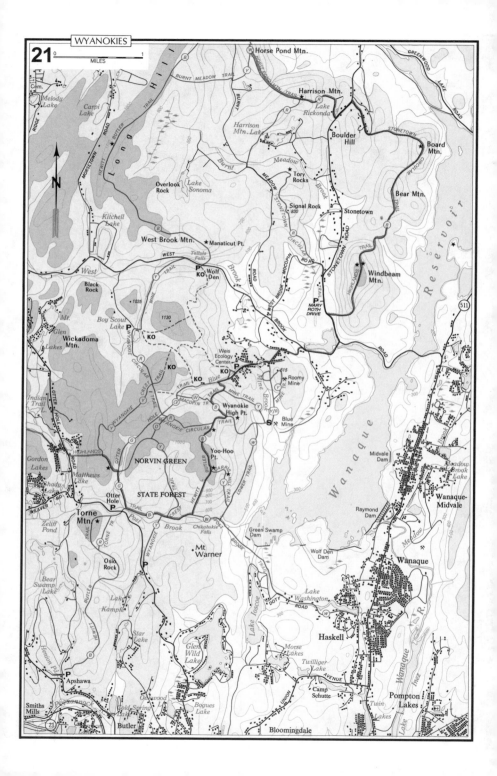